David's Son and David's Lord

Christology for Christ's People

Edited by

Ryan M. McGraw

and L. Michael Morales

EP BOOKS (Evangelical Press)
Registered Office: 140 Coniscliffe Road, Darlington, Co. Durham, UK DL3 7RT

www.epbooks.org
admin@epbooks.org

EP Books are distributed in the USA by:
JPL Books, 3883 Linden Ave. S.E.,
Wyoming, MI 49548

www.jplbooks.com
orders@jplbooks.com

First published 2019

British Library Cataloguing in Publication Data available

ISBN 978-1-78397-260-9

Table of Contents

List of Contributors

Michael Barrett is Vice President for Academic Affairs/Academic Dean and Professor of Old Testament at Puritan Reformed Theological Seminary in Grand Rapids. He is a minister in the Heritage Reformed Congregations and currently serves as Chairman of the Consistory of the Heritage Reformed Church in Grand Rapids. He earned his doctorate in Old Testament Text with a special focus on Semitic languages (Bob Jones University, 1977). For almost thirty years, he was Professor of Ancient Languages and Old Testament Theology and Interpretation at Bob Jones University and then served as President of Geneva Reformed Seminary. He has published numerous articles in both professional and popular journals and has written several books, including *Beginning at Moses, Complete in Him, Love Divine and Unfailing* (the message of Hosea), and *The Next to Last Word* (message of the Postexilic prophets). He contributed to and served as Old Testament editor for *The Reformation Heritage KJV Study Bible*.

G. K. Beale holds the J. Gresham Machen Chair of New Testament and is Research Professor of New Testament and Biblical Interpretation at Westminster Theological Seminary in Glenside, Pennsylvania. He previously taught at Wheaton College, Gordon-Conwell Theological Seminary, and Grove

City College. He holds a Bachelor of Arts in Humanities from Southern Methodist University, a Master of Arts concentrating in Augustinian and Reformation Studies from Southern Methodist University, a Master of Theology from Dallas Theological Seminary, and a Doctor of Philosophy in Divinity from the University of Cambridge. Since 2012, he is an ordained minister in the Orthodox Presbyterian Church (OPC). Previously, he was ordained by the Conservative Congregational Christian Conference. He has authored or co-authored sixteen books, and published sixty articles. He is a member of the Evangelical Theological Society, the Institute for Biblical Research, the *Studiorum Novi Testamenti Societas*, the Society of Biblical Literature, and the Tyndale Fellowship. He and his wife, Mary, have three grown children, and currently reside outside of Philadelphia, Pennsylvania.

Joel Beeke is President and Professor of Systematic Theology and Homiletics at Puritan Reformed Theological Seminary, a pastor of the Heritage Reformed Congregation in Grand Rapids, Michigan, editor of *Banner of Sovereign Grace Truth*, editorial director of Reformation Heritage Books, president of Inheritance Publishers, and Vice-chairman of the Dutch Reformed Translation Society. He has written or co-authored more than 100 books, edited another 100 books, and contributed 2,500 articles to Reformed books, journals, periodicals, and encyclopedias. His PhD is in Reformation and Post-Reformation theology from Westminster Theological Seminary (Philadelphia). He is frequently called upon to lecture at seminaries and to speak at Reformed conferences around the world. He and his wife Mary are blessed with three children and three grandchildren.

Jonathan Gibson is ordained in the International Presbyterian Church, UK, and is Associate Professor of Old Testament and Hebrew, Westminster Theological Seminary, Philadelphia.

Previously, he served as Associate Minister at Cambridge Presbyterian Church, England. He studied theology at Moore Theological College, Sydney, and then completed a PhD in Hebrew Studies, at Girton College, Cambridge. He is contributor to and co-editor with David Gibson of *From Heaven He Came and Sought Her* (Crossway, 2013), and similarly a contributor to and co-editor with Mark Earngey of *Reformation Worship* (New Growth Press, 2018). His PhD dissertation was published as *Covenant Continuity and Fidelity: A Study of Inner-Biblical Allusion and Exegesis in Malachi* (Bloomsbury, 2016). He is married to Jacqueline, and they have two children: Benjamin and Leila.

Ian Hamilton, a Scotsman and member of the Greenville Presbyterian Theological Seminary Board of Trustees, teaches Historical Theology at Edinburgh Theological Seminary and serves as associate minister in Smithton Free Church of Scotland, Inverness, Scotland. He serves as adjunct professor at Greenville Seminary. He received a BA from the University of Strathclyde, Glasgow; BD from the University of Edinburgh; MPhil from the University of Edinburgh; and DD from GPTS. He is a board member of the Banner of Truth Trust. He is the author of *The Erosion of Calvinist Orthodoxy*; *Let's Study the Letters of John*; *John Calvin's Doctrine of Holy Scripture*; *The Faith-Shaped Life*, *The Gospel-Shaped Life*, and the *Lectio Continua Commentary on Ephesians*.

Ryan M. McGraw is Morton H. Smith Professor of Systematic Theology at Greenville Presbyterian Theological Seminary and Adjunct Professor of Doctoral Studies at Puritan Reformed Theological Seminary. He is the author of nineteen books and numerous articles and reviews, including topics such as John Owen, Reformed Scholasticism, the Trinity, Christology, Scripture, Ecclesiology, and various aspects of personal godliness. He has pastored churches in the PCA and in the OPC. He is an editor of the *Journal for the History of Reformed Pietism*, Assistant Book Review editor for *Puritan Reformed Journal*, and co-editor (with Joel Beeke) of the *Cultivating Biblical Godliness* Series. He is from California, he loves skateboarding and science fiction, and he and his wife Krista have four children (Owen, Calvin, Jonathan, and Callie).

L. Michael Morales is Professor of Old Testament at Greenville Presbyterian Theological Seminary. He has experience in pastoral ministry as well as in teaching at Reformed Theological Seminary, Knox Theological Seminary, and Reformation Bible College, where he served as Provost and Professor of Biblical Studies. Aside from articles, his books include *The Tabernacle Pre-Figured: Cosmic Mountain Ideology in Genesis and Exodus*; *Who Shall Ascend the Mountain of the Lord? A Biblical Theology of the Book of Leviticus*; and forthcoming works on the Exodus and Redemption, and a commentary on the book of Numbers.

Richard Phillips is senior minister of the historic Second Presbyterian Church in Greenville, SC. He has authored thirty-five books, most recently a commentary on Revelation. Dr. Phillips serves as adjunct professor at Westminster Theological Seminary, chairman of the Philadelphia Conference on Reformed Theology, co-editor of the Reformed Expository Commentary series, and Council Member of The Gospel Coalition. His regular blog entries can be read at reformation21.com. Dr. Phillips describes his ministry as centering on three "P"s: preaching, praying, and pastoring and his weekly sermons can be viewed at www.spcgreenville.org.

Joseph A. Pipa is President and Professor of Historical and Systematic Theology at Greenville Presbyterian Theological Seminary; 2018 marked his 20th year as President. He is an ordained Teaching Elder in the Presbyterian Church in America (PCA), and has pastored congregations in Tchula, MS, Houston,

TX, and Escondido, CA. He has taught at Westminster Theological Seminary in Philadelphia (1978–1979), as well as at Westminster Seminary California (1990–1997). He holds degrees from Belhaven University (BA), Reformed Theological Seminary (MDiv.) Westminster Theological Seminary (PhD), and Greenville Presbyterian Theological Seminary (DD). He has authored and edited more than a dozen books, and has contributed both scholarly and popular articles to a number of publications.

Ryan A. Speck graduated from Greenville Presbyterian Theological Seminary in 2005. He was ordained in the James River Presbytery (PCA) to serve as the Associate Pastor at Immanuel Presbyterian Church (PCA) in Norfolk, Virginia, where he served from 2007–2012. In 2012, Ryan was installed as the pastor of Redeemer (PCA) in Columbia, MO, where he currently serves. He is the co-author of the pamphlet: *Is Church Membership Biblical?* Ryan is blessed to be married to Carolina and to be the father of six daughters.

Introduction

CHRISTOLOGY IS THE LIFEBLOOD OF CHRISTIAN FAITH AND practice. John Owen (1616–1683) noted that mediating on the glory of Christ was the key to becoming like Christ and that failing to do so was a sign of Christians becoming "carnal." He wrote,

> This is the principal cause of our unreadiness and incapacity to exercise our minds in and about the great mysteries of the Gospel, 1 Corinthians 3:1–3. And it is so with us, moreover, because we do not stir up ourselves with watchfulness and diligence in continual actings of faith on this blessed object. This is that which keeps many of us at so low an ebb, as unto the powers of a heavenly life and spiritual joys. Did we abound in this duty, in this exercise of faith, our life in walking before God would be more sweet and pleasant unto us — our spiritual light and strength would have a daily increase; we should more represent the glory of Christ in our ways and walking than usually we do, and death itself would be most welcome unto us.[1]

One of the greatest needs of the church in every age is to contemplate, know, and love the glory of Christ in order to promote the spread of the gospel and the holiness of God's people.

Yet this all-encompassing vision of Jesus Christ in Christian faith and life is not always common and it is often missing today. Sinclair Ferguson places his finger on the pulse of much contemporary preaching when he observes,

> We must learn to avoid the contemporary plague of preaching the benefits of the gospel without proclaiming Christ himself as the benefactor in the gospel. We do not offer people abstract blessings (peace, forgiveness, new life) as commodities. Rather we preach and offer Christ crucified and risen, in whom these blessings become ours and not otherwise. We preach the person in the work, never the work and its blessings apart from the Saviour himself.[2]

For this reason, Greenville Presbyterian Theological Seminary invited a team of excellent scholars and pastors to unfold the unsearchable riches of Christ for the edification of today's church at their 2018 Spring Theology Conference.

This book, which includes the addresses from this conference, attempts to provide a glimpse into the full breadth of Christology in a short space, and its authors aim at a broad audience. It includes a mature mix of biblical theology and systematic theology, as well as heart-oriented application. While some recent volumes, such as the excellent *Oxford Handbook of Christology*,[3] present comprehensive treatments of the person and work of Christ, fewer books seek to make such rich reflections accessible to pastors and church members. This present book seeks to provide this audience with a window into Christology that will stretch their thinking, bolster their faith, enrich their preaching, and warm their affections for the Savior. It is our aspiration that this work will also help spawn additional works on biblical theology and Christology that will cover the themes and subsets of the themes in much more depth.

The material is divided into eleven chapters. Ian Hamilton opens by treating Christ's prophetic office and his central place in divine revelation for the salvation of sinners. Joel Beeke follows with an exposition of Christ's identity as the pre-existent Son of God. G. K. Beale builds on this picture by answering Anselm's famous question, "Why did God become man?" Richard Phillips next introduces the vital importance of Christ's sinlessness (impeccability). Michael Morales completes this picture by treating Christ's obedience in his role as the true Israel and the obedient Son of God. Ian Hamilton expands for readers the nature of Christ's resurrection, for himself and for his people. Ryan Speck then complements Christ's resurrection by highlighting the redemptive significance of his ascension into heaven. Michael Barrett helps readers understand the integral connection between Christ and his bride, which is the church. Joseph Pipa details what it means for Christ to be King. Jonathan Gibson illustrates Christ's priestly office under the theme of the Suffering Servant Songs from Isaiah. Ryan McGraw then concludes this sketch of the beauty of Christ by showing the biblical emphases related to Christ's return. He demonstrates that the primary emphasis in Scripture on this theme is a call to personal holiness in union with Christ as believers wait for him to appear from heaven.

These chapters together do not exhaust the riches of Christology. Neither are they a complete introduction to all that could be said. Instead, they provide pastors and church members with the key ideas surrounding the person of Christ. As the Puritan Isaac Ambrose (1604–1664) wrote, "The most excellent subject to discourse or write of, is Jesus Christ ... Indeed all we say is but unsavory, if it be not seasoned with this salt."[4] Jesus Christ is also the most excellent subject to read and to prayerfully savor and meditate on. Doing so is the true path to the blessedness of the world to come and of joy and personal holiness in this life. Every glimpse we have of Christ on earth brings heaven down to us so that we might long to appear in heaven where Christ is seated. The

editors hope that this book is a small but meaningful contribution
to this end.

Ryan M. McGraw
and L. Michael Morales
Greenville Presbyterian Theological Seminary

I

Christ our Prophet

Ian Hamilton

ONE OF THE MOST BASIC AND FOUNDATIONAL TRUTHS OF THE
Christian religion is that God is simple. That does not mean that
God is mentally deficient; it means that he is neither a complex
nor an amalgam of parts. He is (Exodus 3:14), and all he is he is
synchronously, not sequentially. The Bible tells us that God is
love (1 John 4:8) and that God is light (1 John 1:5). But he is not
love some of the time and then light at some other point in time.
His nature is love and no less is his nature light. He can never not
be who he is. When we read that God is a consuming fire, for
example, that does not mean that he has suspended his love. God
is, and all he is he is synchronously.

This foundational truth reminds us that while we may speak
about God in discrete ways, those discrete ways are, in one sense,
artificial. They may well be helpful, but they are artificial.

This truth must be kept in mind when we think about our Lord

Jesus Christ as Prophet, Priest and King; namely, in his threefold office (*munus triplex*). It would be a mistake, for instance, to think of our Savior as our Prophet separately from his being our King and our Priest. These are different but coalescing offices, inseparable in their execution and, more significantly, in the one Person who executed those offices. The Lord Jesus Christ is our priestly, kingly Prophet; our prophetic, kingly Priest; our prophetic, priestly King. Because of who he is, our Savior embraces in his theanthropic[1] Person the "triple cure" that antidotes our sin — a Priest to reconcile us to God, a King to rule and reign over us, a Prophet to embody God's word to us, a Prophet who will speak to us the words of life.

As our Prophet, Jesus lives out his saving priestly and kingly calling. Let me develop this for a moment. As our Prophet, Jesus proclaimed himself as the one, final, atoning sacrifice for sin (Mark 10:45). As our Prophet, he proclaimed himself as our King and indeed the King of creation. He died not as a helpless victim but as a King, choosing the very timing of his arrest, arraignment, death and resurrection. Jesus is not just another prophet in a long line of prophets; he is the anointed King, who had come to offer himself, in obedience to his Father, as a sacrifice for sin. In order to understand Christ's prophetic office, we must understand this office in light of his threefold office as Mediator. After briefly describing Christ's prophetic office in relation to his other two offices, I will outline nine reasons why Christ is suited to be God's final prophet.

Christ's Prophetic Office in Relation to his Other Offices

John Calvin made this point well as he began to focus on Christ's threefold office in his *magnum opus*, *The Institutes of the Christian Religion*. He wrote, "Therefore, in order that faith may find a firm basis for salvation in Christ, and thus rest in him, this principle must be laid down: the office enjoined upon Christ by the Father consists of three parts. For he was given to be prophet, king, and priest."[2] Notice what Calvin was saying: the Lord Jesus Christ is not the sum of different parts. He is the God-Man, one Person with two natures. Prophet, Priest and King are not three separate or separable offices. They are three aspects or facets of the one office of Christ as Mediator. Just as a single diamond is one but has a number of brilliant facets, so the Lord Jesus Christ is one, but his oneness is multi-faceted.

Calvin began his rich exposition of Christ's prophetic office with these words,

> Now it is to be noted that the title 'Christ' pertains to these three offices: for we know that under the law prophets as well as priests and kings were anointed with holy oil. Hence the illustrious name of 'Messiah' was also bestowed upon the promised Mediator.[3]

So Calvin would have answered the question, What is a Christian?, by saying that a Christian was, "Someone for whom Jesus is God's last, final and perfect prophetic Word, God's King who rules over all we are by the scepter of his word, God's anointed Priest who is the propitiation for our sins and for the sins of the whole world."

The primary ministry of a prophet was to speak from God. He was, on occasion, a foreteller, but more often he was a forthteller, saying, "Thus says the Lord". In the Old Testament, Israel's history was punctuated with false prophets. God did not send these prophets and the words that they spoke were not God's words. These false prophets had a characteristic in common; they spoke of "peace" when there was no peace (Jeremiah 6:14). They spoke to please men rather than to honor God.

In Deuteronomy 18, we read of Moses looking forward to a day when God would raise up a prophet greater than himself (18:15-18).

In Acts 3:22–23, the apostle Peter recognized that in Jesus Moses' promise-prophecy had come to fulfillment. The opening words of John's Gospel reveal the stunning identity of the Prophet who was greater than Moses. God's final and ultimate Prophet was none other than the eternal Word himself: "In the beginning was the Word, and the Word was with God, and the Word was God" (John 1:1). This "Word", who was in the beginning, who was (literally) face to face with God, and who himself was God, "became flesh" (John 1:14). God's final and best word to humanity was his "face to face Fellow," his own eternally begotten Son (John 3:16).

Christ's Suitability to his Prophetic Office

The New Testament in particular highlights a number of truths that spell out the specific character of Jesus as God's final Prophet. First, we should note the perfect suitability of Jesus to be God's final Prophet. We have noted that Jesus is described in John 1:1–14 as "the Word" who was eternally with God and who was God. John further develops this thought in verse 18: "No one has ever seen God; the only God, who is at the Father's side, he has made him known." Jesus, the Word become flesh (v. 14), is perfectly suited to be God's final, perfect Prophet. As the Word of God who was eternally "with God," Jesus is alone able perfectly to make God known. He is the perfect "exegesis" of the Father (v. 18).

The whole New Testament bears witness to Jesus as the final and perfect revelation of God. Jesus himself testifies to his uniqueness as the incarnate revelation of the Father. In John 14, he told his disciples, "If you had known me, you would have known my Father also. From now on you do know him and have seen him" (John 14:7). One of his disciples, Philip, then said to Jesus, "Lord, show us the Father, and it is enough for us." In reply, Jesus said, "Whoever has seen me has seen the Father" (John

14:8–9). Similarly, the writer to the Hebrews began his pastoral letter to believers who were being tempted to return to Judaism by reminding them of who Jesus is: "Long ago, at many times and in many ways, God spoke to our fathers by the prophets, but in these last days he has spoken to us by his Son" (Hebrews 1:1–2). The antidote to drifting away from Jesus is to grasp that he is the Son in whom God has spoken his best and final word to humanity.

The opening section of the Letter to the Hebrews is a striking example of the native pastoral power of doctrine. Writing to Jewish Christians who were experiencing intense persecution and considering turning back from following Jesus, the writer began his "brief word of encouragement" (13:22) by reminding them of who Jesus is:

In these last days he (God) has spoken to us by his Son, whom he appointed the heir of all things, through whom also he created the world. He is the radiance of the glory of God and the exact imprint of his nature, and he upholds the universe by the word of his power. After making purification for sins, he sat down at the right hand of the Majesty on high, having become as much superior to angels as the name he has inherited is more excellent than theirs (Hebrews 1:2–4).

The Lord of these hard-pressed, struggling Christians was not simply another prophet in a long line of prophets, he is God's final and ultimate word to humanity; "in these last days he has spoken to us by his Son" (Hebrews 1:2). "His Son". These deeply theological words powerfully remind us that the greatest encouragement and comfort we can give to struggling Christians is to remind them of who their Savior is. Every pastor should be persuaded that the greatest good he can do the congregation he serves is to proclaim to them week by week, with faithfulness and passion, "Behold your God".

Some years ago while ministering in Cambridge, I was stopped by two Mormons. I invited them for coffee. Just as they were beginning to launch into their pre-programmed script, I asked them a question: "When I read the testimony of the New Testament to Jesus, I am told he is the perfect revelation of God. I discover that through faith alone in him, God freely and fully forgives all my sin, adopts me into his family, makes me a joint heir with Christ of his glory, sends the Holy Spirit into my life to preserve and sanctify me, and gives me the sure and certain hope of everlasting life. Here is my question: What more can your Joseph Smith do for me, if he truly is God's final word to humanity?" If my memory is accurate, they sat for some moments uncertain of what to say. Jesus alone is perfectly suited to be the final Prophet, the final declarer of God's truth because he is himself the eternal Word, the incarnate "exegesis" (John 1:18) of God.

Third, you cannot read far into the New Testament without being struck by Jesus' unembarrassed egoism. This was both warranted and vital because he is a divine person. Egoism here is not pejorative. It reflects an appropriate self-identity on Jesus' part. He was fully aware that he was in the world as God's final word to men and women dead and lost in their trespasses and sins. In his Gospel, John in particular highlights the self conscious egoism of God's eternal Word: Jesus said, "I am the bread of life; whoever comes to me shall not hunger, and whoever believes in me shall never thirst" (John 6:35). He said, "I am the light of the world. Whoever follows me will not walk in darkness, but will have the light of life" (8:12). He said, "I am the door. If anyone enters by me, he will be saved" (10:9). He said, "I am the good shepherd. The good shepherd lays down his life for the sheep" (10:11). He said, "I am the resurrection and the life. Whoever believes in me, though he die, yet shall he live, and everyone who lives and believes in me shall never die" (11:25–26). He said, "I am the way, and the truth, and the life. No one comes to the Father except through me" (14:6). He said, "I am the true vine … Whoever abides in me and I in him, he it is that bears much fruit, for apart from me you can do nothing" (John 15:1, 5). The unembarrassed egoism is astonishing. His egoism reaches something of a self-conscious climax in Matthew 11, where Matthew recorded Jesus' words, "Come to me, all who labor and are heavy laden, and I will give you rest. Take my yoke upon you, and learn from me, for I am gentle and lowly in heart, and you will find rest for your souls. For my yoke is easy, and my burden is light" (11:28–30). Jesus' uninhibited egoism is breathtaking. He knows who he is. He knows that he is God's final word of grace and mercy to a rebellious world. Here is a Prophet infinitely greater than Moses (Deuteronomy 18:18). As the writer to the Hebrews expressed it, "Moses was faithful in all God's house as a servant ... but Christ is faithful over God's house as a son" (Hebrews 3:5–6).

Fourth, the four Gospels are replete with examples of the penetrating authority of Jesus, God's Prophet-Son. When Nicodemus ("the teacher of Israel", John 3:10) came to Jesus by night to enquire of him, Jesus said to this erudite teacher, "Truly, truly, I say to you, unless a man is born again he cannot see the kingdom of God" (John 3:3). Nicodemus must have been stunned, perhaps even stung, by Jesus' forthright words. With unimpeachable authority, Jesus spoke God's truth as God's ordained Prophet. On another occasion he spoke with equal candor to the Pharisees, who were Israel's appointed spiritual leaders. Quoting words from Isaiah 29:13, Jesus said to them, "This people honors me with their lips, but their heart is far from me; in vain do they worship me, teaching as doctrines the commandments of men" (Mark 7:6–7). No church court had authorized Jesus to speak with such authority. He spoke as he did because of who he was, God's Son, his eternal Word, the final and perfect revelation of who God is. On another occasion Jesus said,

For what does it profit a man to gain the whole world and forfeit his soul? For what can a man give in return for his soul? For whoever is ashamed of me and of my words in this adulterous and sinful generation, of him will the Son of Man also be ashamed when he comes in the glory of his Father with the holy angels (Mark 8:36–38).

Here Jesus identifies himself with the Son of Man prophesied in Daniel 7:13–14. He speaks with the unassailable confidence of One whose word cannot be denied, far less thwarted.

Fifth, the New Testament unambiguously heralds the absolute commitment that Jesus, God's Prophet-Son, demands from people. As God's final Prophet, Jesus spoke with an authority that compelled people to listen, even in their unbelief. At the conclusion of his account of the Sermon on the Mount, Matthew tells us, "the crowds were astonished at his teaching, for he was teaching them as one who had authority, and not as their scribes" (Matthew 7:28–29). This innate authority is seen most strikingly in the absolute demands that Jesus made on would-be followers. Immediately after Peter confessed Jesus to be "The Christ of God" (Luke 9:20), Jesus replied, "If anyone would come after me, let him deny himself and take up his cross daily and follow me" (Luke 9:23). Jesus issued a non-negotiable demand for unqualified allegiance to himself. This demand, of course, flowed out of his grace to sinners. God's grace costs us nothing, but it demands from us everything.

Sixth, Jesus' uniqueness as God's final Prophet is seen not only in his essential divine identity, but also in his redemptive self-disclosure and accomplishment. Jesus was deeply conscious of why he had come from heaven: "For even the Son of Man came not to be served but to serve, and to give his life as a ransom for many" (Mark 10:45). He knew he was "the way, and the truth, and the life" (John 14:6). He knew he was the "I am" (John 8:58). At every stage in his earthly life, Jesus marched relentlessly into the future ordained for him by his Father. He understood that he had not come into the world merely to speak God's word authoritatively, but also and supremely to lay down his life for his sheep (John 10:11). His office of prophet in relation to his threefold office shows his uniqueness as prophet in light of his redemptive work. In Jesus, we see the self-conscious coalescing of the threefold dimensions or facets of his office as Mediator. He is the Prophet who speaks the word of God; he is the Priest who lays down his life in fulfillment of that word; he is the King who marches regally to his saving destiny, repulsing every enemy who attempts to turn him aside.

Seventh, the Gospel accounts overflow with the breathtaking tender mercy of Jesus our Prophet. The first Servant Song in Isaiah (42:1–4) depicts the tenderheartedness of God's final Prophet, "a bruised reed he will not break, and a faintly burning wick he will not quench." The broken, weak and marginalized need not fear coming to this Prophet. It is remarkable that on the only occasion when Jesus self-consciously refers to his own character, he says, "Come to me ... for I am gentle and lowly in heart, and you will find rest for your souls" (Matthew 11:28–29). We see this tenderness wonderfully illustrated in Jesus' encounter with the woman caught in the act of adultery (John 8:1–11). Over against the heartlessness of her accusers, Jesus reveals to the woman his gospel grace in all its glory. He tells her to "go and sin no more." But prior to that he says, "Where are your accusers? Is there no one to condemn you? Neither do I condemn you." The woman must have been bewildered and overwhelmed by the words Jesus spoke. Augustine beautifully commented, "And there remained but two, misery and mercy" (*Relicti sunt duo, misera et misericordia*).[4]

Eighth, the Scriptures highlight the saving accomplishment secured by Jesus our Prophet. At every step from Mary's womb to Calvary's cross, our Lord Jesus Christ gave his unceasing "Amen" to the will of his Father. At every phase, indeed at every moment in his earthly pilgrimage, our Savior lived out in perfect obedience his prophetic ministry. His greatest word as our Prophet reached its crescendo when he cried in victorious weakness, "It is finished" (John 19:30). God the eternal Word, who had become flesh for us, now on the cross was made sin for us (2 Corinthians 5:21) and became a willing curse for us (Galatians 3:13). The history of Israel was a history of killing God's prophets (Matthew 23:37). Jesus identified with his prophet forerunners, with this fundamental difference: they died merely martyrs' deaths while he also died a sin-atoning Savior's death. As Paul so simply, and yet so wonderfully, wrote to the church in Philippi, Jesus was obedient unto death, even the death of the cross (Philippians 2:8); the God-cursed death of the covenant Head of a world of judgment-deserving sinners.

Ninth, if Jesus' "It is finished," had been his last prophetic word, he could not have led many sons to glory (Hebrews 2:10). Following his death, God raised him bodily on the third day and then he ascended into his glory as the Redeemer of God's elect. Now at the right hand of God, as our covenant Head and representative he continues his ministry as God's perfect Prophet. Jesus did not cease his prophetic ministry after his ascension. He continues to be our final and perfect Prophet through the ministry of his prayers, and through the Spirit using his inscripturated Word. Through the Holy Spirit blessed reading and ministry of his word, he proclaims himself, offers himself, and gives himself to be our Prophet, Priest and King.

Conclusion

Jesus is God's best and final word to this world. God has nothing more to say to us than he has said in the coming, living, speaking, dying and rising of his Son. This present life and the life to come will be an endless and inexhaustible exploration of "the Word made flesh" and of the entire Trinity in and through him. This is why Christians cannot countenance anything or anyone who would seek to add to Christ in any aspect of Christian faith and life. Paul's reiterated anathema in Galatians 1:6–9 highlights how seriously the early church regarded the attempt to add to Christ. Not only would any addition destroy the hope of salvation for a judgment-deserving world; it would rob Christ of the glory that wholly and alone belongs by right to him.

2

The Lord from Heaven

The Deity and Pre-existence of the Son of God

Joel R. Beeke

"Jesus said unto them, Verily, verily, I say unto you, Before Abraham was, I am." John 8:58

"Before Abraham was, I am!"[1] With these words of solemn affirmation, Jesus of Nazareth sums up His claim to be the eternal Son of God, "begotten of the Father before all worlds" (Nicene Creed). He forges an unbreakable link between the Old Testament Jehovah, the God of Israel, and the New Testament's Jesus of Nazareth, whom "God hath made ... both Lord and Christ" (Acts 2:36). He extends the reach of His work as the Son of God back to the very dawn of time, anchors it in the measureless stretches of eternity past, and embeds it in the whole history of redemption from beginning to end.

Hence it follows that Jesus Christ is to be received, trusted, loved, called upon, worshiped and served as God; that He is able to save to the uttermost all who come unto God by Him; that His words are true and trustworthy, His promises cannot fail, and His commands are to be obeyed by all. In short, He alone is worthy to be the Mediator of the covenant of grace, the Savior of the world, and the King whose dominion will never cease. He is that God and Savior who was "manifest in the flesh, justified in the Spirit, seen of angels, preached unto the Gentiles, believed on in the world, received up into glory" (1 Timothy 3:16).

All this we learn as we consider four aspects of this great, simple, yet profound text: "Before Abraham was, I am!" These aspects are the speaker, the form, the context, and the content.

The Speaker of This Saying

The speaker is Christ Himself! These are not the words of an admiring disciple, who might be accused of fond delusion or excessive partisan zeal. These are not the words of an "impartial" third-person observer, merely doing the job of a reporter and commenting on the sayings and doings of our Lord. They are not even the derisive, taunting words of a spiritual adversary or unbelieving bystander. These are the words of Christ Himself who, as the great Prophet-Priest-King of the covenant, identifies Himself as the great God of the covenant.

It is often alleged that Jesus never claimed to be God. These words alone would suffice to disprove such an allegation, although many other statements of our Lord could be adduced. Jesus could not have found a clearer, more absolute, or more dynamic way to identify Himself as both God and God's Son, sent of the Father into this world for us and for our salvation.

It is also alleged that the idea of the deity of Christ was added to the gospel as an afterthought, something imposed on the essentially Jewish moral or ethical message of Rabbi Jesus of

Nazareth by the apostle Paul and his fellow enthusiasts. Some even dare to say that this recasting of the faith of Jesus was inspired by pagan mythology! Such allegations are crushed by this rock of truth, fixed forever in place by these words which fell from Christ's own lips, "Before Abraham was, I am."[2]

The Form of This Saying of Jesus

Christ takes care to cast His words in a particular form by prefacing them with the words, "Verily, verily, I say unto you." Literally, Christ says, "Amen, Amen, I say unto you." Amen is the Hebrew word for truth, denoting something that is sure, fixed, and firm. Here it is used as a redoubled adverb calling attention to the truth and trustworthiness of what Christ is about to say.

We might call it "Amen Squared" or "Truth Times Two." Here truth is attested and confirmed by truth, thus placing it beyond all doubt or question, assuring us that it is absolutely true. Such a solemn affirmation is what the apostle Paul calls "a faithful saying, and worthy of all acceptation" (1 Timothy 1:15).

The redoubled form "Amen, Amen" appears only in John's Gospel and is used no less than twenty-five times. As a literary device, it highlights these particular sayings of Christ and calls the reader's attention to them. As William Hendriksen notes, "It often introduces a statement which expresses a conclusion to what has preceded."[3] Here in John 8 it appears at the end of a long, acrimonious debate between Christ and the Pharisees. Christ's use of this formula gives His words a ring of authority, certainty, and finality: "Forever settled in the heav'ns, Thy word, O LORD, shall firmly stand!" (Psalm 119:89).[4]

"Before Abraham was, I am." Clearly this is Christ's final answer to the question, "Who art thou?" (John 8:25). It is intended to stand as the summing up of all that He has said about Himself from the beginning of His public ministry. He does not retract or modify this great claim but bears it to the cross, the grave, and ever afterwards, even as He rises from the dead and ascends into heaven to be enthroned at the right hand of the Majesty on high.

The Context in which These Words are Spoken

Christ is seated in the temple, early in the morning, with "all the people" coming to Him and being taught by Him (John 8:2). He is in the holy temple where God dwells among His people; the place of "judgment's royal seat, Messiah's kingly throne," where "the people of the Lord … come to learn Jehovah's will" (Psalm 122).[5] He is dispensing the chief means of grace, "the preaching of the Word" (*Westminster Larger Catechism*, Q. 155), feeding the sheep of God.

But He does so under the watchful, menacing eyes of "the scribes and Pharisees," who regard Him with loathing and hostility as a rival and a foe. As the day wears on, they assail Him with objections, accusations, and pointed questions. Where are His credentials and attestations (John 8:13)? Who is this Father He speaks of (v. 19)? And finally, they bluntly ask, "Who art thou?" (v. 25), or rendered more literally and emphatically, "You! Just who do you think you are?"

So the battle ensues over this most important question: *Who was and who is Jesus of Nazareth?* In the dialogue that follows, Christ draws upon the entire witness of the Old Testament and the history of redemption. He appeals to what B. B. Warfield calls "the Christology of pre-Christian Judaism,"[6] derived from "all things … which were written in the law of Moses, and in the prophets, and in the Psalms" (Luke 24:44) concerning the person, work, sufferings, and subsequent glory of Israel's Messiah.

In particular, at every point, Jesus identifies Himself as the Son of a heavenly Father, fulfilling the prophecy of Psalm 89:26: "He shall cry unto me, Thou art my father, my God, and the rock of my salvation." He says:

- "I know whence I came, and whither I go" (John 8:14);

- "Ye are from beneath; but I am from above: ye are of this world; I am not of this world" (v. 23);

- "He that sent me is with me: the Father hath not left me alone; for I do always those things that please him" (v. 29);

    and

- "I proceeded forth and came from God; neither came I of myself, but he sent me" (v. 42).

Having identified Himself in this way, Christ makes a bold declaration: "Whosoever committeth sin is the servant of sin" (v. 34), and "If the Son therefore shall make you free, ye shall be free indeed" (v. 36). The Pharisees reject both the charge of being in bondage to sin and the promise of emancipation through faith in Christ as the Son of God: "We be Abraham's seed, and were never in bondage to any man" (v. 33); "Abraham is our father" (v. 39).

Christ responds by distinguishing between mere biological descent and the deeper spiritual kinship and sonship of justifying faith, which He expresses here as doing "the works of Abraham" (v. 39). The Pharisees, however, are doing the will and works of the devil by fighting against God's Word and seeking to kill God's Messenger, so Jesus says, "Ye are of your father the devil, and the lusts of your father ye will do" (v. 44).

The debate over Abraham continues until Christ brings it to an end with this sweeping declaration, "Before Abraham was, I am." The Pharisees have nothing more to say. They understand only too well what Jesus is saying; they regard His words as blasphemous and worthy of death. In anger they resort to violence, confirming

Christ's witness against them: "Ye seek to kill me" (v. 37). But while they look about for stones to cast at Him, Jesus draws his prayer shawl down around His face and slips away, leaving the temple unnoticed among the throngs of people coming and going.

The Content of This Declaration

In five simple words, Christ identifies Himself as the ever-living and everywhere present Jehovah, God of Israel, the Rock of our salvation, and the only Savior. The saying falls into two parts. The first part ("Before Abraham was ...") pinpoints a particular moment in time. The second part ("I am") positions Christ in relation to that particular moment in time, indeed, in relation to all of time: past, present and future.

"Before Abraham was ... "
What an extraordinary claim to an extraordinarily long pre-history! So far as the history of the nation of Israel is concerned, everything began with Abraham. Christ declares that He was there before Israel's history began, and, by implication, long before; likewise, that He had been there throughout that history.

In this way Christ connects Himself with every generation of the children of Israel and with every chapter in the long history of Israel's establishment, unfolding, and fulfillment of the covenant of grace made with Abraham and his seed forever. The riches of grace enshrined in this covenant are the riches bestowed by Christ. The promises of this covenant are Christ's promises; its requirements are His requirements; and the power, both to perform these promises and to enforce these requirements, is the divine omnipotence of Christ Jesus the Lord.

"... I am"
With these two simple words, Christ unmistakably refers to the words of Jehovah recorded in Exodus 3:14: "And God said unto

Moses, I AM THAT I AM: and he said, Thus shalt thou say unto the children of Israel, I AM hath sent me unto you." This is His distinctive name, which He shares with no other (Psalm 83:18). Who but Almighty God, Maker of heaven and earth, the only true and ever-living God, can say such a thing?

But here is Jesus of Nazareth, identifying Himself as Jehovah, the God of Abraham, Isaac, and Jacob and thereby asserting the continuous, unlimited, present tense activity and the indicative reality of His being. Notice how He lets these words stand alone and unqualified as His final answer to the question, "Who art thou?" "I AM."

Christ is only summing up in five crystal-clear words what He has been saying all along. When they ask, "Who art thou?" He first replies, "Even the same that I said unto you from the beginning" (John 8:25). He is not saying this for the first time,[7] or as a mere implication of other things He has said, or as a sideline of no great significance, but He is saying this as the central, foundational truth of the good news He has proclaimed during the previous three years of His public ministry.

In similarly astonishing words, John found the starting point for his account of the gospel of Jesus Christ: "In the beginning was the Word, and the Word was with God, and the Word was God" (1:1). From start to finish, John sets out to show "that Jesus is the Christ, the Son of God" (20:31). It is clear that John understands these words to be an assertion of infinite, eternal being, as one "having neither beginning of days, nor end of life" and exercising "the power of an endless life" (Hebrews 7:3, 16), a mode of being unique to Jehovah, the God of Israel, the great I AM.

The great I AM has also manifested Himself as Lord from heaven in the Old Testament. Theologians call such an appearance a Christophany, which is a visible rather than verbal anthropomorphism. Michael Barrett summarizes this well, saying that a Christophany is

> an effective means of revealing that God is a person. That it was the Second Person of the holy, eternal Trinity who made these special appearances reveals something of the mystery of the Godhead. These Christophanies introduce to man extremely profound theology concerning Christ and His place in the Trinity.[8]

Allow me to elaborate on this concept of a Christophany in just one way — its most common way, reflected in the title, "the Angel of the Lord." Throughout the Old Testament, the Angel of the Lord is one way the eternal Son of God speaks and appears to men. The Son of God comes in human form as the Angel of the Lord prior to His coming in human flesh as Jesus Christ.

The term *angel of the Lord* appears over fifty times in the Old Testament, and the similar phrase *angel of God* occurs nine times. While some of these references speak of ordinary angels (Genesis 28:12; 32:1), many refer to a special Angel. It is helpful to note that the Hebrew word angel is not limited in scope as we would normally use it — that is, it does not always refer strictly to a created spirit sent from heaven. The word often means simply a *messenger,* as when Jesus Christ is called "the messenger of the covenant" who will come later into His temple (Malachi 3:1).

The Old Testament portrays this special Angel as *divine* (that is, He is the Lord) and yet *distinct* (that is, He is unique from the Father). These two points harmonize with the biblical understanding of the Trinity: one Lord with three distinct Persons. The Old Testament demonstrates these two truths about the Angel of the Lord in five ways:

1.   The Angel of the Lord *claims divine authority.* He speaks as God and swears by Himself to fulfill His covenant (Genesis 16:10; 22:15–16).

2. The Angel of the Lord *exhibits divine attributes and performs divine actions.* He has knowledge that only God possesses (Genesis 16:7–8, 11, 13). He judges and redeems as God (Genesis 48:15–16; Judges 5:23; 2 Samuel 24:14–17; 2 Kings 19:35).

3. The Angel of the Lord *receives divine worship.* He is treated as God Himself, receiving sacrifices and homage paid to His Person (Exodus 23:20–21; Judges 6:20–21, 24). No ordinary angel would accept man's worship (Revelation 19:10).

4. The Angel of the Lord is *identified explicitly as God.* He is distinctly said to be the Lord (Genesis 16:13; 22:11–12, 15–18; 31:11–13; 48:15–16; Exodus 14:19; 23:21; Judges 6:11–23; 13:19–22; cf. Isaiah 42:8).

5. *The Angel of the Lord is a distinct, divine Person.* He is evidently divine and yet carefully distinguished from the Lord (Genesis 24:7, 40; 32:24–30; Exodus 3:4–5; 23:20; Numbers 20:16; Joshua 5:14–15; Judges 2:1; 6:11–24; 13:2–24; 2 Samuel 24:16; Isaiah 63:9; Zechariah 1:12–13).

Consequently, the Old Testament portrays this Angel as one of the Persons of the Godhead. The Angel of the Lord should be identified as the second person of the Trinity because He is the sent One who appears bodily, both in the Old and in the New Testaments. He cannot be the Father, who is the Sender. He cannot be the Spirit, who is sent from both the Father and the Son and whose work is to testify to the Son as the only Mediator between God and man. Further, the divine Angel of the Lord no longer appears after the Son of God comes in the flesh at His incarnation. New Testament writings reveal continuity between the Son of God's activity as the Angel of the Lord and His work as the incarnate Jesus Christ. In both His form and His flesh, the Son of God performs a redemptive, messianic work.

The presence of the Angel of the Lord in the Old Testament

communicates two important truths. First, the appearances of the Angel of the Lord prepare the church for her Christ. The temporary form of the Angel arouses a deep love and longing within the people of God for the coming of Jesus Christ in the flesh. The church in the Old Testament searches earnestly for her Beloved to bound over the hills and dwell with her (Song 2:8). Second, the appearances of the Angel of the Lord prepare Christ for His church. His ministry in alleviating His people's misery throughout the Old Testament is a foretaste of His messianic mission. The Son of God's appearances can be seen as expressions of holy impatience prior to the irrupting of His presence on earth when He takes up His threefold role as prophet, priest, and king of His people.[9] These Christophanies were foretastes of His prophetic, priestly, and kingly missions (Malachi 3:1; Zechariah 1:6–17; Exodus 14:19–20).[10]

Time would fail us to survey and discuss the further witness of both Testaments to the central claim of the Lord Jesus Christ that He is the Lord from heaven. It was the opinion of Charles Hodge that, "It is absolutely impossible to present a tithe of the evidence which the Scriptures contain of the truth of this doctrine."[11] Suffice it to say that all the Scriptures bear witness to the fact that "God so loved the world, that he gave his only begotten Son, that whosoever believeth in him should not perish, but have everlasting life" (John 3:16).

Applications for Christians

As they stand, these words of Christ, "Before Abraham was, I am," bristle with implications for Christian faith, Christian worship, Christian living, and Christian witness.

Christian Faith

Ours is a sure Redeemer because He is a divine Redeemer. That Christ is the eternal Son of God who came down from heaven reveals, among other things, the irresistible and almighty power that undergirded "the man Christ Jesus" in His redemptive labors and sufferings. "Why must He in one person be also very God?" asks the Heidelberg Catechism. "That He might by the power of His Godhead sustain in His human nature the burden of God's wrath; and might obtain for, and restore to us, righteousness and life" (Q. 17).

The task set before Christ would have been impossible on any other terms. "The wrath of God against sin is so great, that (rather than it should go unpunished) He hath punished the same in His beloved Son Jesus Christ, with the bitter and shameful death of the cross."[12] The burden of our sins was so great that nothing less than divine omnipotence could bear it.

Nor could the benefits of Christ's perfectly obedient life and substitutionary death, that is, the forgiveness of sins and inheritance of eternal life, be secured in any other way. As Paul says, "For what the law could not do, in that it was weak through the flesh, God sending His own Son in the likeness of sinful flesh, and for sin, condemned sin in the flesh: that the righteousness of the law might be fulfilled in us" (Romans 8:3–4). In the death of Christ, as John Murray wrote, "the righteousness of God" meets "the wrath of God."[13]

Through Christ's blood, all satisfaction for sin is completed. Faith understands that there is nothing to be added nor can be added to Christ's blood for our salvation. That is illustrated well by an aged friend of mine who recently passed on to glory. A few hours before he died, a nurse walked into his room and said, "I'm afraid that I need to do some more blood work on you." My friend replied, "All the blood work I need was done for me on the cross by my eternal Savior who came down from heaven two thousand years ago to shed His blood for me!"

Nor will the promises of Christ be of real and lasting comfort to us unless the truth and trustworthiness of an Almighty God stands behind them, assuring us that, "These things saith the Amen, the faithful and true witness." (Revelation 3:14). We can "hold fast the profession of our faith without wavering" only because we know that "he is faithful that promised" (Hebrews 10:23).

And who is better equipped to declare the grace, truth, and the will of God for our salvation, than the Son of God who from all eternity has lain "in the bosom of the Father" (John 1:18)? And how can the risen and ascended Lord Jesus Christ be sustained in His work of constant intercession for us if not by "the power of an endless life" (Hebrews 7:16), a life that, like His Father, He has in Himself as the Son of God (John 5:26)? If our King is not divine, how can His kingdom be "an everlasting kingdom," and how can His dominion "endureth throughout all generations" (Psalm 145:13)?

Similar things can be said for the ways in which the divine attributes empower Christ to be our all-sufficient Savior and Lord. Christ's "I am" title teaches us about His self-existence. We are dependent beings. He alone is independent and self-existent. Only He can say, "I am God, and there is none else" (Isaiah 46:9).

The glorious name "I am" also implies His unchangeableness. Change is written upon everything earthly, but Christ is immutable. He is "the same yesterday, and to day, and for ever" (Hebrews 13:8).

The name "I am" also teaches us of Christ's all-sufficiency. There is no need which we shall ever face, for which Christ is not the ultimate answer. He is the law-keeper for law-breakers like us (Matthew 5:17). He was forsaken of His Father that we might never be forsaken of Him (Matthew 27:46). He is the all-righteous Savior for unrighteous sinners like us (Isaiah 61:10). He is Wisdom for foolish sinners (Proverbs 8). Do you feel filthy? Christ is "holy, harmless, undefiled" (Hebrews 7:26). Are you tempted? Christ was "in all points tempted like as we are, yet without sin" (Hebrews 4:15). Christ is everything you need. He is strength for your weakness (1 Samuel 15:29), the praying High Priest to intercede for you as you battle prayerlessness (Romans 8:34), and the Shiloh who grants rest in your restlessness. He is the Prophet who teaches you everything you need to learn, the Priest who pays all your debts, and the King who rules over every detail of your life for good. There is no end to His all-sufficiency for your insufficiency.

"I am!" — what a comfort when Christ, though His Word, speaks to us, as it were: "I am light to your darkened intellect. I am purity for your depraved affections. I am pardon for your penitent heart. I am power for your enfeebled will. I am your best Friend when you feel friendless. I am the only Physician who can heal you when you are backsliding or spiritually diseased. I am your justification, sanctification, and full redemption." Jesus Christ is your "all, and in all" (Colossians 3:11).

In summary, the great name "I am" begins to unveil the unfathomable mystery of Christ's being and character. There is a depth in Christ, and His leading of us by His Spirit, that eternity alone can reveal. Like Asaph, we learn much about Christ's being and character in the sanctuary of God, which teaches us to cry out, "So foolish was I, and ignorant: I was as a beast before thee. Nevertheless I am continually with thee: thou hast holden me by my right hand. Thou shalt guide me with thy counsel, and afterward receive me to glory" (Psalm 73:22–24). There in glory we shall know our great "I am" far better and more richly than we have ever known Him on earth.

Do you rest upon Christ in His divine nature and do you marvel at His incomprehensible glory? Are you able to exercise your faith by meditating on His being both God and man? Do not content yourself with a superficial knowledge of our Lord. There are riches to be discovered here in His being the great "I am" — riches that will delight and sustain you throughout every moment of this life because He is an ever-present Savior in all the fullness of His love and power; and riches that will overwhelm you with His glorious being forever in eternity.

Christian Worship

From at least the days just prior to Christ's ascension into heaven, His disciples worshiped Him as the great "I am." He did not reject their worship, but on the contrary, accepted and confirmed it, declaring that "All power is given unto me in heaven and in earth" (Matthew 28:17–18). Nothing less was anticipated by the prophets: "All the ends of the world shall remember and turn unto the LORD: and all the kindreds of the nations shall worship before thee. For the kingdom is the LORD's: and he is the governor among the nations" (Psalm 22:27–28).

Since that time, Christians have been constrained to worship Jesus Christ and to serve Him as Lord. His is the name we call upon for salvation (Joel 2:32), the strong tower into which we may run and be safe (Proverbs 18:10), the one who received the title, "Lord," which is the name above all names (Philippians 2:9), and the name unto which we give all glory for His mercy and His truth's sake (Psalm 115:1).

Such worship and service would be idolatry on any other terms than those set before us by this saying of Jesus, "For it is written, Thou shalt worship the Lord thy God, and him only shalt thou serve" (Matthew 4:10). If there is no link or identity between Jesus and Jehovah, then we Christians are of all men most idolatrous!

Do you give Christ your heart in worship every day, and especially during Lord's Day services? To worship Him is to recognize that He is the One who meets all your needs and brings us true happiness. He is worthy of your adoration and worship. Tell Him, therefore, in public worship, as well as in private, that He is your highest love, your only Beloved without any competitors.

Christian Living

As the "I am," Christ is both our Sovereign Lord and the One who guides us now in His covenant faithfulness. Let's consider both of these comforts briefly.

First, He is our Sovereign Lord, the "I AM WHO I AM" (Exodus 3:14). Here too we see the practical implications of this name when the Lord says to Moses, "Thus shalt thou say unto the children of Israel, I AM hath sent me unto you." God grounds Moses' prophetic ministry upon the divine authority inherent in "I AM." This shows the irony of Pharaoh's statement, "Who is the LORD, that I should obey his voice?" (Exodus 5:2). God thus appeals to His name along with His redeeming work as the basis of His right to bind Israel with His moral law: "I am the LORD thy God, which have brought thee out of the land of Egypt, out of the house of bondage" (Exodus 20:2). Israel's confession, "The LORD our God is one LORD," is the foundation of the great commandment, "Thou shalt love the LORD thy God with all thine heart" (Deuteronomy 6:4–5). Therefore, Jesus can say to His disciples, "If ye love me, keep my commandments" (John 14:15). Who else could make such a statement? Only the One whose name is Jehovah, the great "I AM," could make such a claim. Thus, the name of the Lord is a name of supreme authority, and the Word of the Lord bears that authority.

Does His Word have this kind of authority in your life? Are you careful to study and learn His commandments, especially in their breadth, for His "commandment is exceeding broad" (Psalm 119:96)? In our day, too many appear to turn the glorious truth of justification, as in the phrase, "Jesus plus nothing is everything," into a kind of practical antinomianism. Their emphasis on justification leads them to give too little attention to sanctification and the honoring of Christ through careful keeping of His commandments. To be sure, a settled conviction of your justification by faith alone in Christ alone is foundational for all obedience, but are you pursuing the holiness without which no one will see God (Hebrews 12:14) because of the grace of free justification that you have received?

Furthermore, do you strive to obey Christ solely because of His mercy to you? If you understand what has been said about Christ being Jehovah, the sovereign Lord, then you must also motivate yourself to lovingly serve Him because of His great authority over you. To neglect His authority as Lord by emphasizing His mercy as Savior is to dishonor Him. It is also a form of antinomianism, since it neglects the authority of His law as a ground for obedience.

Second, the name Jehovah also reflects Christ's covenantal faithfulness: "I will be with thee" (Exodus 3:12). Although God's name, "I AM," signifies the transcendent glory of His being, it also indicates He is close to His people in order to keep the promises of His covenant. The Most High is not a God who is far away, but near at hand to do what He said He would do in salvation and judgment. That our Lord Jesus Christ is the great "I AM" teaches us that the incarnation was not the beginning of His involvement with mankind as our Mediator and Savior, but was the culmination of His many "goings forth have been from of old" (Micah 5:2) for the salvation of His people.

So Paul, in his survey of the history of the Exodus and of the wilderness wanderings of the children of Israel, can say, "They drank of that spiritual Rock that followed them: and that Rock was Christ" (1 Corinthians 10:4). Hodge explains what Paul's words mean:

Not that Christ appeared under the form of a rock. ... Christ was the rock in the same sense that he is the vine [John 15:1]. He was the source of all the support which the Israelites enjoyed during their journey in the wilderness. This passage distinctly asserts not only the pre-existence of our Lord, but also that he was the Jehovah of the Old Testament. ... He is called, therefore, in the Old Testament, an angel, the angel of Jehovah, Jehovah, the Supreme Lord, the Mighty God, the Son of God — one whom God sent — one with him, therefore, as to substance, but a distinct person.[14]

We should read Paul's declaration in the light of the Song of Moses (Deuteronomy 32). Moses announces his purpose in writing this great hymn of praise: "I will publish the name of the LORD: ascribe ye strength unto our God. He is the Rock, his work is perfect" (Deuteronomy 32:3–4a). Paul simply draws a straight line from Jehovah, God of Israel, to Jesus of Nazareth, Savior and Lord. "He is the Rock!" The Song of Moses has become the Song of Moses and the Lamb (Revelation 15:3).

So when we read the account of creation in Genesis 1, we hear the voice of Christ speaking those mighty words that summon all things into being out of nothing. The Father's will stands behind all that is said and done. It is the Spirit's wisdom and power that produce the spectacular results, but it is the Son's voice that heralds and evokes them by His word of command.

Likewise, when we read the words of Jehovah summoning Abram to leave his native land to go in search of another country (Genesis 12:1–3), we hear the Son of God speaking in His office as the angel or messenger of Jehovah. And likewise, through the long record of Abram's journey to justifying faith (Genesis 15:6), and onward to the glorious day when Jehovah appears to him saying, "I will make my covenant between me and thee … and thy seed after thee" (Genesis 17:2, 7). Time and again the eternal Son of God appears on earth speaking words of truth, grace, and life, but also executing the judgments of God among the nations.

To be in covenant with Him and the Father and Holy Spirit is to belong to the Holy Trinity. It is to say, "I am my beloved's, and my beloved is mine" (Song 6:3). Because "I am my beloved's … his desire is toward me" (Song 7:10). As one who has savingly embraced the covenant by faith, you can comfort yourself in all your trials and troubles with the truth that God has chosen you for Himself: "For the LORD's portion is his people; Jacob is the lot of his inheritance" (Deuteronomy 32:9). If you are a sincere believer, you are his peculiar treasure, which is evidenced by your obedience to His voice and the keeping of His covenant (Exodus 19:5). Meditate often upon the value the Triune God has put on you. Of all the things He could desire in this universe that He made, you are what He wants. You are the portion He has chosen for Himself.

The fact that Christ has been faithful to His covenant and to His covenant people throughout the ages proves that He will be faithful to you now. Can you recount the many times when Christ has shown Himself faithful to you? The fact that Christ has been faithful to his covenant and covenant people throughout the ages proves that He will be faithful to you now and forever more. Can you recount the many times when Christ has delivered you from trouble? Sometimes doubts arise within us because of various trials we encounter. Are you prepared to counter these doubts by recounting His many deliverances? Keep a record of the ways God has brought you through difficulties in the past. There is wisdom in the children's song, "Count your blessings, name them one by one." Memory is treacherous; write them down and refer to them often, especially when doubts occur. And then, hear His voice: "Now therefore, if ye will obey my voice indeed, and keep my covenant, then ye shall be a peculiar treasure unto me above all people: for all the earth is mine" (Exodus 19:5).

Christian Witness
When people complain bitterly against God when terrible things happen in life, they often ask, "Where is God? What is God doing?" Usually they are criticizing God as if He were negligent and uncaring, or attempting to justify their atheism since calamities must prove that God does not exist. On the other hand, we have,

as true believers, the awesome privilege of proclaiming to everyone we meet that God is not far away or inactive. On the contrary, He has come to earth and has accomplished everything necessary to overcome the curse upon our world and us. He is redeeming a people for Himself and will turn everything to their good. Not only that, He will create a new heavens and a new earth in which there will be no sorrow, tears, calamities, disease, disasters, or death. We can tell people that they can see what God is truly like by looking to the great "I am" — the Lord Jesus Christ — as God in the flesh. He is the ultimate manifestation of the compassion of God. All who endure the miseries of this life are invited to come to our divine Christ to find forgiveness, healing, and eternal life.

There is an awesome wonder in the fact that God the Son puts aside His glory and assumes our humanity because He loves people and is determined to bring about their great deliverance from sin and sorrow. Likewise, we can declare to the world that God the Father loves us with an eternal love and is calling all men everywhere to cast aside their worthless idols, to turn from the sins that are destroying and will destroy them, and to enter into His infinite love. If they will respond to the love of the Father and come by faith in Christ through the power of the Holy Spirit, then they will enter into life and that more abundantly (John 10:10). "This is life eternal, that they might know thee the only true God, and Jesus Christ, whom thou hast sent" (John 17:3).

Our witness, therefore, includes, but also extends beyond, the salvation of individuals. It includes the restoration of all things. In our divine Christ, the Triune God is at work to bring an end to everything that has marred and corrupted His creation. The whole purpose of history has been to bring glory to the Father's Son: "All things were created by him, and for him" (Colossians 1:16). To be united to Him by faith is to understand the purpose of our very existence, to be part of the grand plan of creation, and to be part of something that is truly far bigger than ourselves.

Are you so full of love to and joy in the Savior that you regularly speak for the great "I am"? Are you so taken up with the wonders of a holy God who saves sinners from His own judgment that you find ways to tell others? This is your duty, but it is also your privilege. Love not only loves the Beloved, but it also loves to tell others about one's Beloved. You will doubtlessly speak of Christ in your own way, according to your own personality, but, if you find that you do not tell others of your Beloved, then you need to examine your heart and find whatever is a hindrance and obstacle to doing so, remove it, and be enamored with the Christ who loves you and gave His life for you.

Banish every fear to the winds and rejoice in your adorable Savior and Lord, the great "I am" of your salvation. Rejoice in the almighty power of your blessed Redeemer for greater is He that is in you than all who are against you (1 John 4:4). Rejoice in God's precious Son and His covenant faithfulness, and in all the precious promises of God, which are "in him yea, and in him Amen" (2 Corinthians 1:20).

Let me address pastors, elders, and those preparing for the ministry with two verses from the Bible. They are statements describing situations in which pastors and teachers have failed to witness fully to the redeeming work of Christ. The first comes to us from Jeremiah 12:10: "Many pastors have destroyed my vineyard, they have trodden my portion under foot, they have made my pleasant portion a desolate wilderness." The second was spoken by the prophet Hosea: "My people are destroyed for lack of knowledge" (Hosea 4:6). The rest of verse 6 comes with a dire warning: "because thou hast rejected knowledge, I will also reject thee, that thou shalt be no priest to me: seeing thou hast forgotten the law of thy God, I will also forget thy children."

Your responsibility to see that the whole counsel of God is proclaimed from your pulpits and taught in your classrooms is tremendous. The apostle Paul, when departing from the Ephesian elders for the last time, exhorted them in this regard by his own example:

> And now, behold, I know that ye all, among whom I have gone preaching the kingdom of God, shall see my face no more. Wherefore I take you to record this day, that I am pure from the blood of all men. For I have not shunned to declare unto you all the counsel of God. Take heed therefore unto yourselves, and to all the flock, over the which the Holy Ghost hath made you overseers, to feed the church of God, which he hath purchased with his own blood (Acts 20:25–28).

In like manner he exhorted his protégé, Timothy,

> Preach the word; be instant in season, out of season; reprove, rebuke, exhort with all long suffering and doctrine. For the time will come when they will not endure sound doctrine; but after their own lusts shall they heap to themselves teachers, having itching ears (2 Timothy 4:2–3).

You have this glorious gospel of Christ, our divine Savior and Lord, to proclaim. Do it faithfully as unto the Lord. Too many today play the part of hirelings, who are more interested in their own reputations and prosperity than in being faithful shepherds. Do not be afraid of the opposition that will inevitably come. Take to heart what Paul went on to say to Timothy,

> Notwithstanding the Lord stood with me, and strengthened me; that by me the preaching might be fully known, and that all the Gentiles might hear: and I was delivered out of the mouth of the lion. And the Lord shall deliver me from every evil work, and will preserve me unto his heavenly kingdom: to whom be glory for ever and ever. Amen (2 Timothy 4:17–18).

You can be sure that if you are faithful to Christ, He will be faithful to you, and at the last day you will hear those wonderful words, "Well done, thou good and faithful servant; thou hast been faithful over a few things, I will make thee ruler over many things: enter thou into the joy of thy lord" (Matthew 25:21, 23).

To those who sit under the ministry of the Word week by week: do all in your power and position to encourage your pastors and elders in their work. Let them know what kind of fruit their efforts are having in your life so that they know that their witness is not in vain.

In conclusion then, we must see in Jesus of Nazareth the great "I am," the incarnation of the God of our salvation, the eternal and only begotten Son of God, begotten of the Father before all worlds, and sent of the Father into this world to save it and us. We must look to Christ alone, and call upon Him alone for our salvation. That is, for justification from the guilt of all sin, which includes a righteousness that will stand in the great Day of Judgment; for adoption as God's children by which we receive a right to all of the privileges of the sons of God; for the gift of new life, and for growth in holiness in our sanctification, while we live; and for our final transformation into Christ's likeness in our glorification. For He is our life; and even in our deaths, Christ is the anchor of our hope of glory. It glorifies the Father, and it pleases the Spirit, when we have eyes and hearts for none but Christ alone, and can sing from the heart:

> In sweet communion, Lord, with Thee I constantly abide;
> My hand Thou holdest in Thy own to keep me by Thy side.
> Thy counsel through my earthly way shall guide me and control,
> And then to glory afterward Thou wilt receive my soul.
> Whom have I, Lord, in heav'n but Thee, to whom my thoughts aspire?
> And, having Thee, on earth is naught that I can yet desire.[15]

3

Cur Deus Homo:
Why God Became Man

Why Was It Necessary that the Pre-Incarnate Son of God Become Incarnate?

G. K. Beale

Introduction[1]

"Why did the second person of the Trinity, the pre-incarnate Son of God, become a man?" We can discover readily from the New Testament why it was necessary that God become incarnate as a human. The beginning of Matthew's Gospel states straightforwardly, "And she will bear a Son; and you shall call His name Jesus, for it is He who will save His people from their sins" (Matthew 1:21).[2] The Gospels clearly lay out the mission of Jesus. Matthew 9:6 says, "the Son of Man on earth has authority to forgive sins" (so also Mark 2:10; Luke 5:24); Matthew 20:28 affirms:

"the Son of Man did not come to be served, but to serve, and to give His life a ransom for many" (so also Mark 10:45). Luke 19:10 says likewise, "For the Son of Man has come to seek and to save that which was lost." So, by these "Son of Man" statements, the New Testament is clear about why God became man.

The New Testament also refers to Jesus as the "Son of God," and, perhaps surprisingly to some, attributes a similar mission to the "Son of God" as we have seen under the title, "Son of Man," although not as explicitly. John 20:31 says, "but these have been written that you may believe that Jesus is the Christ, the Son of God; and that believing you may have life in His name." Galatians 2:20: "I have been crucified with Christ; and it is no longer I who live, but Christ lives in me; and the life which I now live in the flesh I live by faith in the Son of God, who loved me, and delivered Himself up for me." 1 John 3:8 says, "the one who practices sin is of the devil; for the devil has sinned from the beginning. The Son of God appeared for this purpose, that He might destroy the works of the devil." Similarly, 1 John 5:10–11 asserts: "The one who believes in the Son of God has the witness in himself; the one who does not believe God has made Him a liar, because he has not believed in the witness that God has borne concerning His Son. And the witness is this, that God has given us eternal life, and this life is in His Son." Just as Jesus, as the Son of Man, came to save his people from their sins, so he does as the Son of God.

According to these passages about Jesus' mission, it was necessary that the Son of God become incarnate as the Son of Man in order to forgive believing humanity's sin and to give humanity life, as well as to destroy the works of the devil. We must ask, "How does Jesus' title as 'Son of Man' relate to his title as 'Son of God?'" The fact that the above stated missions of Jesus as "Son of Man" and "Son of God" are related closely shows as well that these two titles are related closely. We can better understand the meaning of these titles by exploring their Old Testament background, especially as they relate to Adamic ideas in Scripture. The New Testament authors relied on and appealed to the Old Testament for their use of these titles. But what does the Old Testament affirm about the necessity of an end-time Son of God and Son of Man coming to forgive humanity's sin and to give them life? One important clue to this question is in Luke 3:38, where at the conclusion of Jesus' genealogy, Luke directs us to the Old Testament by saying that Jesus is ultimately related to "the son of Seth, the son of Adam, the son of God." Yet why does Luke connect Jesus as the "Son of God" to Adam as a "son of God"? After answering such questions, the rest of this chapter treats how the Old Testament helps us better understand the relationship of Jesus' titles "Son of Man" and "Son of God" and how they both relate to his incarnate mission. As we will see, these titles in the Old Testament are sometimes references to someone inheriting an Adamic position and obligation and promised blessings for obedience. Why?

The Old Testament Background of the "Son of Man"

First, let's look at the title, "Son of Man." This epithet alludes to the fact that Jesus is the "son of Adam," who was the first man. One of the clearest references to this fact is found in Psalm 8, where the title, "Son of Man," refers to an end-time ideal Adam, which 1 Corinthians 15:27, Ephesians 1:22, and Hebrews 2:6–9 apply to Jesus. Verses 4–8 of this Psalm state,

> What is man, that Thou dost take thought of him?
> And the son of man, that Thou dost care for him?
> Yet Thou hast made him a little lower than God,
> And dost crown him with glory and majesty!
> Thou dost make him to rule over the works of Thy hands;
> Thou hast put all things under his feet,
> All sheep and oxen,

And also the beasts of the field,
The birds of the heavens, and the fish of the sea,
Whatever passes through the paths of the seas.

This is one of the most explicit allusions to Genesis 1:26–28
found in the Old Testament. This is not a general statement
about fallen humanity's rule over the earth, but more likely is an
ideal eschatological reference to one who would finally rule in the
way Adam should have. This Psalm 8 passage is then reused and
applied to Jesus in the New Testament. This is why Jesus is called
the "last Adam" in 1 Corinthians 15:45 and "second Adam" in
1 Corinthians 15:47.

The most prominent Old Testament background for Jesus' use of
the title "Son of Man" is Daniel 7:13–14, which states:

> With the clouds of heaven one like a son of man was coming ... and
> to him was given dominion ... that all the peoples, nations, and men
> of every language[3] ... [will] serve him ... (his rule will replace that of
> the "beasts" from the sea).

Not only is this an allusion to one of the reiterations of Adam's
Genesis 1:28 commission (which we will see later), but it is likely
an allusion to the Adamic content of Psalm 8, since both Daniel
7:13–14 and Psalm 8 refer to (1) the "Son of Man," (2) as a ruler
over all creation, (3) and particularly over sea beasts, all of which
Psalm 8 draws from Genesis 1. If this is the case, then, the Adamic
associations of Daniel 7:13–14 are enhanced, since Psalm 8:5–8
is one of the clearest developments of Genesis 1:28 in the Old
Testament. Some even see a direct allusion to Genesis 1:26 and
28 (cf. 1:26, "rule ... over all the earth") in Daniel 7:14 ("to him
was given dominion" over "all the nations of the earth").[4] It is
evident in Daniel 7 that the "saints" of Israel share in the Son of
Man's rule, because he represents them as the Adamic King. The
main expression of this is Daniel 7:18, 22, and 27, which says that

Israel ruled in the same kingdom that the Son of Man rules over in 7:13–14. Accordingly, Israel shares in the identity of the kingly "Son of Man" in that as a king he represents them, so that they can even be called a "Son of Man." For example, Psalm 80:17 refers to the whole nation as the "Son of Man:" "Let your hand be upon the man [Israel] of your right hand, upon the son of man whom you made strong for yourself." In the context of the Psalm, this is speaking of the nation Israel. They are sons of Adam, who are destined to inherit the first Adam's dominion because they are represented by and share in the end-time kingly Son of Man's rule, i.e., the end-time Adam's rule.

When Jesus refers to himself as the "Son of Man" in the Gospels, he understands himself as the beginning fulfillment of the Daniel 7:13–14 prophecy that a coming "Son of Man" would rule over the earth.[5] There are three kinds of "son of man" sayings in the synoptic Gospels: (1) those that refer to aspects of Jesus' earthly, pre-passion ministry; (2) those that refer to Jesus' death; (3) those that refer to Jesus' future coming in glory. The clearest references to Jesus as the "Son of Man" of Daniel 7:13 relate to the third category, which includes quotations from Daniel 7:13 (Matthew 24:30; Mark 13:26; 14:62; Luke 21:27). However, it is likely better to see most of these references in category three as fulfilled not at the end of history, but in AD 70 at the destruction of Jerusalem, in which case the Son of Man's coming would be understood as an invisible coming in judgment using the Roman armies as his agent.[6] The reference in Matthew 25:31 to the "Son of Man" who will "come in his glory" and "sit on his glorious throne" is not a quotation, but it is an allusion to Daniel 7:13–14,[7] which is clearly applied to the end of the age at Christ's final coming. Thus, Jesus comes as the "Son of Man," dies as the "Son of Man," judges Israel in AD 70 as the "Son of Man," and consummates history as the "Son of Man."

Many scholars do not see Daniel 7 behind the "Son of Man" references in the synoptic Gospels, except where it is part of a quotation. However, scholars are increasingly recognizing that a number of the references outside of the quotations are indeed allusions to Daniel 7:13. These allusions typically have reference to the "Son of Man" who "comes," which would appear to be sufficient wording to recognize an allusion to the "son of man" who "comes" in Daniel 7:13, though other wording from Daniel 7:13–14 is sometimes found in combination with the "Son of Man."[8] Some of these allusions refer to Christ's post-ascension coming in the future (e.g., Mark 8:38).[9] Many of these allusions are found among various sayings about Jesus' earthly ministry.

The Adamic associations present in Daniel 7:13–14 show that Jesus' application to himself of the Son of Man idea in Daniel highlights Jesus' kingship as the last Adam. However, not only does the title, "Son of Man," have an Old Testament background, but so does the title, "Son of God."

Old Testament Background of "Son of God"

In Scripture, Adam is conceived of as a "son of God," though that exact phrase is not used in Genesis 1–3. In Genesis 1:26, God created Adam and his wife "in the likeness" and "according to the image" of God. Genesis 5:1–2 reiterates the language of 1:26 by referring to Adam as having been "created" in the "likeness of God." Verse 3 then applies this language to the notion of sonship:

> 1 This is the book of the generations of Adam. In the day when God created man, he made him *in the likeness of God.*

> 2 He created them male and female, and he blessed them and named them man in the day when they were created.

> 3 When Adam had lived one hundred and thirty years, he became

the father of a son *in his own likeness, according to his image*, and named him Seth.

In Genesis 5:3, Adam is described as having "become the father of a son in his own likeness, according to his image." This is virtually identical to the language of Genesis 1:26. The import of the wording in Genesis 5:3 is clearly that for Seth to be "in the likeness, according to the image" of Adam indicates that he was born from Adam, that he reflected Adam's nature, and that he was Adam's son. This is sonship language. The explicit sonship notion of this language in Genesis 5:3 should inform our understanding of the same wording in verses 1–2, which refer back to 1:26. If this is the case, then this language about being in God's image in Genesis 1:26 indicates that Adam was a son of God. The genealogy of Christ included in Luke 3 confirms that this is the case by noting that Adam was "the son of God."

The notion of divine sonship occurs again in Exodus, where, for the first time, God refers to Israel as his son: "Thus says the Lord, 'Israel is my son, my firstborn …' So I said to you, 'Let my son go that he may serve me" (Exodus 4:22–23). Elsewhere, Israel is said to be God's "son" (Hosea 11:1; Psalm 2:7;[10] Wisdom 18:13; Song 18:4) or "firstborn" (Deuteronomy 33:17; Jeremiah 31:9; Psalm 89:27;[11] Jubilees 2:20; 4 Ezra 6:58; Sirach 36:12 [17]; Song 18:4).[12]

Why was Israel called God's "son" or "firstborn"? Later Jewish literature said that "Adam was the world's firstborn" (Midr. Rab. Numbers 4:8).[13] We have seen that the concept of Adam being a son of God is deducible from the book of Genesis itself by comparing Genesis 1:26 with 5:1–3. The likely reason that Israel was called God's "son" or "firstborn" is that the mantel of Adam had been passed on to Noah and then to the patriarchs and to their "seed" via Israel. I will discuss below how the Old Testament frequently reiterates Adam's commission in Genesis 1:28 and applies it to Israel, as well as how this commission relates to Christ.

Thus, the commission given to Adam as God's son was passed on to Israel, so that Israel inherited the position of being God's son. This idea was even understood in early Jewish thought: Isaac gave Jacob the following blessings in Jubilees 22:13: "May the Most High God give thee all the blessings wherewith he has blessed me and wherewith he blessed Noah and Adam; may they rest on the sacred head of thy seed from generation to generation for ever."[14] This statement from an early Jewish commentary on the Old Testament provides a good reason for why Israel is repeatedly called God's "son" and "firstborn." We will see that this reflected the teaching of the Old Testament itself.

When one comes to the Gospels, Jesus is called repeatedly the "Son of God." This should likely be understood in light of the Old Testament and the Jewish understanding of Adam and of as Israel as God's son. It is a reference to Jesus being and doing what the first Adam and Israel should have been and done. He is not only a completely obedient human son; he is also a divine son. He obeyed God fully in a way that no mere human could.

As noted earlier, the last verse of Luke 3 is the tip of the iceberg for understanding 'son of God' in terms of Adam, where Jesus' genealogy is concluded with "Seth, the son of Adam, the son of God." This confirms further our analysis of Genesis 5:1–3, where we saw that Seth's being in the "likeness" and "image" of Adam reflected sonship language. It is important that Luke ends his third chapter with this reference, because the subsequent narrative in Luke 4 places Jesus the "Son of God" in the wilderness, being tempted with the same temptations that Adam and Israel experienced, yet succeeding where they failed.

The Further Connection of these Titles in the Old Testament

Both titles considered above refer to Adam in the Old Testament and, therefore, both of them refer to Jesus as the end-time Adam (1 Corinthians 15:45). Furthermore, both titles refer to Israel as being a kind of corporate or national Adam. Thus, not only is Jesus an end-time Adam, but he sums up end-time Israel in himself, fulfilling also the Adamic destiny of Israel.

In the light of the above discussion, it is evident that both titles "Son of God" and "Son of Man" sometimes refer to adopting an Adamic position and undergoing Adamic obligations, looking to promised blessings on obedience. In this regard, it is unlikely coincidental that "Son of Man" and "Son of God" appear to be used interchangeably in early Judaism as well as in the Gospels.[15]

In Daniel 7:13, the clause, "the Son of Man coming on clouds," indicates a divine being because everywhere else in the Old Testament where a figure comes on clouds the reference is to God. Perhaps this is why Daniel 7:13 in the Old Greek says that "the son of man ... came as the Ancient of Days," while the Aramaic canonical text says "the son of man ... came up to the Ancient of Days." This is the earliest example we have of the interpretation that the "Son of Man" referred not only to a human being, but to a divine being. "Son of God" would be a very appropriate title for the Old Greek version's view of the divine "Son of Man," whose father is the Ancient of Days. In fact, the heavenly being in the furnace in Daniel 3 was called one "like the son of the gods," which may have influenced the Old Greek rendering of Daniel 7:13. Other parts of early Judaism also understood the Daniel 7 "son of man" as the "son of God." A Qumran document, referred to as 4Q246 (also designated 4QpDanA), offers an interpretative paraphrase of Daniel 7, including verses 13–14, which interprets the "Son of Man" to be the "Son of God" and "the Son of the Most High." The following italicised text represents interpretative paraphrases of parts of Daniel 7.[16] The following is a part of that text:

4Q246 fii:7 [...] *he will be ruler over the land*

4Q246 fii:8 [...] *will be subject to him and all will obey* (= Daniel 7:14)

4Q246 fii:9 [him. Also his son] will be called The Great, and be designated by his name.

4Q246 fiii:1 *He will be called the Son of God, they will call him the son of the Most High* (= Daniel 7:13) But like the meteors ...

The crucial observation is that where Daniel 7:13 refers to "one like a son of man," this Qumran paraphrase has "the Son of God" and "the son of the Most High." Likewise, the late first century apocalypse, 4 Ezra, refers to the vision of "the form of a man" (4 Ezra 13:1–3), which likely refers to the Son of Man figure in Daniel 7:13. Then, in the following interpretative section of the vision, the "man" in view is called repeatedly "my [God's] Son" (4 Ezra 13:32, 37, 52).[7] Similarly, later Judaism interprets Psalm 2:7 ("You are my Son") corporately by "the children of Israel" who "are declared to be sons" elsewhere in Scripture (Midr. Pss. 2.7). Two of the Scriptures adduced to support this are Exodus 4:22 ("Israel is my son, my firstborn") and Daniel 7:13 concerning the "Son of Man." These Jewish references, of course, are not canonical, but they are interpretative commentaries that well understand the Old Testament equation of the "Son of Man" with the "Son of God" in Daniel 7, which is discernible in Daniel itself.

The Gospels also interchange references to Jesus as the "Son of Man" with the "Son of God." The clearest illustrations of this are Mark 8:38 (9:7); 14:61–62; Matthew 16:13–17; John 1:49–51; 3:14–18; 5:25–27. Similarly, Revelation 1:13 portrays Jesus as appearing as "one like a son of man" and then verse 14 describes him with a description of the Ancient of Days from Daniel 7:9: "his head and his hair were white like wool." Then Revelation 2:18 draws from the initial vision of Jesus in 1:13–15, but now calls him the "Son of God." This title is thus equivalent to "Son of Man" in 1:13.

It is probable that the reason for equating these two titles is because of their virtually synonymous relationship in the Old Testament (which Judaism also reflected). Adam was a "son of God," and Israel, inheriting Adam's mantle, was thus a "son of God" and "son of man [Adam]." Likewise, the eschatological King of Israel prophesied in Daniel 7 would be both the "Son of Man" and the "Son of God," who would represent his people, Israel, so that they could be called a corporate "son of man" and "son of God."

These two titles for Jesus underscore his Adamic identity. However, we should remember that Daniel 7 presents the Son of Man as a divine figure as well. The further theological significance of this for Jesus' mission is, as Kim wrote, that,

> with "the 'Son of Man'", Jesus designated himself in reference to the heavenly figure who appeared to Daniel "like a son of man" … in a vision. Understanding the figure to be the inclusive representative of the ideal people of God, or the Son of God representing the sons of God, Jesus saw himself destined to realize the heavenly counsel revealed to Daniel in advance and create the eschatological people of God. So, as "the 'son of Man'" (= the representative of the ideal people of God), Jesus understood his mission … In short, with "the 'Son of Man'", Jesus intended discreetly to reveal himself as the Son of God who creates the new people of God (the children of God) at the eschaton, so that they may call God the creator "our Father" …[18]

The Relationship Between Adam's Commission in the Old Testament and Jesus' Mission in the New Testament

So far, we have seen that as "Son of Man" and "Son of God," Jesus is the last Adam who has come to rule the nations. His specific mission, as we saw at the beginning of this chapter, was to save his people from their sins, to give them life, and to destroy the devil's work through the first Adam. Where do we find this mission rooted in the Old Testament and connected to Adam's mission?

We must first examine the original commission to Adam in Genesis 1–3 to begin to answer this question. The commission of Genesis 1:26–28 involves the following elements, especially as summarized in 1:28:

1. "God blessed them;"

2. "be fruitful and multiply;"

3. "fill the earth;"

4. "subdue" the "earth;"

5. "rule over … all the earth" (so Genesis 1:26, and reiterated in 1:28).

Some commentators have noticed that Adam's role in Eden is part of the initial carrying out of the mandate given to him in Genesis 1:26–28. Just as God, after his initial work of creation, subdued the chaos (cf. Genesis 1:2), ruled over it, and further created and filled the earth with all kinds of animate life, so Adam and Eve, in their garden abode, were to reflect God's activities in Genesis 1 by fulfilling the commission to "subdue" and "rule over all the earth" as a king and to "be fruitful and multiply" (Genesis 1:26, 28).[19] Thus, the focus of the divine image in Adam in Genesis 1–2 is upon how Adam's activities copy God's, though there is the underlying assumption that Adam was created with attributes that were reflective of God's attributes. Adam was thus to "fill the earth" by "multiplying" image bearers who would reflect God's glory, so the goal was to fill the entire earth with divine glory. This includes rather than excludes noetic and ethical aspects of the image of God, as we will see below.

Adam's commission to "cultivate" (with connotations of

"serving") and to "guard" in Genesis 2:15 as a priest-king is probably part of the commission given in 1:26–28.[20] Hence, 2:15 continues the theme of subduing and filling the earth by humanity created in the divine image, which has been placed in the first temple.[21]

God created Adam to be an obedient servant in maintaining both the physical and spiritual welfare of the garden, which included dutifully keeping evil influences from invading the arboreal sanctuary. In fact, the physical and spiritual dimensions of Adam's responsibilities in relation to the Genesis 1 commission are apparent from the recognition that Adam was like a primordial priest serving in a primeval temple. He was to be like Israel's later priests who both physically protected the temple and who were to be experts in the recollection, interpretation, and application of God's word in the Torah.[22] Accordingly, essential to Adam and Eve's raising of their children was spiritual instruction in God's word that the parents themselves were to remember and pass on.

In this respect, it is apparent that knowing and being obedient to God's word was crucial to carrying out the task of Genesis 1:26, 28 (and disobedience to it led to failure: cf. Genesis 2:16–17 and 3:3–4). Thus, knowing God's will as expressed in his word of command (Genesis 2:16–17) is part of the functional manner in which humanity was to reflect the divine image (Genesis 1:26, 28), which assumes that Adam was created with the rational and moral capacities to comprehend and carry out such a command. The first couple were to think God's thoughts after him, and teach their progeny God's word, so that they would learn to reflect the glory of God's image. Thus, Adam and his wife's "knowledge" of God also included remembering God's word addressed to Adam in Genesis 2:16–17, which Adam's wife failed to recall in Genesis 3:2–3. After God puts Adam into the Garden in Genesis 2:15 to serve him, he gives Adam a positive command, a negative command, and a warning to remember: Genesis 2:16–17 says, "From any tree of the garden you may eat freely; but from the tree of the knowledge [in LXX, it is the infinitive "knowing"] of good and evil you shall not eat, for in the day that you eat from it you shall surely die."

When confronted by the satanic serpent, Adam's wife responded to him by quoting Genesis 2:16–17, but she changed the wording in at least three places. It is possible that the changes were incidental and that they were a mere paraphrase that retained the meaning of God's words. It is more likely, however, that she either failed to remember God's word accurately, or that she intentionally altered them for her own purposes.[23] The telltale sign that at least one of these options was the case is that each change appears to have theological significance. First, she minimized their privileges by saying merely "we may eat," whereas God had said "you may eat freely;" second, Eve minimized the judgment by saying, "lest you die," whereas God said, "you shall surely die;" third, she maximized the prohibition by affirming, "you shall not ... touch it," for God had originally said only that they "shall not eat ... it." Lowering the guard of God's word let sin flood in, and they disobeyed God.

If Adam had faithfully obeyed the commission, the following escalated end-time, consummative blessings would have been bestowed on him and on his progeny: (1) his "subduing" of the Serpent would have given eternal security and rest from outside threats of satanic evil; (2) "filling the earth" by reflecting God's glory throughout the earth as an image bearer is a goal that would be reached, which presupposed Adam's producing and raising faithful children who would be faith image bearers; (3) Adam would have been able to partake of "the tree of life" and have received "eternal life" (Genesis 3:22), which is the positive antithesis to the judgment of "surely dying" because of disobedience in Genesis 2:17; (4) the earth would have also become incorruptible and everlasting; (5) if Adam were in God's image, then he should rest from his work, reflecting God, since God also had already rested from his work.[24] Just as God had achieved heavenly rest after overcoming creational chaos and constructing the beginning of his creational temple, so Adam presumably would achieve unending physical and spiritual rest after overcoming the opposition of the Serpent and the opposing temptation to sin; (6) Adam and Eve's "nakedness" at the end of Genesis 2 is meant to point to the need for clothing, the bestowal of which would have been part of their later escalated blessing and final kingly inheritance. They grasped for their reward in the wrong way and at the wrong time. They ineptly tried to provide clothing for themselves (Genesis 3:7), but true clothing was provided subsequently for them by God to signify their inaugurated restoration to fellowship with him in Genesis 3:21. This second set of clothing was not the full clothing originally designed for them but only symbolically represented their future consummate inheritance as kings of the earth. This second set of clothing symbolized a permanent inheritance that they would receive at some consummative point in the future, which would entail a greater glorious kingly investiture of clothing when they would completely fulfill the mandate to rule as kings over the earth.[25]

The first Adam would have experienced all these heightened conditions and irreversible blessings, if he had been faithful to the covenant obligations imposed upon him by God. Theologians have traditionally referred to this arrangement as a covenant of works.

As we know well, Adam failed to fulfill this commission. Therefore, God raised up other Adam-like figures to whom his kingly and priestly commission was passed on. We find that some changes in the commission occurred as a result of sin entering the world. Adam's descendants, like him, however, all fail and sin "in the likeness of Adam's offense" (Romans 5:14). Failure will continue until there arises a "last Adam," who will finally fulfill the commission of the first Adam on behalf of humanity. The reason that all of Adam's descendants fail is that they are all represented by him in his initial act of failure, so that when Adam "sinned" it meant that "all sinned" in him. Only a sinless human could come and undo the effects of Adam's sin and faithfully obey and represent all believing humanity in doing so.[26]

It can be helpful to see how Adam's commission was passed on to others in the Old Testament epoch in a way that purposely fell short and was never fulfilled:[27]

Genesis 1:28 "And God blessed them; and God said to them, '*Be fruitful and multiply, and fill the earth, and subdue it; and rule* over the fish of the sea and over the birds of the sky, and over every living thing that moves on the earth.'"

Genesis 9:1, 7 "And *God blessed Noah and his sons* ... '*Be fruitful and multiply, and fill the earth ... be fruitful and multiply; populate the earth abundantly and multiply in it.*'"

Genesis 12:2–3 "And I will make you a great nation, and *I will bless you*, and make your name great; and so be a *blessing*; and *I will bless those who bless you*, and the one who curses you I will curse. And in you *all the families of the earth* shall *be blessed.*"

Genesis 17:2, 6, 8 "And I will establish My covenant between Me and you, and *I will multiply you exceedingly* ... And *I will make you exceedingly fruitful* ... And I will give to you and to your descendants after you, the land of your sojournings, all the land of Canaan ..."

Genesis 22:17–18 "Indeed, *I will greatly bless you, and I will greatly multiply your seed* as the stars of the heavens, and as the sand which is on the seashore; and *your seed shall possess the gate of his [sg. pronoun] enemies*. And in your seed *all the nations of the earth shall be blessed*, because you have obeyed my voice."

Genesis 26:3 "Sojourn in this land and I will be with you

and *bless you*, for to you and to your descendants I will give all these lands, and I will establish the oath which I swore to your father Abraham."

Genesis 26:4 "And *I will multiply your descendants* as the stars of heaven, and will give your descendants all these lands; and by your descendants *all the nations of the earth shall be blessed ...*"

Genesis 26:24 "And the Lord appeared to him the same night and said, 'I am the God of your father Abraham; do not fear, for I am with you. *I will bless you, and multiply your descendants*, for the sake of my servant Abraham.'"

Genesis 28:3–4 "And may *God Almighty bless you and make you fruitful and multiply you*, that you may become a company of peoples. May He also give you the *blessing* of Abraham, to you and to your descendants with you; that *you may possess the land* of your sojournings, which God gave to Abraham."

Genesis 28:13–14 "I will give it [the land] to you and to your seed. *Your seed shall also be like the dust of the earth*, and you shall spread out to the west and to the east... and in you and in your seed shall *all the families of the earth be blessed.*"

Genesis 35:11–12 "God also said to him, 'I am God Almighty; *be fruitful and multiply*; a nation and a company of nations shall come from you, and *kings shall come forth from you*. And the land which I gave to Abraham and Isaac, I will give it to you, and I will give the land to your descendants after you.'"

This commission is repeated, particularly, to Abraham: (1) "I will greatly bless you, and (2) I will greatly multiply your seed ... and your seed shall possess the gate of their enemies [= 'subdue and rule']. And in your seed all the nations of the earth shall be blessed ..." (Genesis 22:17–18).[28] God placed Adam in a garden, and he promised Abraham a fertile land. God expresses the universal scope of this commission by underscoring that the goal is to "bless" "all the nations of the earth."[29] It is natural, therefore, that in the initial statement of the commission that God gave him in Genesis 12:1–3 that God commanded Abram, "Go forth from your country … and so be a blessing … and in you all the families of the earth shall be blessed." Gordon Wenham observes in this respect that "the promises to Abraham renew the vision for humanity set out in Genesis 1 and 2," so that "he, like Noah before him, is a second Adam figure"[30] or a "new Adam."[31] The commission is reapplied to Isaac and to Jacob as well. The difference between the commissions of Adam and Noah and that of the patriarchs is that, while the command of Adam's and Noah's commission continues, now a promise of a Seed is given, who will eventually fulfill the commission (see Galatians 3:16).

After the patriarchs were not able to fulfill the commission, it passed on to Israel, who fulfilled it in part, but failed to do so ultimately. Consider the following passages of Scripture:

Genesis 47:27 "Now Israel lived in the land of Egypt, in Goshen, and they acquired property in it and *were fruitful and became very numerous.*"

Genesis 48:3–4 "God… *blessed me,* and He said to me, 'Behold, *I will make you fruitful and numerous,* and I will make you a company of peoples, and will give this land to your descendants after you for an everlasting *possession.*'"

Exodus 1:7 "But the sons of Israel *were fruitful and increased* greatly, and *multiplied,* and became exceedingly mighty, so that *the land was filled* with them."

Exodus 1:12 "The more *they multiplied* …the more *they spread out.*"

Exodus 1:20 "The people *multiplied,* and became very mighty."

Numbers 23:10–11 "Who *can count the dust* of Jacob, *or number* the fourth part of Israel? ... Then Balak said to Balaam ... behold, you have actually *blessed them!*"

After the events surrounding Israel's rebellious attitude in Egypt and, particularly, their apostasy with the Golden Calf, it became clear that the promise was not consummated in Israel, since they did not obey the commission fully. Moses prays that, nevertheless, God would fulfill the promise (Exodus 32:13). The promise that the nation, as a corporate Adam, would fulfill the commission at some point in the future was reiterated again, just as it was to the patriarchs in Genesis:

Leviticus 26:9 "I will turn toward you and *make you fruitful and multiply you*, and I will confirm my covenant with you."

Deuteronomy 7:13 "He will love you and *bless you and multiply you; he will also bless the fruit of your womb* ... in the land which he swore to your forefathers to give you" (cf. also Deuteronomy 6:3; 8:1).

Deuteronomy 15:4, 6 "*The Lord will surely bless you* in the land which the Lord your God is giving you as an inheritance *to possess* ... *For the Lord your God shall bless you* as he has promised you ... and *you will rule over* many nations ..."

Deuteronomy 28:11–12 (LXX) "And the Lord your God *will multiply you* with respect to good things concerning *the offspring* of your womb ... *to bless* all the works of your hands ... and *you will rule over* many nations ..."

Deuteronomy 30:16 "In that I command you today to love the Lord your God, to walk in his ways and to keep his commandments and his statutes and his judgments, that *you may live and multiply*, and that the Lord your *God may bless you* in the land where you are entering *to possess it*" (cf. 30:5).

2 Samuel 7:29 (LXX) "And now *rule and bless* the house of your

servant ... and now from your *blessing* the house of your servant *will be blessed forever*."

Despite the promise of future blessing, at various points throughout the succeeding history of Israel the language of the commission detailed in Genesis 1:28 was again reapplied to individual Israelites, or the nation as a whole, in order to indicate its initial fulfillment in some measure:

1 Chronicles 4:10 "Now Jabez called on the God of Israel, saying, 'Oh that you would *bless me indeed, and enlarge* my border, and that your hand might be with me, and that you would keep me from harm that it may not pain me!' And God granted him what he requested."

1 Chronicles 17:9–11, 27 "And I ... will plant them [Israel] ... And *I will subdue* all your enemies (LXX adds here, '*I will cause you to increase*') ... and I will establish his *kingdom*;" but then note verse 27, affirming initial realization: "And now it has pleased you to *bless* the house of your servant, that it may continue forever before you; for you, O Lord, have *blessed, and it is blessed forever*."

Psalm 107:37–38 "And sow fields and plant vineyards, and gather a fruitful harvest. Also *He blesses them and they multiply greatly*, and he does not let their cattle decrease."

Isaiah 51:2–3 "Then I *blessed him* [Abraham] and *multiplied him* ... her [Israel's] wilderness he will make like Eden, and her desert like the garden of the Lord" (note that the concluding wording is a promise for the future, which is repeated below).

However, sinful events occurred that made it clear that the king and the nation only partly accomplished this commission. Ultimately, they failed in attempting to do what Adam and their forefathers had failed to do as well. Therefore, the promise that eschatological Israel and her end-time King will finally succeed in fully accomplishing the Adamic commission was reiterated later:

Psalm 8:5–8 "Yet you have made him a little lower than God, and you do *crown him with glory and majesty! You do make him to rule over the works of your hands; you have put all things under his feet,* all sheep and oxen, and also *the beasts of the field, the birds of the heavens, and the fish of the sea,* whatever passes through the paths of the sea."

Psalm 72:8, 17, 19 "May he [the end-time king] also *rule* from sea to sea, and from the river to the ends of the earth ... And let men *bless* themselves by him; *let all nations call him blessed* (allusion possibly to Genesis 12:2–3, 28:14, and above all to 22:18) ... And *may all the earth be filled* with his [God's] glory."

Isaiah 51:2–3 "Then *I blessed him* [Abraham] and *multiplied him* ... her [Israel's] wilderness he will make like Eden, and her desert like the garden of the Lord."

Isaiah 54:1–3 "... the sons of the desolate one will be more numerous ... Enlarge the place of your tent; stretch out the curtains of your dwellings ... Lengthen your cords, and strengthen your pegs. *For you will spread abroad to the right and to the left.* And *your seed will possess the nations*" (allusion to Genesis 28:4, 13–14).

Jeremiah 3:16, 18 "And it shall be in those days when you are *multiplied and increased* in the land... the land that I gave your forefathers as an inheritance."

Jeremiah 23:3 "Then I myself shall gather the remnant of my flock out of all the countries where I have driven them and shall bring them back to their pasture; and *they will be fruitful and multiply*" (cf. 29:6; 30:19; 33:22).

Ezekiel 36:9–12 "You [the promised land] shall be cultivated and sown. And *I will multiply men on you* [the land] ... And *I will multiply on you* [the land] man [Israel] and beast; and *they will increase and be fruitful* ... and *possess you* ..." (cf. 36:27).

Daniel 7:13–14 "With the clouds of heaven one like a son of man was coming ... and to him was given *dominion* ... that *all the* peoples, *nations*, and men of every language[32] ... [will] serve him ..." (his rule will replace that of the "beasts").

Hosea 1:10 "Yet the number of the sons of *Israel will be like the sand of the sea, which cannot be measured or numbered* [allusion to the Abrahamic promise] ... 'You are the sons of the living God.'"

The Significance of the Repetition of Genesis 1:28 in Scripture[33]

We can speak of Genesis 1:28 as the first "Great Commission" that was repeatedly applied to humanity and especially to the patriarchs, Israel and her descendants. This commission was to bless the earth. Part of its essence included God's salvific presence. Before the "Fall," God commanded Adam and Eve to produce progeny who would fill the earth with God's glory, reflected through their bearing of the image of God. After the "Fall," a remnant, created by God in his restored image, were to go out and spread God's glorious presence among the rest of darkened humanity. This "witness" was to continue until the entire world would be filled with divine glory. Thus, Israel's "witness" was reflective of her role as a corporate Adam, which highlights the notion of missions in the Old Testament.[34]

Without exception, the reapplications of this Adamic commission throughout Scripture are stated positively in terms of what Noah, the patriarchs, Israel, eschatological Israel, or her King should do or were prophesied to do. Always the reapplication is that of actual conquering of the land, increasing and multiplying population, and filling the promised land and the earth with people who will reflect God's glory. While texts like Isaiah 53, Daniel 9, and Zechariah 12 (and a handful of typological Davidic texts like Psalm 22) prophesy the Messiah's death is crucial to achieving Israel's restoration, they are never directly associated with the repetitions of the Adamic commission. Never is there a hint that this commission is to be carried out by what we might call a negative act, that is, by death. Therefore, the Adamic expectations and promises of obedience for Israel's patriarchs, the nation, and her king are always stated in positive terms of what they were to do or were promised to do.

As we observed at the beginning, the upshot of this is that that aspect of Jesus' mission of dying for sin is certainly a fulfillment of Old Testament prophecy. However, that aspect of his mission in giving righteousness leading to "life" for his people is especially expressed by Adam's original commission, and its repetition throughout the Old Testament, which in essence was faithfully to obey in order to receive eternal life for him and his progeny. We may say that Jesus as the unique representative last Adam faithfully obeyed where the first Adam was disobedient, thus causing his progeny to be declared to be imputed with this righteousness and the life he inherited in his resurrection. This is exegetically apparent through observing that Christ is said to have inherited the reward and promise of the first Adam's eternal irreversible rule because of his obedience, which was promised in Psalm 8:6: "you have placed all things under his feet," which is applied to the result of Christ's resurrection in 1 Corinthians 15:27 and Ephesians 1:22. Though many evangelicals, and some Reformed among this group, deny there is any biblical basis for the imputation of Christ's positive righteousness, once one understands Christ as accomplishing what the first Adam should have done, then there is a substantial basis for this doctrine. One cannot say that Jesus' righteousness only qualified him to be a perfect sacrifice for sin, since Genesis 1:28 and its reiterations entail an obedience

that is oriented toward inheriting the reward of eternal life, and
there is no connection with that obedience qualifying one as a
perfect sacrifice, though, of course, this was also true of Jesus, and
predicted in Isaiah 53. But Jesus went even further than the first
Adam was obligated to do — Jesus was faithful as a servant even
to death in order to pay the penalty for Adam's sin, as Philippians
2:6–8 affirms, where allusions to the Son of Man and Isaiah 53 are
probably combined.

   Thus, why was it necessary for the pre-incarnate Son of God and
Son of Man to become incarnate? It was to faithfully obey God
by dying for the penalty of sin and perfectly keeping the Adamic
commission, thus inheriting life. Consequently, he bestowed his
righteousness and life on those who believe in him. My attempt
in this chapter has been to try to provide a more robust Old
Testament basis for this mission of Jesus, which is not often
recognized.

4

Spotless Lamb of God

The Impeccability and Obedience of Christ

Richard D. Phillips

For if the sprinkling of defiled persons with the blood of goats and bulls and with the ashes of a heifer sanctifies for the purification of the flesh, how much more will the blood of Christ, who through the eternal Spirit offered himself without blemish to God, purify our conscience from dead works to serve the living God (Hebrews 9:13–14).

An image that is central to the message of Christianity is that of the blood of Jesus Christ. We sing of being "washed in the blood," or "saved by the blood of Jesus," and even exult in a "fountain filled with blood." To critics of Christianity this seems bizarre and primitive. Bishop John Shelby Spong, for instance, complains that this image of Jesus as crucified and shedding his blood for our sins is so pervasive "that one can hardly view Christianity apart from it."[1] He is right about that, but he therefore proposes that we need a new kind of reformation — not one that recovers the truths of the Bible, but one that jettisons the blood of Christ. "I would choose to loathe" he writes, "rather than to worship a deity who required the sacrifice of his son."[2]

People who share Spong's view will not think much of Hebrews 9:11–14, because if there is one passage in the Bible that exults in the blood of Jesus Christ it is this one. The blood of Jesus is the emblem of his sacrificial death for the sins of believers. Hebrews 9 shows why the crucifixion of Jesus Christ is not only necessary but also a source of great joy and power; it shows not a cruel and twisted heavenly Tyrant, but a God of love who makes the most costly provision so that we can draw near to him. For those aware of their great need to be forgiven their sins, the blood of Christ is something to sing about: "O precious is the flow that makes me white as snow; no other fount I know, nothing but the blood of Jesus."

As has been the case all through Hebrews, the writer is interested in a comparison between Christianity and old covenant Israel. He has shown the supremacy of Jesus to Moses, Christ's priesthood to Aaron's, the new covenant to the old covenant, and the heavenly tabernacle to the earthly tabernacle. All these comparisons are summed up in the phrase: "the good things that have come" (Hebrews 9:11) in Christ, as compared to the provisional and shadowy order of the earlier time.

Jesus Christ has brought in an entirely new order. Before was the time of shadows and types. But now that Christ has gone "through the greater and more perfect tent" (Hebrews 9:11) — that is, into the tabernacle of heaven as our high priest — all the good things of the promised new order have been inaugurated. Verses 1–10 symbolized this new situation by comparing it to the tabernacle, with the curtain removed so that the Holy of Holies was opened to the sight of the priests in the outer room. Our access to God and the sending of the Holy Spirit is at the heart of this new order. But what is the source of these staggering changes? Verse 12 answers: "[Jesus] entered once for all into the holy places, not by means of the blood of goats and calves but by means of his own blood, thus securing an eternal redemption." Three things about Christ's blood secure this redemption: its impeccability, its power, and finally, its purpose.

The Impeccability of Christ's Blood

The superiority of Christ's shed blood is seen by comparison with the blood shed under the old covenant: "The sprinkling of defiled persons with the blood of goats and bulls and with the ashes of a heifer sanctifies for the purification of the flesh" (Hebrews 9:13). "The blood of goats and bulls," is a general expression pointing to the whole Old Testament sacrificial system for dealing with sin. The last phrase, "the ashes of a heifer," refers to a ritual described in Numbers 19, in which the ashes of a red heifer were mixed with water for the purification of those rendered unclean by contact with a dead body. Sin and death were the things that defiled; these sacrifices dealt with the two great problems that separated man from God. The blood of bulls and goats succeeded in restoring the unclean to ceremonial cleanliness and therefore to the religious life of the nation. But there was a better blood to which they pointed, a blood that in its shedding would actually cleanse the whole man, and therefore restore people to real fellowship with the holy and ever-living God.

What we see here is called a "how much more" argument. The writer of Hebrews is showing the superiority of Christ's blood because it is able to do much more than the old sacrifices could do. Christ's blood is superior and truly purifying — able, as verse 12 says to "secure an eternal redemption" once and forever — because it is a better and impeccable sacrifice.

The old covenant required sacrificial animals to be without

spot or blemish, and we see in verse 14 that Jesus offered himself "without blemish to God." For symbolic purposes, Old Testament priests would select animals that possessed no outward defect. But these animals could never serve for a sacrifice that would actually deal with human sin. Instead, they were placeholders and signs pointing to the true and better sacrifice that would be offered in the impeccable nature of Jesus Christ.

The doctrine of Christ's impeccability shows the infinite superiority of Christ's blood in that his nature was not only sinless but beyond even the possibility of sin. W. G. T. Shedd notes:

> the holiness of the God-man is more than sinlessness. The last Adam differs from the first Adam, by reason of his impeccability. He was characterized not only by the *posse non peccare*, but by the *non posse peccare*. He was not only able to overcome temptation, but he was unable to be overcome by it.[3]

It is important for us to mine the full riches of Christ's sinless suitability to be sacrificed for us, since the writer of Hebrews bases Christ's ability to provide an eternal and spiritually-penetrating redemption to this unblemished nature. Yet the impeccability of Christ is denied in many quarters, so let us consider why we hold that Christ presented himself as our spotless lamb in a nature that was beyond the possibility of sin.

First, Christ's human nature was beyond the possibility of sin by virtue of the hypostatic union, by which the one person was possessed of two natures — one divine and one human — both of which communicated their properties to his person. Paul wrote of the incarnate Jesus: "in him the whole fullness of deity dwells bodily" (Colossians 2:9). As a result, the mutability of Christ's human nature was upheld by the immutable holiness of his divine nature. Herman Bavinck notes Jesus

> is the Son of God, the Logos, who was in beginning with the God

and himself God. He is one with the Father and always carries out his Father's will and work. For those who confess this of Christ, the possibility of him sinning and falling is unthinkable.[4]

Some would argue that if the incarnation involved a true humanity, then a real ability to sin and err must be involved. This same argument is used by liberal scholars to argue from the incarnational analogy against the inerrancy of Scripture. "To err is human," they say, so that a man-produced Bible cannot lack errors. What they fail to note is that the divine will and purpose is determinative in the production of Scripture, so that Psalm 19 can say of the Bible: "The law of the LORD is perfect, ... the testimony of the LORD is sure, ... the precepts of the LORD are right, ... the commandment of the LORD is pure" (Psalm 19:7–8). The same principle applies to the holiness of the incarnate Christ. To err and sin is integral to fallen humanity, but not to the eternal divine Son who took up human flesh in the Bethlehem manger.

Second, Christ's humanity was furnished and empowered by the fullness of the Holy Spirit. Isaiah 11:2–3 states: "the Spirit of the Lord shall rest upon him, the Spirit of wisdom and understanding, the Spirit of counsel and might, the Spirit of knowledge and the fear of the LORD. And his delight shall be in the fear of the LORD." Such a human nature, infused by the Holy Spirit, is beyond the possibility of sin. We should not underestimate the intimate relationship between the Holy Spirit and the human nature of Christ. The angel told Mary: "The Holy Spirit will come upon you, and the power of the Most High will overshadow you; therefore the child to be born will be called holy — the Son of God" (Luke 1:35). Then, in inaugurating Jesus' messianic ministry in his baptism, the Spirit of God descended like a dove to rest on him (Matthew 3:16). Indeed, the first words that Jesus spoke on taking up his ministry in the Nazareth synagogue were these: "The Spirit of the Lord is upon me, because he has anointed me" (Luke 4:18). Speaking of himself in John 3:31–34, Jesus said: "He who comes from above is above all. ... For he whom God has sent utters the words of God, for he gives the Spirit without measure." In Jesus, we not only have the eternal divine Son who has taken upon himself a perfect human nature, but that nature is then upheld throughout his earthly life by the fullness of the Holy Spirit. Such a person is not only sinless but impeccable: beyond the very possibility of sin. It is this nature that the writer of Hebrews considers in the offering of Jesus to be our sacrifice.

Another argument against Jesus' impeccability holds that unless he possessed the ability to sin then his victory over temptation had no meaning. Christ's temptations, therefore, must involve the triumph of his will over a real quandary with respect to sin. Otherwise, it is argued by no less than Charles Hodge, Hebrews 4:15 could not speak of Jesus' sympathy for us by his shared burden of temptation.

The problem with this argument is that not all temptation arises from a sinful human nature. James 1:14 says that in our case, "each person is tempted when he is lured and enticed by his own desire." But Jesus possesses no sinful inclinations or desires. There is no concupiscence in his nature. His temptations were rather assaults of the devil and the world against his humanity, and against these Jesus truly suffered. Bavinck notes that "although real temptation could not come to Jesus from within but only from without, he nevertheless possessed a human nature, which dreaded suffering and death."[5] Shedd adds that we would not say that "because an army cannot be conquered it cannot be attacked. ... [Likewise,] Jesus Christ was open to all forms of human temptation excepting those that spring out of lust, or corruption of nature."[6] Moreover, we should never suppose that our Lord's temptations were incidental because he was sinless. Rather, "the innocent temptations of Christ were made more stringent and powerful by reason of the steady resistance which he offered to them."[7] Far from saying that Jesus' impeccability preserved him from the fullness of temptation, it is rather that he alone experienced the fullness of temptation for the reason that he never yielded.

By virtue of his impeccable nature, Christ presented himself as our sacrifice in an infinitely spotless nature that was truly able to stand stead for all his people. Moreover, he came as one who offered perfect obedience to God the Father. Possessed of a perfectly holy nature, Jesus exercised his will in perfect conformity to the will of God. It is because we differ from him so greatly in this respect that we need a substitute and sacrifice: we "all have sinned and fall short of the glory of God" (Romans 3:23). Therefore Jesus came to fulfill the Law with his own perfect obedience. He stood unblemished before God, able and willing to bear our sin, for he was himself infinitely and immutably acceptable to God.

The greatest act of obedience rendered by Christ was his voluntary suffering and death for believers on the cross. When Jesus struggled in prayer in the Garden of Gethsemane, it was not because of inward sinful desires that had to be sanctified but rather the human dread of such awful torment. His obedience, expressing a holy will in perfect yieldedness to his Father, formed a part of the sacrifice that he offered for us. By willful, spiritual obedience, Jesus did what "the blood of goats and bulls" could never do: he "through the eternal Spirit offered himself without blemish to God, purify[ing] our conscience from dead works to serve the living God" (Hebrews 9:14). Hebrews 10:5–7 makes the point of how Christ's obedience makes his sacrifice so acceptable to the holy Father: "Sacrifices and offerings you have not desired," (referring to the Old Testament rites), "but a body have you prepared for me. ... I said, 'Behold, I have come to do your will, O God, as it is written of me in the scroll of the book.'"

Here, then, is the question: How could one man take the penalty for so many people? The answer is that Jesus was more than a mere man; he was the very Son of God, possessing a nature of infinite and impeccable holiness, expressed in an offering of perfect obedience. When we say that Jesus redeemed us with the coin of his own precious blood, we refer to a perfect human nature, joined to the person of the only begotten Son of God, offered up on our behalf in an act of efficacious obedience for our redemption:

> Not all the blood of beasts on Jewish altars slain,
> Could give the guilty conscience peace, or wash away the stain:
> But Christ, the heav'nly Lamb, takes all our sins away;
> A sacrifice of nobler name and richer blood than they.[8]

The Power of Christ's Blood

Hebrews 9:14 emphasizes that, as the blood of the Anointed One, Jesus offered his sacrifice "through the eternal Spirit." In other words, his sacrifice was offered up not merely bodily but in spirit. We should always remember that Christ's physical sufferings were nothing compared to the spiritual agony of his alienation from the Father as God's wrath poured down upon his soul. It was the spirit of Christ, not just the body of Christ, that drank up the penalty for sin; his infinite and divine spirit absorbed all the wrath of an infinitely holy God. Since his spirit is divine and is, as chapter 7:16 says, "indestructible," he survived and emerged to enter into heaven as our perfect high priest.

Because his was a spiritual sacrifice, Jesus' blood is applied to us spiritually, whereas the blood of animals could only be applied ritually to the flesh. The whole point of this passage is that Christ's blood applies to the heart, a spiritual sacrifice that is spiritually applied, actually restoring us to fellowship with God, who is spirit (John 4:24). Christ's blood was offered to "purify our conscience from dead works to serve the living God" (Hebrews 9:14).

This spiritual nature of Christ's death notes the writer's second main point about the superiority of Christ's blood. Not only was his the offering of an impeccable nature in perfect obedience, but the blood of Christ has power to cleanse the conscience.

We do not often think about our conscience as a serious problem when it comes to God. The problem is what he thinks about us, not what we think about ourselves. But even after God has accepted us in Christ, our unclean conscience can keep us far from God. Christ's intent as high priest is to bring us to God. Therefore, he not only reconciles God to us, but also cleanses our consciences so that we may enter into his service.

The conscience serves to tell us about ourselves. It communicates to us what we are. Charles Haddon Spurgeon, in his sermon on this text, pointed out three problems revealed by our conscience: a knowledge of past sinful acts; a knowledge of our sinful nature, with its thoughts and desires; and our ongoing contact with evil in this world. All of these conspire, unless cleansed, to keep us from serving the Lord. About the first of these, Spurgeon writes:

> Upon our consciences there rests, first of all, a sense of past sin. Even if a man wishes to serve God, yet until his conscience is purged, he feels a dread and terror of God, which prevent his doing so. He has sinned, and God is just, and therefore he is ill at ease… "God is angry with the wicked every day, if he turn not he will whet his sword; he hath bent his bow, and made it ready"; and the sinner, knowing this, asks, "How can I serve this terrible God?" He is alarmed when he thinks of the Judge of all the earth; for it is before that Judge that he will soon have to take his trial.[9]

Christ's blood, however, possesses power to cleanse this great fear from our hearts, this great condemnation from our consciences. His death preaches to us that the debt has been paid for all our sin; an infinite atonement has been made to relieve us of the burden of so great a guilt. This is what causes Christians to sing about the shedding of Christ's innocent blood, for in it we see our own guilt washed away.

There is no greater burden in this world than the guilt of our sin. Other burdens weary the feet or the back; this burden wearies the soul. People who abhor the idea of a blood-shedding God may write platitudes about the goodness of man. People may say that we are finding our destiny out of a Darwinian soup. Perhaps we are not yet what we might be, but we are certainly not guilty, they insist. But for the real man and woman in this world, such words will not wash. They will not wash away the knowledge of things we have done in a universe with moral reality over which stands a real and holy God.

If you come to recognize how your words have torn the hearts of others as knives tear the flesh; if you think for just a moment how your neglect of duty and selfish pursuit of gain has meant sorrow and woe for real people; if you merely ask how many men and women in this world have real cause to resent you and wish you had never crossed their paths, if you take stock of God's holy and unyielding Law and your incessant violation of it, then your conscience will speak against you about what you really are and deserve. You will crave a cleansing such as Christ alone can give.

How, then, can robes be washed in blood and come out white? The answer is that Christ's shed blood, representing the spiritual sacrifice of his perfect life upon the cross, is the cleansing agent provided by God for the stain of the guilt of our sin. For this reason, Christ's blood preaches forgiveness of sin: "Though your sins are like scarlet," it says, "they shall be as white as snow" (Isaiah 1:18).

What about the second problem of the conscience, the awareness of sinful desires and thoughts, the knowledge not merely of our sinful deeds but also of our sinful nature? This, too, is cleansed by the blood of the Lamb. We feel unclean and this keeps us from God. Like Isaiah, we see the seraphim praising God in his temple, singing, "Holy, holy, holy is the Lord of hosts." At such a sight we cry, "Woe is me! For I am lost; for I am a man of unclean lips!" (Isaiah 6:5). But Jesus, like the angel in Isaiah's vision, flies to grasp a coal from the altar on which his own blood was shed and presses it to our lips. "Behold," he says, "your guilt is taken away, and your sin is atoned for." Our conscience tells us what we must think of ourselves, but the blood of Christ tells us what God thinks of us in Christ. God sees his sinless, impeccable, obedient Son, standing stead for us, having offered his life as our sacrifice. What a message this sends to the troubled conscience! And Jesus stands with basin and towel in hand and says, "You are clean" (John 13:10). As our heavenly high priest, he sends his Holy Spirit to work within us, his blood having procured the resources of heaven for the cleansing of our hearts.

Finally, our conscience recoils as we walk through this world, brushing against all kinds of sin and evil, which bring defilement as contact with death did to the Israelites of old. Just as Israel's priests sprinkled the blood of bulls and goats upon the skin, we have in Christ a ready cleansing: "If we confess our sins," 1 John 1:9 tells us, "He is faithful and just to forgive us our sins and to cleanse us from all unrighteousness." We have cleansing through the blood of Jesus. His superior blood has power to do what no bull or goat could ever offer. As Isaac Watts writes:

> Jesus, my great High Priest,
> offered his blood and died;
> My guilty conscience seeks
> no sacrifice beside.
> His powerful blood did once atone,
> and now it pleads before the throne ...

Behold my soul at freedom set;
my Surety paid the dreadful debt.[10]

The Purpose of Christ's Blood

Finally, what is the purpose for this grace that is offered in the
blood of Christ? There are many reasons, of course: God's love and
Christ's glory head of the list. But one purpose is directly tied to
the high priestly office of our Lord and tabernacle setting in which
this passage fits: "How much more will the blood of Christ, who
through the eternal Spirit offered himself without blemish to God,
purify our conscience from dead works to serve the living God"
(Hebrews 9:14).

We are called into God's priestly service. As John wrote in his
great doxology, he "loves us and has freed us from our sins by his
blood and made us a kingdom, priests to his God and Father"
(Revelation 1:5–6). Peter wrote, "You are a chosen race, a royal
priesthood, a holy nation, a people for his own possession, that
you may proclaim the excellencies of him who called you out of
darkness into his marvelous light" (1 Peter 2:9). Again, it is what
we see pictured in the worship scenes of heaven, as Revelation
says of those who have washed their robes in the blood: "They
are before the throne of God, and serve him day and night in his
temple" (Revelation 7:15). This eternal service begins in the present
life which is our preparation for heaven and the beginning of that
for which we are destined in glory.

When we consider the wonderful work of grace that has brought
us salvation, the shedding of Christ's precious blood, we need to
ask, "What is this for?" The purpose is not simply our own benefit.
It is not merely that we should escape a deserved judgment, much
less that we should have a nice, quiet, affluent Christian existence.
The purpose is that the living God might have a fitting priesthood,

for the service and praise of his glorious Name. This cleansing in Christ's blood is not the end, but the means for the Christian.

The Greek word "to serve" (*latreuein*) has a specifically priestly connotation. It is the service of the priests in the tabernacle we are called to perform, not outwardly but spiritually. The priests entered into the holy place to light the lampstand and we too are to serve as light-bearers for all the world. They came and sent incense up before God's throne, and so, too, we are ministers of intercessory prayer with real access to the throne of God. Unlike the Old Testament priests, our service takes place with the veil torn asunder, with God's presence unhindered and our service readily accepted in Christ.

We were made and redeemed to serve God, and it is in the service of him that we discover our true freedom. Spurgeon says:

> To serve the living God is necessary to the happiness of a living man: for this end we were made, and we miss the design of our making if we do not honor our Maker. 'Man's chief end is to glorify God, and enjoy Him forever.' If we miss that end we are ourselves terrible losers. The service of God is the element in which alone we can fully live.[11]

Hebrews 9:14 speaks of our cleansing from "dead works." This is what this world is busy about, works that if not sinful are certainly pointless and dead from the perspective of eternity. Building empires that will fall, buying things that do not satisfy or last, serving ambitions that are destined for the grave. How crushing such a life is for those made in the image of God! Humanity was fashioned for God and his pleasure. To neglect God, to refuse his service, to deny his presence and rule is to shrink into the dust. It is to be ruled by the flesh, as beasts rather than as the men and women God made in his image. Is not this just what our secular, unbelieving society is discovering?

But not so the Christian. We are priests with a holy calling, a service of joy born of gratitude, for a God who loves us enough to have shed the precious blood of Christ. What we do for him will carry beyond the grave, lasting forever in heaven, where Christ reigns now as the priest upon the throne at the right hand of the living God.

Cleansed by the Blood

Of course, none of this is possible until we have first been cleansed by the blood of Jesus Christ — the precious blood of the impeccable Son of God that is superior to that of bulls and goats, that has power to cleanse the conscience, and that has the purpose of sanctifying us for God's own priestly service. Until then we may not serve the Lord, for he is a holy God and we must be kept as lepers outside the camp of Israel, as those defiled by death and unclean before his throne. What Joshua told Israel is also true for us, until we have turned to Christ's cleansing blood: "You are not able to serve the LORD. He is a holy God; he is a jealous God" (Joshua 24:19). But what a difference it makes to be cleansed by Jesus' blood! Hebrews says, "You are able to serve him!" Not because of deeds we have done to cover our sins or silver coins we have given to procure God's favor. But because of what God in his love has given for us: "the blood of Christ, who through the eternal Spirit offered himself without blemish to God, purify our conscience from dead works to serve the living God" (Hebrews 9:14).

5

Jesus the Obedient Son

The Life that Glorifies God (Matthew 4:1–11)

L. Michael Morales

THE OPENING QUESTION AND ANSWER OF THE *WESTMINSTER Shorter Catechism* teaches us that Man's chief end — that is, humanity's highest purpose and pursuit — is to glorify God, and to enjoy him forever. This is *Soli Deo Gloria* in its full sense, encompassing our justification, to be sure, but working through it into a life that is lived to the glory of God. Those who are saved, Paul writes in Ephesians 1:12, "should be to the praise of his glory." Based upon this and similar biblical passages, Sinclair Ferguson wrote that the essence of the Christian life is "living in such a way as to glorify God."[1] But just here the question comes: How does one live so as to glorify God? What is the sort of life that renders God glory? The Scriptures offer us a clear answer: namely, we render glory to God by obedience to his word. Indeed, "to obey is better than sacrifice" (1 Samuel 15:22).[2] The life that glorifies God, then, is none other than the life of obedience to his word. Such a life, it must be said, can only be lived in Christ by the power of the Holy Spirit. And this means that if we are going to learn how to glorify God in our lives, we need to be conformed by the Spirit to the one human life that has been lived fully to God's glory. We need to look to him, Christ Jesus, to see what a life that glorifies God looks like — to see what obedience to God looks like. The passage before us, the Testing of Christ in Matthew 4:1–11, offers a summary of Jesus' life of obedience.[3] Immeasurably beyond anything else accomplished in human history, this life — Jesus' self-denying span of days on earth — is what has brought God glory.

Christians often use 'SDG' (for *Soli Deo Gloria*) as a signature line, or attach SDG to works of accomplishment like musical compositions or published books. This is well and good. But may we also understand that trusting and submissive obedience, like Jesus' obedience, whether as a child to his parents or when finally he laid down his life in submission to God's will — this life of total obedience is of infinitely higher worth and esteem to God than any works of art, music, or literature we can accomplish for the sake of his Name. Eric Liddell understood this principle: he would not forsake his regular Sabbath-keeping for the sake of winning a race — his ordinary obedience to God's word rendered God more glory and pleasure than any gold medal won in his Name.

In the verse that comes right before our passage, Matthew 3:17, God the Father proclaimed that he was well pleased with Jesus. While some tend to relegate this statement to being a mere descriptor of Jesus' status as God's Son, the Father's expressed approval and praise was, rather, the outcome already of Jesus' thirty years of quiet, trusting obedience. Matthew 4 is set within a larger presentation of Jesus as analogous to Israel. Jesus functions as the true and faithful remnant of Israel; he represents Israel and so his life parallels the history of Israel. In Matthew 2, like Israel's Exodus, Jesus is brought out of Egypt by God; in Matthew 3, like Israel's crossing of the sea, Jesus is brought through the waters of baptism; and here in Matthew 4, like Israel's wilderness experience for forty years, Jesus is tested in the wilderness for forty days and nights. Jesus' obedience in the wilderness, then, is meant to be understood particularly by way of contrast to Israel's failure to do so. This means that we need to grasp the theology of Israel's wilderness experience in order to understand the profound significance of Jesus' own testing — and so we will begin with Israel in the wilderness.

Israel's Failure in the Wilderness

The wilderness period began as soon as Israel was delivered out of Egypt and crossed through the sea. Beginning in the middle of Exodus 15, after the LORD destroyed the Egyptian hosts in the sea, we find a series of stories relating Israel's failure to glorify God in the wilderness. These accounts are carefully crafted as progressive lessons — together they form a theology of Israel's failure in the wilderness. The first story, related in Exodus 15:22–27, lays the foundation for Israel's life in the wilderness. In this account, the people are thirsty and find only bitter waters; they complain to Moses. YHWH heals the water and then instructs Israel on how to live in the wilderness (vv. 25–26):

> ...There he [God] made a statute and an ordinance for them, and there he tested them, and said: 'If you diligently obey the voice of the LORD your God and do what is right in his sight, give ear to his commandments and keep all his statutes, I will put none of the diseases on you which I have brought on the Egyptians. For I am the LORD who heals you.

This instruction, again, is the foundation, the path set out before Israel. God has explained to Israel the paradigm, the key to glorifying the Lord God in the wilderness, which is also the path of enjoying God: obedience to his word. Israel's ensuing failure, then, is not merely a matter of grumbling in the midst of privation; rather, it is a particular failure to glorify God through obedience to his word. As we will see, Israel's failure in the wilderness may be traced in three steps.

Israel's First Step in Failing to Glorify God in the Wilderness: Disregard for God's Word

The next wilderness episode begins in Exodus 16, and it is an immediate application of yhwh's previous ordinance and lesson. The Israelites are hungry and the Lord tests them as to their adherence to his word. Exodus 16:4–5 recounts (emphasis added):

> Then the Lord said to Moses, 'Behold, I will rain bread from heaven for you. And the people shall go out and gather a certain quota every day, that I may test them, *whether they will walk in my law or not*. And it shall be on the sixth day that they shall prepare what they bring in, and it shall be twice as much as they gather daily.

The test of obedience to God's word, then, is twofold: only gather what you need for each day — trusting the Lord himself to provide on the next day; on the sixth day gather enough for the seventh — the Sabbath — day, trusting the Lord that, on this occasion, the extra bread gathered will not rot. In the midst of their hunger, God tests their hearts in relation to his word. He gives them specific instructions that will gauge their priorities: which does Israel value more, God's word or daily bread? Notice that the wilderness testing and Israel's failure is quite specific: the issue concerns their disposition to the word of God. God tests his people to uncover their hearts. As it turns out, Israel's appetite for food took priority over obedience to God's law in their lives: they went out on the seventh day to gather bread. The Lord says in verse 28: "How long do you refuse to keep my commandments and my laws?" The stories in Exodus 15 and 16 combine, then, to demonstrate that Israel, like Esau, valued physical sustenance over God's living and eternal word; momentary hunger took priority over God's eternal promises. Distrusting God himself, they did not believe his word. The first step in Israel's failure, then, is that they disregarded the word of God.

Israel's Second Step in Failing to Glorify God in the Wilderness: Testing the LORD

The second step along the path of Israel's failure in the wilderness is found in Exodus 17:1–7. Here, Israel turns the tables and, we are told, they test the LORD. Because they thirst, they contend against Moses, ready to stone him, and they call YHWH himself into question. The concluding statement in verse 7 declares that they tested the LORD, saying, "Is the LORD among us or not?" That is, "If the LORD doesn't intervene miraculously when we are thirsty, then he is not among us — he must not be our God." Israel assails God's being and character by the measuring rod of their own wellbeing — if we suffer thirst, then something must be amiss with God. Regrettably, we do this, too, so often in the midst of our trying circumstances, or, for example, when we hear about the horrific persecution of God's people — we question God's character. The Israelites want to force God's hand: "Prove yourself, God, by intervening miraculously on our behalf — and if you don't, if your people suffer then the LORD fails the test." The people act as if God is in the wilderness to serve Israel rather than the reverse: Israel is in the wilderness to serve God. And so, the narrative states twice that Israel 'tested the LORD' (vv. 2, 7), and then the place itself is named Massah, meaning "tested." Instead of waiting upon the LORD with quiet trust, the people stubbornly follow the dictates of their own hearts, and then they presume on God's faithfulness, testing him. There is a development, then, a digression from disregarding God's word to testing God's presence and provision — rather than obeying his will, they try to bend his will to their own.

Israel's Third Step in Failing to Glorify
God in the Wilderness: Idolatry

Upon the previous two steps, the path's trajectory is firm, so it hardly comes as a surprise that the third step of Israel's failure in the wilderness is full-blown apostasy: they commit idolatry in Exodus 32. Growing impatient, in a heinous act of self-will, they exchange the glory of God for an image made in the likeness of a beast — they bow down to a golden calf. In doing so, it should be noted, Israel abandons its status and calling as God's son; they forsake God himself. This, then, is the road to apostasy in the wilderness, in three steps: (1) disregarding God's word, leads to (2) testing God, which then leads to (3) abandoning God, apostasy and idolatry. This pattern repeats itself in the book of Numbers. Numbers 11–25 presents the testing of Israel in the wilderness after they set out from Mount Sinai, and this testing ends in Numbers 25 with the second generation committing the same sort of apostasy as the first generation: they commit idolatry with Baal of Peor.

Before returning to Matthew 4, we need to answer two questions to deepen our theology of the wilderness.

Why Test Israel in the Wilderness at all?

The first question is: Why test Israel in the wilderness at all? Presumably, if he had wanted, the LORD could have led Israel immediately into the land without any period of trials or privation in the wilderness. And he could have so provided food and water that his people would never have experienced hunger pains or thirst to begin with. So, what is the purpose of such testing in the wilderness? Clearly, in Deuteronomy 8:2 the LORD says he had tested Israel "in order to know what was in your heart," yet, even so, why in the wilderness — what was God's purpose for the wilderness experience? The basic answer is that the wilderness was Israel's training ground for public ministry in the land. Remember that Israel was created and redeemed for the sake of public ministry among the nations. Israel will be brought into the land to be a royal priesthood between God and the nations; Israel is called to be a servant of God and a light unto the nations. As Jesus put it in Matthew 5:16, Israel was called to let the nations "see your good works and (so) glorify your Father in heaven." Israel was called to live as an obedient son, bringing honor to God the Father among the nations. The wilderness serves as a secluded training ground for learning obedience. Somewhat similarly, parents train and discipline their children in the seclusion of the home, so that in public the children will bring honor to them and to God, rather than shame. Israel was called into being by God not merely to become another ethnic, political entity; no, Israel was brought forth out of Egypt for public ministry among the nations. Before setting Israel upon the pedestal of Zion, as a city on a hill, Israel needed to be trained, disciplined — as every beloved son is disciplined by his father — and that training was primarily in terms of glorifying God by obeying his word. The goal, the great end of Israel's existence, was *Soli Deo Gloria*. By covenant bond, YHWH's Name and reputation among the nations was linked to Israel's faith and obedience — Israel's love and loyalty. And this is why, when the first generation of Israelites rejected their calling, YHWH God destroyed them in the wilderness. Not only did Israel refuse to the enter the land of Canaan in Numbers 13–14, but they had determined to reverse the Exodus itself — "let us appoint a leader," they say, "and return to Egypt" (Numbers 14:4). When this happens, God makes a curious statement, a statement that can only be understood within the context of Israel's calling. In Numbers 14:21–24, we read these words from YHWH:

> Truly, as I live, all the earth shall be filled with the glory of the LORD — because all these men who have seen My glory and the signs which I did in Egypt and in the wilderness, and have put Me to the test now these ten times, and have not obeyed My voice, they certainly shall

not see the land of which I swore to their fathers, nor shall any of those who rejected Me see it. But My servant Caleb, because he has a different spirit in him and has followed Me fully, I will bring into the land where he went, and his descendants shall inherit it.

The agenda for Israel's public ministry was to fill all the earth with the glory of the LORD. Israel's failure in the wilderness, the failure to glorify God through obedience to his word, makes the prospect of their life in the land worse than pointless, because Israel would then bring shame and dishonor to God — and so that generation will not be allowed into the land for public ministry. But notice what sort of Israelite is allowed in the land; Caleb, who is described as God's servant and as one who follows YHWH obediently.

Deuteronomy follows the book of Numbers. The whole point of the book of Deuteronomy is to bring these lessons to bear upon the second generation of Israel. Deuteronomy is essentially comprised of Moses' pleading with Israel: "When the LORD brings you into the land, heed his word — his word is your life!" He pleads with Israel to live as an obedient son to YHWH, namely, to love the LORD your God with all your heart, soul, and strength (6:5), and this is how you will be a light of blessing to the nations. So that was the first question, why test Israel in the wilderness? The answer is because the wilderness was the secluded training ground for Israel's public ministry in the land.

Why do the Nations need Israel?

The second question is this: Why do the nations need Israel? Part of the answer is that the nations are the target of God's redemptive acts in history, and Israel was brought forth as God's means to that end. This question brings us back to the Tower of Babel episode in Genesis 11. There we read of how all the people of the earth had gathered together for a grand building project, to build a city with a ziggurat, whose summit would reach into the heavens.

Their deepest motivation and highest aspirations are summed up by their words, "Let us make a name for ourselves" (Genesis 11:4). "Name" refers here to reputation, fame, and glory. The whole drama of human history and God's redemption of the nations turns around this subject of glory. The heart of humanity is bent upon boasting in self, filled with the desire to publish and promote one's own name, to bring glory to oneself. Well, as the story continues, the LORD brings judgment upon these tower builders. Having confused their language, he divides them into separate nations and scatters them into the darkness and hopelessness of exile. The nations are separated from YHWH God, cut off from his covenants of promise; they are without God and without hope in this world. But God had called out Abram and created Israel to undo the curse, to bring blessing to all the families of the earth. He promised in Isaiah 2 that one day the Tower of Babel scattering would be reversed, and all the nations would be regathered together, streaming to God's holy Mount Zion — to the house built for YHWH's Name — for his reputation, his fame, and his glory. The nations would magnify the glory of YHWH and sing praise to his Name.

Within this context, Israel's calling is to bring blessing to the nations, to reclaim the nations for YHWH. Israel is to shine the light of the knowledge of God and his glory into the darkness of the nations' plight. Israel was to be a living catechism for the nations — that is their public, international calling. By observing Israel, the lost nations were to understand that man's chief end is to glorify God and enjoy him forever. And this reality is what makes Israel's utter failure so profoundly devastating — why create a separate nation if it's just going to leap headlong into the idolatry and sexual immorality and pollution of all the other nations — and, what's worse, Israel will actually heap shame upon God's holy name in the process. That was the verdict: "the name of God is blasphemed among the Gentiles because of you," wrote Paul in Romans 2:24;

and he was merely quoting the ancient verdict of the prophets before him (see Isaiah 52:5; Ezekiel 36:22).

Let us summarize our considerations so far. First, Israel's calling is to glorify God among the nations, by obeying his voice — like the exceptional Caleb, Israel is to follow YHWH closely. Secondly, the wilderness was Israel's training ground for the life that brings God glory, where Israel was to learn how to heed God's word faithfully. Thirdly, Israel failed to glorify God in digressive steps: Israel dismissed God's word for bread; then Israel tested the LORD; and then they abandoned the LORD God in idolatry. Finally, we have seen that Israel's election was part of God's agenda for bringing salvation to the nations.

Jesus' Testing in the Wilderness

Keeping the theology of the wilderness in mind, let us return to Jesus' testing in the wilderness (Matthew 4:1–11) and make several observations.

Jesus' Testing follows the Threefold Paradigm of Israel in the Wilderness

First, notice that Jesus' testing follows the threefold paradigm of Israel, replacing Israel's faithless disobedience each time with his own faithful obedience. In response to the first temptation, Jesus says (v. 4), "It is written, 'Man shall not live by bread alone, but by every word that proceeds from the mouth of God.'" Obeying God's will is more important than feeding one's body, which means there's simply no greater priority for God's people than to heed and obey his word. This point is underscored in all three responses inasmuch as every response of Jesus to temptation is a quotation from Scripture. Each response, more particularly, is a quotation from the book of Deuteronomy, Israel's charter for how to live the life that glorifies God. Rather than disregarding God's word as Israel of old did, Jesus clung to God's word as unto life. In the second testing, when tempted to force God's hand of deliverance for a presumptuous act, Jesus responds (v. 7), "It is written again, 'You shall not test the LORD your God.'" Deuteronomy 6:16, from which Jesus quotes, includes a direct reference to the Massah incident of Exodus 17. Jesus will not presume upon God, nor try to force his hand or bend his will. In the third temptation, when promised all the kingdoms of the world and their glory in exchange for idolatry, Jesus, full of holy indignation, cries out, "Away with you, Satan! For it is written, 'You shall worship the LORD your God, and him only you shall serve.'" This last temptation is not prefaced with the phrase 'If you are the Son of God,' because it would have amounted to forsaking Jesus' Sonship, abandoning his status and calling as God's beloved and obedient Son — precisely what Israel had done. Moreover, this temptation unveils Satan's deepest desire, to deflect glory from God onto himself. Because it is obedience that brings God glory, Satan's highest desire is to lead God's people in disobedience, and so to rob God of the glory due his Name. Here in the wilderness, he uses every possible means to deflect Jesus from obedience to God; horribly, he tries to drive a wedge between Jesus, the beloved Son, and God, his faithful Father. Yet the bond of love would not be severed. In this way, we find the threefold paradigm of Israel's failure here inverted: a refusal to disregard the word of God, a refusal to test the power of God, a refusal to exchange the glory of God. Where Israel had failed, Jesus the true Israelite and the obedient Son, denies himself for God's honor, rendering glory unto God the Father.

Jesus' Testing was a Prelude to his Public Ministry

The second observation to make, in keeping with wilderness theology, is that Jesus' testing in the wilderness is a prelude to his public ministry. In fact, Jesus' testing actually functions as a summary preview of the rest of Matthew's Gospel. Notice, for example, the geography of testing: it moves from the wilderness, to the holy city and temple, and finally to a high mountain. This is precisely the sequence of Jesus' ministry recounted in the rest of Matthew. Notice as well how the three tests involve a pattern: the first two tests question Jesus' identity as the Son of God, and the third is an offer of the kingdoms of the world, which is related to worship. The first section of Matthew ends in chapters 14–16 with Jesus feeding bread to God's people in the wilderness, after which Peter declares him to be the Son of God. Jesus proves he is the Son of God, not by feeding himself, but by feeding others in the wilderness. The second section ends at Jerusalem in chapters 26–27 and with an allusion to Psalm 91, which is the very Psalm Satan had quoted to him in the second temptation. In the Garden of Gethsemane, Jesus refused to call upon the Father to deliver him with more than twelve legions of angels. Then as he hangs tortured on the cross, Jesus hears the devil's echo amidst the taunts of the crowd: "If you are the Son of God, then come down from the cross — save yourself" (27:40). Yet upon his death, the centurion declares him to be the Son of God. Jesus proves he is the Son of God not by angelic deliverance, but by suffering and dying for God's people — and for God's glory. The third section of Matthew then ends on a mountain in chapter 28 with Jesus himself — who is of one substance with the Father — being worshiped, and declaring that the nations have been granted to him by God (vv. 17–20). In the third temptation, Jesus had refused all the kingdoms of the world and their glory, for he was not seeking their pomp and boasted glory — he is seeking the glory of God. Far from committing idolatry to gain the nations, Jesus' aim is for the nations themselves to worship God the Father, yielding him glory. Upon his resurrection, Jesus the obedient Son is given all authority in heaven and on earth, and he commissions the apostles to go forth and to disciple those nations into obedience — through their obedience, the nations will render God glory. Having redeemed the nations with his own blood, Jesus will now train them to glorify God with his own Spirit.

Cleary, then, Jesus' wilderness testing was both the training ground for and a summary of his public ministry. Jesus' faith and obedience were proved in the wilderness. He demonstrated his willingness to deny himself for the Father's sake; he demonstrated his utter faithfulness to God; he demonstrated the priority of obedience to God's word in his life, and so he brings Israel's calling to fruition — he reveals the knowledge of the glory of God to the nations.

Jesus' Obedience Glorifies God because it is a Loving Godward Obedience

A third observation to make is that Jesus' obedience glorifies God because it is a loving Godward obedience. Deuteronomy, once more the main backdrop of our text, establishes that true obedience is animated by Godward love. This is not merely outward conformity to a standard, nor is it comprised only of the horizontal refusal to give in to temptation. No, Deuteronomy describes obedience as Godward love, and this is what we find in Jesus' obedience. Have you ever noticed how every response Jesus gives to Satan amounts to a defense of his Father's honor? He does not just say, 'No' to Satan — rather, he zealously defends God's reputation. Man lives not by bread alone but by every word of God's mouth. That is, "I will not disregard what proceeds from God's mouth — that is what is precious to me, God is my life." He does not simply refuse to leap from the pinnacle; he declares, "You shall not test the LORD your God" — that is what would have made leaping from the temple so heinous. In effect he says, "God is my loving and Holy Father — I will not put him to the test; I will not question God's goodness; I will not force God's hand." Then, of course, his refusal to bow down to Satan is a zealous guarding of the exclusive devotion owed to God alone: "Away with you, Satan! It is written, 'You shall worship the LORD your God and him only [him only!] you shall serve.'" Each of Jesus' refusals centers upon true adoration and obedience to God the Father.

Now consider that the Son's love of the Father is eternal, his seeking the Father's honor springs from an eternal, ever-flowing wellspring. Imagine how the annals of human history must have grieved the Son — not one single human life ever lived utterly to God's glory! From Adam's downward plunge and onward, even the highlights of humanity's saints had all their works tinged with human pride and self-will. Think of David, one of the Old Testament's central figures, a man whose heart was after God's own heart, and yet consider how he dishonored God's favor upon him, committing adultery and then murder. Even as God's people, our disobedience really does dishonor and displease God. Remember all the daily sins of all humanity, committed in thought, word, and deed, every sin a slander against the honor and reputation of God. We know what it is like when someone slanders or mistreats a person we love. Imagine, for example, a mother spending time with her son and his family, only to discover that her son's wife doesn't value and care about her husband. We can understand the grief that would cause a mother. Perhaps she overhears a conversation where her son tells his wife how he needs to set out early in the morning on important business, and her daughter-in-law responds by saying, "Fix your own breakfast then, and don't wake me up." You and I know precisely what this mother will do the next morning, don't we? Her son will arise to discover that she, his mother, had woken up much earlier and, out of both love and sorrow, she had prepared him a grand feast. She will do for her son what her daughter-in-law would not do for her husband. Even as sinful humans, we understand this. But, now, think of the Son's care for his Father's honor throughout human history. No one righteous, no not one (Romans 3:10; Psalm 14:1; 53:1; 143:2) — how humanity had blasphemed the Name of the Son's dear Father! We can almost picture the Son's grieved heart, zealous over his Father's glory, and how that desire itself would blossom forth into the Incarnation — "Here am I, send me! Prepare for me a body, I come to do your will, O God!" (cf. Isaiah 6:8; Hebrews 10:5, 7; Psalm 40:7). He comes not only to fulfill Israel's vocation, but humanity's creation — he becomes a human being to render glory to God on behalf of humanity. What we would not do for our Maker, he, out of an eternal love for his Father, took upon himself to do. This, this is the loving adoration with which he here renders trusting submission and comprehensive obedience to the Father. This is the Son's driving aim and motivation, which comes out in everything he says. When asked by the disciples for instruction in prayer (see Matthew 6:9–13), he sets before them the first petition: "Father, may your Name be hallowed" — which means, "May you receive the honor due your Name." The second and third petitions flesh out this desire: for God's kingdom to come by his will being done on earth, as it is in heaven. The Father's Name will be hallowed, honored, glorified, through the earth's obedience — it is for this that the Son yearns, for this that he prays, for this that he preaches and lives, and for this that he died.

As evident from Jesus' responses to the devil, Deuteronomy 6–8 is the main background to Matthew's Testing of Christ; and Deuteronomy 6:4–5 (the "Shema") is the heart, not only of Deuteronomy 6–8, but of the whole book of Deuteronomy. There is a rich history of Jewish interpretation that connects Israel's three tests to loving God with the heart, soul, and strength, respectively (see, for example, Targums Neofiti and Onkelos). So, loving God with an undivided heart meant choosing his word above bread. Secondly, loving God with one's whole soul meant you should be willing to lose your soul (which means "life" in Hebrew) for God; that is, you will not forsake God even if he determines to withhold protection from death. Thirdly, "strength" is understood as wealth and property. In Deuteronomy 6 and 8, Moses warns Israel, "When you enter the land and enjoy its riches, take heed you do not forget the LORD, and worship and serve other gods;"

rather you should love him with all your strength. Israel, then, had demonstrated little love for YHWH God; Israel had a divided heart, soul, and strength. By contrast, in the wilderness Jesus loved his Father fully. He loves God with all his heart, with all his soul, and with all his strength — as he does this, he loves, through his obedience.

The Cross is at the Center of Each of the Three Wilderness Tests

This leads us to our fourth and final observation, namely, that the cross is at the center of Christ's obedience (Philippians 2:8). This means that the cross is at the center of each of the three wilderness tests. After fasting forty days and nights, Jesus is hungry with a hunger unto death, but he is submitting to the Father's will. The first temptation is to distrust and reject God and to preserve himself — presumably, to avoid death by feeding himself. Similarly, the second test is not merely about leaping, but rather about calling for angelic deliverance, so that he would not dash his foot upon a stone. We have already noted that on the night of his betrayal Jesus refused his prerogative to claim angelic deliverance from death, and how on the cross of torment, as every pained molecule of his body aimed to submit to God's judgment, the temptation had resounded: "If you are God's Son, then come down from the cross and save yourself." And in the third test, Satan goes to the heart of Jesus' mission, namely, to reclaim the nations for God through the redemption of the cross. Here, the tempter says in effect, "I'll give you the nations now — take the glory without the suffering." In the wilderness, Jesus, out of love for his Father, offers up a threefold embrace of the cross. Already here in the wilderness, he embraces the instrument of his own death. Simply put, loving, Godward obedience requires self-mortification. Through the cross of death, the obedient Son was embracing the Father he so loved. This is why the cross is the act of obedience in human history, which, above all others, has brought and continues eternally to bring God glory. John Owen wrote that the cross "was the most glorious spectacle unto God," and that through the cross, Jesus "set a crown of glory on the head of the law," glorifying the holiness and justice of God so that "God was well pleased, satisfied, and reconciled unto sinners."[4] The heart, soul, and strength with which Jesus loved and lived fully unto God's glory and honor, that life of ever-hallowing his Name in obedience, he then laid upon the altar as a sweet-smelling fragrance. Mark Jones, in his book *Knowing Christ*, writes of a wondrous thought for contemplation: "The sweet aroma of Christ's death pleased and glorified God more than he was dishonored by the sins of all people everywhere."[5]

When the apostle Paul speaks of Jesus' obedience in Philippians 2, he says that Jesus was obedient unto death, even — even — the death of the cross! Fundamentally, the cross was an act of obedience from a son to his Father. Therefore, Paul goes on to say, "God has highly exalted him" — and even this exaltation, Paul states, is "to the glory of God the Father." Everything Jesus does and accomplishes is for this magnificent, breathtaking goal: to the glory of God the Father. And, this is because Jesus is the supremely obedient Son. The wilderness testing revealed, authenticated, and refined Jesus' heart so that he, empowered by the Spirit, might fulfill Israel's mission as God's servant, and so bring the gladness of salvation to the nations. After Jesus' period of testing, God, as a token of his approval and pleasure, sends angels to serve Jesus, a foretaste of the exaltation that would soon follow the obedient Son's completed work on earth.

Conclusion

It would be a mistake to think that the Son's eternal zeal for the Father's honor could ever be satisfied merely by his own singular incarnate thoughts, words, and deeds. This one human body at one definite period in human history, rendering glory unto God was not the end-all of the Son's desire. No, the Son's incarnation was but the beginning of fulfilling his desire to see the Father glorified. The Son's taking upon himself our humanity, as one individual human person who lived to God's glory, is to be but the drop that falls into a placid lake, sending ripple upon ripple to the extent of the entire body of water. The Son will not be satisfied until you and I live in full, loving submission to the Father, rendering unto him glory. Jesus, in other words, was an obedient Son in the wilderness not only as our substitute (and praise God he is that), but also as our forerunner and leader in the life that glorifies God. By the empowering Holy Spirit, Jesus obeyed God in the wilderness through faith. Relying on the power of the Holy Spirit, he trusted and obeyed God's word. Similarly God's people are called to live — in Christ, by the power of the Holy Spirit — self-denying lives in obedience to God. Indeed, the indwelling Holy Spirit is the Spirit of Christ, who conforms our lives to Christ and to his obedience. Uniting us to Christ, the Spirit takes Jesus' history, his obedient self-denial, and makes it ours, refashioning us after him — conforming our lives to his. But we must be convinced that mundane obedience to God's word on Monday morning, submission to God's will in our ordinary daily lives (in marriage, family, church, work and world), brings God glory above anything else we can accomplish from the world's perspective. Through his Spirit, Christ purposes to brand 'SDG' on our ordinary daily lives and callings — this is the sphere of obedience.

At the end of the Bible, in Revelation 21, we read that the kings of the earth will bring the glory and splendors of their nations into the New Jerusalem unto God. The nations, walking in the light of Christ, will stream into the city of God to glorify and honor him — his Name, his reputation, his fame. It was for that day, that Jesus had first refused the kingdoms of the world and their glory. It was for that day, he had embraced the cross of suffering. It was for that day, Matthew's Gospel ends with Jesus sending out the apostles into all the world, to disciple the nations, baptizing them into the Name of the Father, Son, and Holy Spirit, and teaching them to obey all he had commanded (Matthew 28:19–20). May God be pleased to speed that day, for Christ's sake and for God's glory (Revelation 22:20)!

For of him, and through him, and to him, are all things, to whom be glory forever and ever. Amen (Romans 11:36).

6

Christ's Resurrection

Ian Hamilton

JESUS' RESURRECTION FROM THE DEAD ON THE THIRD DAY belongs to the heart of God's salvation as much as his sin-atoning death on the cross. In his Letter to the Romans, Paul declares that God's saving righteousness belongs to those who, "believe in him who raised from the dead Jesus our Lord, who was delivered up for our trespasses and raised for our justification" (Romans 4:24–25). Our Savior himself understood the saving centrality of his resurrection and he expressed this when he said, "Because I live, you also will live" (John 14:19).

For the early church, Jesus' resurrection was not simply a supernatural fact to rejoice in and to proclaim; it stood at the very heart of the gospel. In 1 Corinthians 15, Paul dwelt at length on the centrality of Christ's resurrection to the Christian faith. He began the chapter by affirming that the resurrection belongs to those gospel truths that are of "first importance" (1 Corinthians

15:3–4). He proceeded to highlight the many witnesses who bore testimony to the fact of Jesus' bodily resurrection on the third day (1 Corinthians 15:5–8). He then affirmed that, "if Christ has not been raised, then our preaching is in vain and your faith is in vain" and "If in Christ we have hope in this life only, we are of all people most to be pitied" (1 Corinthians 15:14, 19). Christ's resurrection from the dead was not a doubtful or dubious fact; rather, it was an undeniable fact: "Christ has been raised from the dead" (1 Corinthians 15:20). The Scriptures had foretold it (1 Corinthians 15:4) and many eyewitnesses affirmed it (1 Corinthians 15:5–8).

Christ's Resurrection and the Trinity

However, the historical and undeniable fact of Jesus' resurrection is presented in the New Testament as the concerted act of the Holy Trinity. Jesus spoke of his power to lay down his life and to take it up again (John 2:19; 10:18). More often, the New Testament identifies the Father as the One who raised Jesus from the dead (e.g. Acts 2:24; Romans 8:11; 2 Corinthians 4:14). But no less is the Holy Spirit seen to be vitally active in Jesus' resurrection: he was "declared Son of God in power by his resurrection from the dead, according to the Spirit of Holiness" (Romans 1:4). The concerted engagement of the entire Trinity in Jesus' resurrection highlights, perhaps as nothing else does, the profound significance of the resurrection. Just as Jesus' death on the cross was the concerted act of the Trinity (see Hebrews 9:14), so no less did Jesus' bodily rising from the dead involve the agreement, will, and purpose of the Triune God.

This cardinal and salvific truth highlights a theological aphorism common among the early church Fathers: "*Opera ad extra trinitatis indivisa sunt*", which means, "the works external to the Trinity are indivisible;" that is, one divine person cannot act apart from the others, even though each person works appropriately to the eternal order of processions. Jesus' resurrection stands in the midst of history as a testimony to the concerted activity of the Trinity, the personal sinlessness of Jesus ("It was not possible that death should keep hold of him," Acts 2:24), and the secure salvation of everyone who has put their self-abandoning trust before God in the sin-atoning risen Lord Jesus Christ.

Christ's Resurrection and Theology

It is imperative, however, that we understand that the resurrection of Christ is not merely a powerful apologetic confirming who Jesus is. Too often the multi-witnessed bodily resurrection of Christ (1 Corinthians 15:1–9) is relegated to an "evidence" that "proves" who Jesus is and that highlights the saving significance of his death on Calvary's cross. No doubt there is evidential value in the undeniable fact of Jesus' resurrection. However, Richard Gaffin rightly maintains that the resurrection belongs to the "structure of redemption."[1] Far from simply being a powerful, even compelling, apologetic, Jesus' resurrection, along with his incarnation, perfect life of covenant obedience, and substitutionary penal atonement, belongs to the essential heart of the salvation that Jesus accomplished.

With this in mind, we will consider three pivotal passages in the New Testament that highlight the "structure of redemption" embedded in Jesus' resurrection.

Romans 1:4
Of all the statements in the New Testament regarding Jesus' resurrection, Paul's words here are the most immediately arresting. The first thing we need to consider is the Greek verb ὁρισθέντος ("*horisthentos*"). The ESV translates this word as, "declared." However, ὁρισθέντος rarely has this meaning or force in the New Testament. It would be more accurate to translate the Greek verb as, "appointed," or, "constituted." The resurrection "appointed"

Jesus the "Son of God in power." What is Paul saying? We can be sure that is not saying that Jesus only became the Son of God at his resurrection. This is clear from what we read in verse 3. The gospel of God concerns "his Son." The Son of God "predated" his incarnation. Later in Romans 8:32, we read, "[God the Father] did not spare his own Son but gave him up for us all." It was the Son, his own Son, that the Father delivered up for us on Calvary's cross; his pre-existent Son, the Son he loved from times eternal. It was this Son who was "appointed Son of God in power by his resurrection from the dead according to the Spirit of holiness." The key words are "in power." The contrast Paul is making in verses 3 and 4 is not between the Lord's divine and human natures, as might at first be supposed, but between the "two successive stages of the historical process of which the Son of God became the subject."[2] The same idea is found in 2 Corinthians 13:4: "he (Jesus) was crucified in weakness but raised (and is now living) by the power of God." The resurrection unveiled the Lord Jesus Christ as the all-powerful Son of God. In other words, the resurrection concerns Christ's human nature. No longer is that nature clothed in weakness; now the Son of God in our flesh is "appointed Son of God in power, according to the Spirit of holiness."

We now need to ask what Paul means by the explanatory clause, "according to the Spirit of holiness?" In verse 3, "according to the flesh," defines the phase that came to be through God's Son being born of the seed of David. So, in parallel, "according to the Spirit of holiness" characterizes the phase that came to be through the resurrection.[3] And what was that new phase? It is the new phase of mediatorial sovereignty and power. Murray captured Paul's thought well: "the lordship in which he was instated by the resurrection is one all-pervasively conditioned by pneumatic powers."[4] What Paul is contrasting is not a phase in which Jesus is not the Son of God and another in which he is. He is the Son of God both in his humiliation and in his exaltation, but in his humiliation his eternal Sonship was marked, even hidden, by weakness; in his risen exaltation, his Sonship is marked by "the Spirit of holiness."

In 2 Corinthians 3:17–18, Paul makes a statement that on first reading seems odd, but that gives clarity to the meaning of the idea that the Father raised Christ "according to the Spirit of holiness:" "Now the Lord is the Spirit ... For this comes from the Lord (Jesus) who is the Spirit." Paul is not confusing or blending in any way the persons of the Lord Jesus and of the Holy Spirit. He has been highlighting the comparative excellence of the new covenant over the old covenant (vv. 6–16). Through Christ, who is the risen, reigning Lord, the spiritual darkness that "veils" God's old covenant people and prevents them from seeing his truth concerning his Son, is "taken away" (v. 14). How is this veil taken away? In his earlier letter to the church in Corinth, Paul had answered that question (1 Corinthians 2:6–14). It is the special new covenant ministry of the Holy Spirit to bring glory to Christ (John 16:14). So when Paul writes, "the Lord is the Spirit," (v. 17) he is not confusing two divine persons; he is highlighting their new covenant functional unity. As with justification and sanctification, so with the cross and the resurrection Jesus and the Spirit are never to be confused, far less conflated, but they are to be understood as being "one." When Jesus said to his disciples, "I and the Father are one ... Whoever has seen me has seen the Father" (John 10:30; 14:9), he was not teaching "modalism," that is, the idea that God has different "modes," at one time "the Father" and at another "the Son." No. He was teaching them the unity that lies behind the diversity in the Godhead, and also the unity of purpose that coheres between the Father and the Son. This divine unity pervaded Jesus' resurrection, which was accomplished by the power of the Spirit.

Romans 4:25

What did Paul mean when he wrote that Jesus "was raised for our justification" (Romans 4:25)? Is this not surprising? Does this not appear to conflict with what Paul writes in Romans 3:24, that we are justified by God's grace as a gift "through the redemption that is in Christ Jesus;" and what he says in Romans 5:9, that we are "justified by his (Christ's) blood?" If it was the sin-bearing, sin-atoning death of Christ that justifies us, and this justification comes to us from the grace of God and is received by us through faith alone (Romans 3:27–28; 4:1–8), then what does Paul mean in Romans 4:25? In particular, what does the word "for" (διὰ, *dia*) mean?

We first must say that without the resurrection the cross would have been an unmitigated tragedy (1 Corinthians 15:3–4, 14, 17; Romans 6:4–5). Jesus' death and resurrection are seen in the New Testament as essentially one event or two halves of the one whole, which is Paul's point in Romans 4:25. Consider the following:[5]

1. Only as the "living" Lord can Jesus be the object of faith. Saving faith is directed to the Saviour who rose on the third day and now reigns at the right hand of his Father. This is why faithful Bible Christians do not fix their thoughts, far less their jewelry, on a still crucified Christ, but on a risen, living, reigning Lord.

2. It is in union with Christ that we are justified (Romans 8:1), and that union is with the risen and reigning Savior.

3. The righteousness of Christ by which we are justified is the righteousness of the risen, living Christ (1 Corinthians 1:30). He was "obedient to the point of death" and, in consequence, "God has highly exalted him and bestowed on him the name that is above every other name, so that at the name of Jesus every knee should bow, in heaven and on earth and under the earth, and every tongue confess that Jesus Christ is Lord, to the glory of God

the Father" (Philippians 2:8–11). Jesus' resurrection culminates and perfects his mediatorial obedience as the last Adam, God's second Man (1 Corinthians 15:28). It is this perfect, resurrected righteousness that is the justifying righteousness of believers. This is what the phrase "the Lord is our righteousness" signifies (Jeremiah 23:6; see also 1 Corinthians 1:30; 2 Corinthians 5:21; Philippians 3:9). The whole course of our Lord's life, from his incarnation in the womb of the Virgin Mary to his ascension to the right hand of God, is the righteousness by which we are justified before God. Faith takes us "into" Christ our righteousness; that is, the risen and living Christ.

4. **The death and resurrection of Christ are inseparable.** Christ's death could have no efficacy for us in isolation from his resurrection. We must always distinguish Jesus' death and resurrection, but we must never separate them. The Christ we receive in the gospel is "a whole Christ." This further accents that the death and resurrection of God's Son in our flesh were not two separate events, but one event that occurred in two phases. Jesus died according to the Scriptures and he rose from the dead according to the Scriptures (1 Corinthians 15:1–4). This accounts for the emphasis in the preaching of the early church, especially in Acts, on Jesus' resurrection.

5. It is through the mediation of the risen Savior that we come into the grace of acceptance with God (Romans 5:2). We rightly think of Jesus' "finished work," the finished work of making atonement for sin, but we must never forget his "continuing work" as our interceding Mediator at his Father's right hand. Jesus' resurrection initiated him into a new phase in God's eternal plan. Now as the risen Lord, he has "all authority in heaven and on earth" (Matthew 28:18). He is the King whom God has established on his holy hill (Psalm 2:6). As the risen and now regnant King, he "ever lives to make intercession" for his people

(Hebrews 7:25; Romans 8:34). Our justification is eternally secure because our righteousness is at God's right hand. As John Bunyan so memorably wrote, 'My righteousness is in heaven ... my good frames cannot make it any better, my bad frames cannot make it any worse.'[6]

1 Corinthians 15:20–23

1 Corinthians 15 is a stunning exposition of Jesus' resurrection. The whole chapter is a *tour de force*, highlighting first the historical fact and then the profound theological, spiritual and cosmic implications of Jesus' resurrection. In verse 20, Paul calls Jesus "the firstfruits (*aparche*) of those who have fallen asleep." Paul used Old Testament cultic language and imagery to highlight a glorious gospel truth. In the Old Testament, the "firstfruits" represented the complete harvest, the visible assurance that the beginning of the whole harvest had arrived. In Exodus 23:19, Moses told the Israelites, "The best of the firstfruits of your ground you shall bring into the house of the Lord your God." God commanded Jeremiah to tell God's people that, "Israel was holy to the Lord, the firstfruits of his harvest" (Jeremiah 2:3). The idea is that God is the Creator of everything and giving him the "firstfruits" acknowledged this fact. Doing so symbolized that everything was his by right. When Paul called Jesus "the firstfruits," he was not simply saying, "Jesus is our Pioneer, his resurrection is the assurance of our resurrection." He was saying, "In our Lord Jesus Christ, our representative, our resurrection has begun!" We belong to him and therefore like him belong to God. Richard Gaffin makes the point succinctly: "'Firstfruits' expresses the notion of organic connection and unity, the inseparability of the initial quantity from the whole."[7] In Paul's understanding, then, our resurrection and Jesus' resurrection are not two separate events; they are "two episodes of the same event."[8] Just like justification and sanctification, they are never to be confused, but neither can they ever be separated.

Christ's Resurrection and Salvation

The resurrection, then, is not only the public sign and seal of our Savior's victory over sin and death and hell, it belongs to the essence of our salvation. We are saved, which includes being justified, adopted, sanctified, and, ultimately, glorified by a risen Jesus Christ (Romans 8:29–30). The resurrection actually assures us that Jesus' death secured the rich blessings decreed by God for his people. More than that, because of his resurrection, we share in those blessings by virtue of our union with him, a union decreed and procured by the God of grace and received by faith.

Basic to all this is Paul's doctrine of union with Christ though it is more accurate to say that this doctrine Paul received from the risen Lord on the Damascus Road. When the Lord spoke to Saul of Tarsus and said, "Saul, Saul, why are you persecuting *me*?" (emphasis added), he was identifying himself with his people whom Saul was persecuting (Acts 9:4–5). Our Lord Jesus Christ did not come into this world as a private individual, but as a representative covenant Head (Romans 5:12–21). All he was and all he did he was and did for those given to him in times eternal by his Father (see John 17:2). The classic Pauline statement on the union between Christ and his people is found in Romans 6:

> Do you not know that all of us who have been baptized into Christ Jesus were baptized into his death? We were buried therefore with him by baptism into death, in order that, just as Christ was raised from the dead by the glory of the Father, we too might walk in newness of life. For if we have been united with him in a death like his, we shall certainly be united with him in a resurrection like his (Romans 6:3–5).

Jesus' bodily resurrection from the dead on the third day was an act of God witnessed by hundreds. Yet his resurrection was also the resurrection of everyone united to him by the will and grace of God. We enter into the experience of that resurrection the moment we place our whole unalloyed trust in the Lord Jesus Christ, and will enter into the eschatological fullness of that resurrection when he transforms our lowly bodies to be like his glorious body by the power that enables him to subdue everything to his eternal purpose (Philippians 3:20–21).

Christ's resurrection was a definitive moment in the history of redemption. All that yet awaits those united to Christ is the eschatological completeness of their redemption, the resurrection of their bodies. As Paul unpacks the new life that believers possess by virtue of their union with Christ, he looks forward to the day when what we now possess will come into its decreed perfection:

> And not only the creation, but we ourselves, who have the firstfruits of the Spirit, groan inwardly as we wait eagerly for adoption as sons, the redemption of our bodies. For in this hope we were saved. Now hope that is seen is not hope. For who hopes for what he sees? But if we hope for what we do not see, we wait for it with patience. (Romans 8:23–25).

This final phase in the history of redemption is guaranteed because of the embodied nature of Christ's resurrection. As he is, so we shall be. This is why the "Christian hope" is not the immortality of the soul, but the resurrection of the body.

Risen With Christ

This leaves us asking the question, "How should the Savior's resurrection and my resurrection in him make a difference to how I live?" Much could be said, but one thing stands out. At the conclusion of his exposition of "life in the Spirit" in Romans 8, the new resurrection life that is the present possession of all believers, Paul poses a number of questions: "If God is for us, who can be against us? ... Who shall bring any charge against God's elect? ...

Who is he that condemns? ... Who shall separate us from the love of God?" (Romans 8:31–35). His implied answers, "Nothing and no one," inform us how we are to live in the light of our union with Christ in his death and resurrection. If you are in Christ, then you are in the eternal sphere of the love of God. This, then, is how you are to live, as God's beloved son or daughter, knowing that nothing and no one can condemn you, overcome you, or separate you from his love because of your indissoluble union with your Savior. Even in your trials and troubles, live thankfully, even joyfully, because "in Christ" you have been blessed with every spiritual blessing (Ephesians 1:3–14).

Here is the sum of the matter,

> If then you have been raised with Christ, seek the things that are above, where Christ is, seated at the right hand of God. Set your minds on things that are above, not on things that are on earth. For you have died, and your life is hidden with Christ in God. When Christ who is your life appears, then you also will appear with him in glory" (Colossians 3:1–4).

Let us look to Christ's resurrection as an act of the entire Trinity. Let us understand that it has more than mere apologetic value. Let us recover the necessity of the resurrection for Christian faith and life. And, above all, let us live as those whose lives are hidden with the resurrected Christ in God in heaven.

7

Rejoice! The Triumphant Lord Jesus

Ascends to and Is Seated in Heaven

Ryan Speck

WHILE READING THE GOSPEL ACCOUNTS, HAVE YOU EVER LONGED to be there with Jesus as He ministered?[1] To be on that boat, for example, in the midst of the raging storm among terrified disciples, to hear Jesus Himself rebuke the howling wind and the buffeting waves, and to see with your own eyes the tumultuous storm immediately cease and suddenly to be standing in abrupt calm — what an astonishingly wonderful experience (e.g., Luke 8:24)! Or, to see with your own eyes the brightness of Christ's face, shining as the sun, and His clothes bursting forth in brilliant light, to see Moses and Elijah speaking with Jesus on that mountain, and to hear the voice of God express love for His Son, falling down on your face and then opening your eyes to see Jesus standing alone as glorious — what an experience the Transfiguration would have been (e.g., Matthew 17:2)! Or, to stand outside under the midday sun but enveloped in complete darkness, hearing Jesus upon the cross as He cried out, "*Eloi, Eloi, lama sabachthani!*" (e.g., Mark 15:33–34). To feel the earth tremble under your feet, to know the veil of the Temple was rent asunder, and to hear the centurion say, "Truly, this was the Son of God!" (e.g., Matthew 27:54) — what a profound experience that would have been! How many astonishing and breathtaking events those disciples who walked the earth with Jesus experienced — events that we will never experience but would have been thrilled to witness personally. Don't you long to be there, as you read the Scriptures? Don't you even wish that you were born at that time or could return to that ministry? When will we ever see such things again?!

However, while we rightly value such experiences, we should not long to return to the "good old days" of Christ's ministry on this earth. We should not lament the fact that Jesus has departed from this earth. In fact, we should rejoice greatly that Jesus has departed! Why? How can we rejoice that Jesus has left? When Jesus first told His disciples that He would depart, they were sorrowful (John 16:6–22). Yet, when Jesus actually departed, they were not sorrowful but responded with "great joy" (Luke 24:52). The very same disciples who witnessed His earthly ministry rejoiced at His departure. What did they come to understand about the departure of Jesus that we need to understand also — that we may rejoice as they did? Why rejoice to see Jesus depart? As their New Testament writings demonstrate, these disciples had come to understand that the Lord Jesus ascended to be exalted and to be seated above in order that He might bless His people from that exalted position. They rejoiced at this exaltation both for Christ's sake and for their own sake as those united to Christ. Therefore, I will first explain why we too should rejoice that Christ ascended, and, second, I will explain why we should rejoice that Christ is seated in heaven at the Father's right hand.

Rejoice in the Ascended Christ!

Why should we rejoice in the ascension of Christ? The manner in which Jesus ascended into heaven speaks volumes about the nature of His ascension, explaining in large degree why we should rejoice that Jesus has departed.

Our Blessing High Priest Ascends Heavenward

First, Jesus ascended into heaven *while blessing* His disciples (Luke 24:50–51). This benediction was our Lord's last ministerial act in His earthly ministry and how He chose to ascend. What does this blessing mean, and why did Jesus ascend while blessing His people?

In order to explain this blessing we must understand that the Old Testament background for Christ lifting His hands is the priestly blessing revealed in Numbers 6:22–27.[2] When Aaron pronounced this blessing upon the people, he lifted his hand toward the congregation (Leviticus 9:22). However, unlike a prayer in which the minister lifts his hands *towards God* in heaven, the priest lifted his hand high but with his palm stretched out *towards the congregation*. Why? The minister is reaching high (to call down from the exalted God a heavenly blessing) and reaching towards the people (to place that blessing upon the people). Thus, his hand "put the name of God upon" the people (Numbers 6:27).[3] Christ, likewise, lifted His hands to put this blessing upon His disciples as He ascended. For this reason the disciples of Christ were not bowing down (as they might in prayer), but they were looking up at Him while He blessed them (Acts 1:9ff). Thus, when Jesus departed, He departed as the High Priest fulfilling His priestly office, while His disciples look up at Him (watching Him depart). John Calvin noted, "In the lifting up of the hands is described an ancient ceremony which, we know, was formerly used by the priests."[4] As Norval Geldenhuys wrote,

Like the high priest when he came forth from the temple on great feast days, He lifts up his hands and blesses His disciples as the eternal High Priest (cf. Psalm cx and Hebrews vii-ix). And so, with outstretched hands, while the disciples look up to Him with receptive and worshipful hearts (Acts 1:9), He is parted from them and He, who had from all eternity been with the Father in divine glory, had again entered the Invisible World, and had returned to Him, but now with a human though glorified and heavenly body (cf. Acts 1:11)."[5]

Jesus departed not merely wishing His disciples well but efficaciously blessing His people as their High Priest. The priestly blessing (as is clear in Numbers 6:27) was a means of grace that not only declared God's intention but conveyed God's actual grace to those with faith to receive it (e.g., Luke 10:5–6). As William Hendriksen wrote: "This act of blessing is more than mere well-wishing. It is an effective impartation of welfare, peace, and power."[6] Or, as John Calvin put it, "When men bless one another, it is nothing else than praying in behalf of their brethren [unless endued with God's authority]; but with God it is otherwise, for he does not merely befriend us by wishes, but by a simple act of his will grants what is desirable for us."[7]

Furthermore, this efficacious blessing did not end with the ascension, but it continues today. In fact, to indicate the continuation of this blessing, Christ ascended, "while He blessed them" (Luke 24:51). He did not bless them, stop blessing them, and ascend. He did not finish His blessing in the ascent. He ascended into heaven as He was in the process of blessing them, which means His work of blessing was not finished but continues in heaven. As Matthew Henry wrote,

While he was blessing them, he was parted from them; not as if he were taken away before he had said all he had to say, but to intimate that his being parted from them did not put an end to his blessing them, for the intercession which he went to heaven to make for all his is a continuation of the blessing. He began to bless them on earth, but he went to heaven to go on with it.[8]

This point is clear not merely by implication from the manner of His ascent. The Scriptures establish this idea from the clear declaration of Hebrews 7:25, which reveals that Christ ever lives to make intercession for us. Jesus ever lives to secure divine blessing for us by His intercession for us in heaven. As Heidelberg Catechism Question 46 states, we should understand the words, "He ascended into Heaven," to mean, "that He continues there for our intercession." Dear friends, the Lord Jesus Christ is seated at the right hand of God our Father and from that glorious height He intercedes in order to send His greatest blessings to us. His parting from us is for no other reason than to bless us from heaven. Is this not exactly how the disciples understood Christ's ascension? They were not sorrowful and downcast at His parting (as they had been upon first hearing that He would depart, e.g., John 16:6–22). Rather, they rejoiced because their blessing Lord Jesus ascended to heaven in order to bless them from there. He says, by this manner of departure, in effect, the ministry of blessing you that I began on earth, I continue in heaven.

Yet, you might ask, why did Jesus need to ascend into heaven in order to intercede for us, in order to secure blessings for us (Hebrews 9:24)? Didn't He intercede for me while on earth? Yes (e.g., John 17:6–26; cf. Zechariah 3:1–5). However, by presenting Himself before the Father, our Lord Jesus intercedes for us directly and personally. As *Westminster Larger Catechism* Q. 55 puts it,

> Christ maketh intercession, by his appearing in our nature continually before the Father in heaven, in the merit of his obedience and sacrifice on earth, declaring his will to have it applied to all believers; answering all accusations against them, and procuring for them quiet of conscience, notwithstanding daily failings, access with boldness to the throne of grace, and acceptance of their persons and services.[9]

To put it another way, since God accepted Christ's work and exalted Him to this position, how could God refuse Christ's intercession? Because Jesus is there showing the Father the holes in His hands, feet, and side, having completed the work God sent Him to do, how can the Father refuse Him? Why would He want to, when He loved us and sent His Son to save us? If even doubting Thomas could not deny Christ when shown the evidence of His love (John 20:27–28), then how could the Father? Jesus sits in heaven near the Father, presenting Himself as the Lamb of God slain (e.g., Revelation 5:6, 12) — the very reason that the Father should favor and bless us. Jesus, our great High Priest, entered the holy of holies with His own blood, ascending there to secure our blessing forevermore (Hebrews 9:24). Truly, this is the great fact of Christ's personal, heavenly intercessions — presenting Himself as our slain Redeemer to secure our blessing. Upon the basis of His sacrificial presence in heaven, Jesus secures many and various blessings for us by this heavenly intercession. What are those blessings?

First, note that Jesus continues to bless us from heaven through His earthly ministers who pronounce biblical benedictions today. In order to continue blessing His people with efficacious authority, Christ sent ministers of the Word as a gift to His church, calling these ministers to pronounce His benediction (e.g., Ephesians 4:8–16).[10] As you may hear Christ, the Good Shepherd, speak to you in the preaching of His Word, so too you may receive Christ's blessing to you at the end of the service. Jesus Christ may be gone, no longer bodily present; but He has well-equipped His people with ministers who continue to bless in His Name. As Aaron blessed the people and God promised that He Himself would bless them (e.g., Numbers 6:27), so too Jesus calls His ministers to bless His people with the implicit promise that He Himself from heaven will bless them. Thus, Christ's blessing continues through the means of His church. Accordingly, when we receive the minister's benediction by faith, we may be well assured that we are blessed indeed because Christ ever lives in heaven to secure that blessing for us (e.g., Hebrews 7:24; 12:24).

Second, our Advocate with the Father (1 John 2:1–2) pleads for the Father to hear our prayers,[11] which fulfills the Old Testament type of incense. As the priests in the Old Testament not only offered blood sacrifices for the people but also were responsible to offer the incense (e.g., Exodus 30:7; 1 Samuel 2:28; 1 Chronicles 23:13; 2 Chronicles 26:18), so too Jesus our High Priest pleads His sweet aroma as the reason our prayers should be heard. Namely, the sweet aroma of the incense signified the sweet aroma of Christ (that propitiates God), which propitiation was accomplished by His sacrifice (Ephesians 5:2; cf. Genesis 8:21). Therefore, the incense was offered at the same time as the burnt offering, since propitiation is based upon the blood sacrifice of Christ (e.g., 2 Chronicles 13:11; cf. Psalm 141:2). Yet, this incense was combined with the prayers of the saints (e.g., Luke 1:10; Revelation 8:3–4), making those prayers acceptable. Therefore, the incense of Christ and the prayers of the saints are not easily disentangled but can be spoken of as one and the same (e.g., Revelation 5:8). For, what God has joined together, no man may put asunder! Thus, when God's people pray, Christ's own propitiatory intercessions accompany those prayers. Christ pleads His sweet aroma as cause for accepting the prayers of His people. When Abel was murdered by Cain, Abel's blood cried out for vengeance against his wicked brother (e.g., Genesis 4:10–11). Yet, Christ's blood speaks better things than the blood of Abel (e.g., Hebrews 12:24), namely, Christ's blood pleads for mercy. Thus, when you pray to the Father as a Christian begging mercy and grace in time of need, Christ sits at the right hand of God to make your requests sweet to the Father!

Third, Christ intercedes for us with His own petitions.[12] As

Christ interceded for us on earth with specific petitions (e.g., Luke 22:32; John 17:6–16), so too He intercedes for us in heaven. Why would His intercessory work of actual petitions on earth change when in heaven? Therefore, when we are offering our petitions to God, Christ is interceding for us by offering His petitions also. To learn how Christ intercedes for us in heaven, simply consider how Christ prayed on earth. For example, Christ interceded for Himself in the Garden of Gethsemane by saying, "Not My will but Yours be done" (Matthew 26:39). That is, He submitted even His human will to the Father, desiring the Father's good will to override His own. Jesus prayed for Himself (as the Spirit likewise intercedes) "according to the will of God" (e.g., Romans 8:26–27). For, the will of our Father is truly what is good for us. Thus, whatever our desires, as Christ prayed for Himself so Christ likewise prays for you, by adding this caveat, "Not the believer's will but Yours be done." Likewise, for example, when we pray for some difficult trial to cease (longing, perhaps, to depart this world even), Christ will no doubt add (if it is not God's time for us to depart this earth), as He prayed on earth, "I do not pray that You should take them out of the world, but that You should keep them from the evil one" (John 17:15). In other words, whether God causes that painful trial to end immediately (as we request), Christ intercedes for us so that this trial will not lead us to apostasy but will lead us to be sanctified by the Word (e.g., John 17:17; cf. Luke 22:31–32).

Accordingly, in John Bunyan's book, *Holy War*, the godly captains of war, seeking to save the city of "Mansoul," plead with King El Shaddai to send them help that they might save the city. They send their petitions by the hand of "Love-to-Mansoul," but who should receive that letter and make appropriate intercession for them? Bunyan explained,

> When this petition was come to the palace of the King, who should it be delivered to but to the King's Son? So he took it and read it,

and because the contents of it pleased him well, he mended, and also in some things added to the petition himself. So, after he had made such amendments and additions as he thought convenient, with his own hand, he carried it in to the King; to whom, when he had with obeisance delivered it, he put on authority, and spake to it himself.[13]

Have you ever, in frustration, screamed in your mind, "That's not what I prayed for!" Yet, perhaps, that irritating outcome resulted from Christ's editorial work in your prayers, which means that unexpected and undesired answer is the best answer to your (edited) prayer. Christ ever lives to intercede for us, taking our petitions, making them acceptable, and pleading our cause in heaven with our Father. In this way, the Father truly blesses us according to the intercessions of Christ. Rejoice, therefore, trusting that Christ's intercessions bring you — far above your own wisdom, far above what you can think or imagine to ask (e.g., Ephesians 3:20) — the greatest blessings, even when you cannot see how!

Our Divine Savior Returns Home

Second, when Jesus ascended to heaven, received by a cloud (e.g., Acts 1:9ff), this ascension and reception reveal Christ's inherent glory as God and imply He is returning home (to where He belongs). Thus, we should rejoice for Christ's sake because this ascension is a homecoming for our Lord Jesus. That is, this ascension was the answer to our Lord's prayer in John 17:5, namely, that He would be glorified with His Father with the glory He had before the world was. Where else would our Lord of Glory belong except in heaven! As Charles Hodge put it, "Heaven was his home. It was the appropriate sphere of his existence."[14] Jesus is God and He belongs in heaven, deserving to be exalted and worshiped continually by glorified souls and sinless angels.

Accordingly, the Scriptures make explicitly and abundantly clear that Jesus was exalted to heaven in His ascension. In J. R. R.

Tolkien's book, *The Lord of the Rings*, Bilbo Baggins gave a speech at his 111th birthday party, disappearing suddenly (after putting on his ring of power), to the shock and amazement of all. What a remarkable exit! Nobody knew where he went, and all were amazed. Have you ever asked, "Why did Jesus not simply disappear like that? Why was Jesus not standing on the ground and then, suddenly, 'poof,' He was gone?" That would have been impressive and shocking to all present. Yet, simply disappearing (while standing on the ground) would not have conveyed the appropriate truth. As with Bilbo, people might wonder where Jesus went. Rather, by ascending (not immediately disappearing), Jesus revealed pointedly and clearly where He was going — He was being exalted up to heaven. He clearly ascended, demonstrating his upward trajectory, so that His disciples would know exactly where He went — to heaven, where He, as God, belongs.

Likewise, when He ascended, "a cloud received Him out of their sight" (Acts 1:9). Why is this fact (of the cloud) noted in the inspired Word of God? Being received in a cloud reveals Christ's divine glory. For, the control and use of clouds is associated with divinity. For example, God often uses the clouds as a chariot. Who else can use the clouds as a chariot but God? In Daniel 7:13, for example, the Son of Man comes with the clouds. In Scripture, when someone comes on the clouds, it implies deity.[15] In fact, Jesus Christ applied this imagery of coming with or on the clouds to Himself several times,[16] which is one reason the Sanhedrin condemned His words as blasphemous. As the Son of Man, He claimed that they would see Him coming on the clouds, which God alone could do (Matthew 26:64–65)! As C. F. Keil wrote, "The clouds are the veil or the 'chariot' on which God comes from heaven to execute judgment against His enemies."[17] Likewise, Isaac Ambrose observed,

> Hereby he shows that he is the Lord of all the creatures; he had

already trampled upon the earth, walked upon the sea, vanquished hell or the grave, and now the clouds received him, and the heavens are opened to make way for this King of glory to enter in.[18]

The way in which Jesus ascended assured His disciples that the Word Who became flesh, Who was with God and Who was God (John 1:1, 14), returned to His rightful position through the clouds as the glorious God Who is over all. For this reason, "they worshiped" Him (Luke 24:52). They recognized that Jesus was God Himself and that He deserved their worship. As Leon Morris noted, "Whatever their view of His Person during His ministry, the passion and resurrection and now the ascension had convinced them that He was divine ... They were understanding more than they had previously."[19] You see, brethren, the Lord Jesus was opening the understanding of His disciples to comprehend Who He is and how to respond to Him rightly (Luke 24:45). While they still did not understand all things (e.g., Acts 1:6), they finally understood that Jesus is their High Priest Who blesses them and is their God who was worthy of worship. They understood this from His teaching (e.g., Luke 24:44–49), which was confirmed by the way He ascended to heaven (e.g., Luke 24:50–51). What a joy to understand more and more Who Jesus is! Yet, what happens after Jesus ascended adds to that joy. What happened on the other side of the veil?

Rejoice in the Seated Christ!

When Jesus ascended into heaven, He was installed as King over all (e.g., Mark 16:19; Ephesians 1:19–21; Hebrews 1:2–4; 1 Peter 3:21–22). He was seated at the Father's right hand and began His "session." The word "session" simply refers to being seated for a specific purpose (until that purpose is completed). Thus, you might have a business session in which you sit to discuss specific business decisions, not rising until those seated have made the necessary decisions. So, what was Christ's "session"? It is a session (He was seated) in order to rule and to reign. His disciples rightly rejoiced because they loved Jesus Christ (John 14:28). Therefore, they rejoiced for His sake because Jesus ascended to be seated as the King of kings and Lord of lords — to whom all authority has now been given.[20]

Yet you might ask, since Jesus is God, doesn't He already have "all authority"? We must differentiate between "authority" and "power." Namely, power refers to the ability to do something, but authority refers to the right to do it. A bully may have power to hit someone, but he does not have the authority (the right) to do so. A parent has the authority to discipline his children and (with few exceptions) the power to do so also. Jesus had all power by virtue of being divine. However, Jesus did not have every right (all authority) to work good for sinners by simple fiat. It is not right to justify sinners, unless atonement is made for them (e.g., Hebrews 9:22). Thus, Jesus received this authority as our Savior once He earned this authority by completing His work of salvation (e.g., Daniel 7:13–14; Matthew 28:18; Philippians 2:8–11; Hebrews 1:4; 1 Peter 3:22).

Accordingly, Scripture speaks clearly of Christ's rightful authority as King over the Kingdom of God being given to Him. God does not have the authority, the right (without earning it, without acting to gain it), to create for Himself a Kingdom of redeemed people from fallen sinners! Why? It is because God's own character — an inward constraint (not an outside, external rule greater than God!) — does not allow Him unjustly to justify and bless sinners, which would be an abomination (e.g., Proverbs 17:15). God is just, and He cannot simply dismiss someone's sins without just cause and bring that person into His kingdom ruled by His dear Son. It would be just only to condemn that sinner to hell forever — unless atonement is made for him. God does not have the authority, the right to be un-just. Therefore, in order for God to create for Himself this Kingdom of redeemed living stones (1 Peter 2:5), He sent His Son to shed His precious blood so that, having atoned for their sins, Christ could be exalted as the new King over this Kingdom of the redeemed. Christ, by virtue of His atoning work, has the authority, the right to redeem His people and build His Kingdom. God, His wrath and justice having been satisfied, gives Christ the right fully to reign as the King of the Kingdom of heaven. God is both the just and the justifier of the ungodly (Romans 3:26). Accordingly, when Jesus ascended into heaven, He ascended as the King Who now has all authority to bless His people![21] Thus, Christ is now exalted as the Lord of Glory and as the King of kings (e.g., Revelation 5:9–10). He is now seated and reigns above, having all authority to rule for our good.

His Position

Accordingly, Jesus sat down at God's right hand.[22] What does this act of sitting at God's right hand mean exactly? First, this position signifies the highest authority and honor. Since most people are right-handed, to be at the right hand of someone is to be at his favored side (e.g., Genesis 48:13–14; Leviticus 14:17). This is the favorite position, then (e.g., 1 Kings 2:19; Psalm 45:9; Psalm 118:15–16; Matthew 20:21). There is no one greater than God. Therefore, to sit at God's right hand is the most exalted position in the universe. Search anywhere and everywhere, and you will not find a more exalted position. Jesus is exalted "far above" everything and everyone else (e.g., Ephesians 1:20–21; 3:10; 6:12).

What power or authority is there that is not under the authority and power of Jesus Christ? What government official? What nation? What person? What terrorist? What angel? What demon? Everywhere and at all times, all things are under Jesus Christ, the Supreme Head of all. Beloved brethren, how we need the eyes of our heart opened to see this is true! How we need to believe this is so! For, this authority and power of Jesus Christ He wields especially for our good. Is that not what Paul says in Ephesians 1:22? Paul makes clear that all things are put under His feet "to the church," or "for the church." It is to the good of the church, to the blessing of the church — for the sake of the church — that this is so. The universal authority and almighty power our Lord Jesus exercises in this world are for the good of His own people, His treasured possession. Everything whatsoever that happens under His watch (Who neither slumbers nor sleeps, Psalm 121) is bringing to pass blessing upon the church. Yes, even the challenging, trying, painful events of providence are for this purpose. May God open the eyes of our heart to see and know that this is true! As William Cowper put it in his hymn, *God Moves in a Mysterious Way*: "Ye fearful saints, fresh courage take; the clouds ye so much dread are big with mercy and shall break in blessings on your head."[23]

When Joseph discovered that his betrothed, Mary, was pregnant, without knowing him intimately, did he imagine this would lead to great blessing (Matthew 1:18–19)? When Joseph and Mary discovered their 12-year-old boy, Jesus, was not with them so that they returned in alarm to the Temple in search of Him, did they think in their panic and fear that this was a real blessing (Luke 2:42–46)? When Jesus hung on the cross dying, did His mother and His disciples believe this was a blessing while they stood at the foot of the cross (John 19:26–27)? Yet, the cross proved to be the greatest blessing of all. Do we understand this principle in our own lives? Jesus rules and directs difficult and painful providences for our good. For, God designs every trial to lead to our blessing. Our faith is strengthened to endure (e.g. James 1:2–4). We are humbled (e.g., 2 Corinthians 12:7). We grow in our understanding of God's sufficient grace, relying on Him more and more (2 Corinthians 12:9). We are brought to know dear friends we may never have otherwise met (e.g., Acts 9:8ff; Acts 9:26–27). Therefore, rejoice!

Jesus Christ is seated with authority over all in order to bring blessings upon us, His people, His church![24] If He has shed His blood for us, then what good thing will He withhold from us (Romans 8:32)? As Edward Griffin exhorted,

> What could you wish for more? What change can you desire? In what single circumstance would you move for an alteration? Our blessed Jesus governs all. Would you take the government of a single event out of his hands? To whom then would you commit it? To angels? They never loved like Jesus. To chance? There is no such love in chance. To men? Men never died to save your lives. To yourselves? Jesus loves you better than you love yourselves, and knows infinitely better what is for your good. Come then [to Christ] ... and rejoice that this redeemed world is governed by the matchless love of him who died to deliver it from Satan's oppression. Come and give up your souls to this dear exalted Saviour.[25]

Second, this position of sitting at God's right hand signifies a settled position. We cannot stand for long in one place. Standing is a posture that lends itself to activity and movement (such as singing or walking). Furthermore, lying down is a posture of inactivity that may last a long time so that we might be refreshed by that rest, rising as those strengthened for more activity. Sitting, however, speaks of a settled position for a settled purpose. We sit down for a time in order to do something specific. We sit down to eat a meal. We sit down to read. We sit down to watch a movie. Jesus sat down to rule. He sat down on His throne in order to reign over all things. He will not cease sitting (figuratively speaking, at least, cf. Acts 7:56) until that reign is completed — until all things are put under His feet (Psalm 110:1; Matthew 22:44; 1 Corinthians 15:25). Rejoice, for Christ our King reigns, and He will sit until He subdues all the rebel elements and conquers all His and our enemies (*Westminster Shorter Catechism* Q. 26)!

Furthermore, beloved brethren, since Jesus is exalted in heaven, so are we by virtue of our union with Christ (e.g., Ephesians 2:6). Our hearts are with Christ in heaven (Colossians 3). Our happiness is secure in Him there. For, there is our treasure — the gracious Savior, Jesus Christ. As Augustus Toplady put it in *A Debtor to Mercy Alone*, "Yes, I to the end shall endure, as sure as the earnest is giv'n; more happy, but not more secure, the glorified spirits in heav'n."[26] Those glorified in heaven are happier than we are on earth, but they are not more secure than we are! We are equally secure in Christ, Who is seated above. As Derek Thomas put it, "Our vision is too earth-bound, too restricted. The doctrine of the ascension forces us to lift up our heads and look up ... [to] gaze on Jesus in his glory."[27]

Do you not feel, at times, as if you are drowning? This sinful world in which we live is likened in the Scriptures to a sea — an ever-churning, tumultuous, inhospitable sea (e.g., Isaiah 57:20; Revelation 13:1; Revelation 21:1). How can we live here without drowning? John Newton explained:

> He is the head of his body the church: and though the church, while in this world, is in a suffering perilous state; yet as the body of a man is not in danger of drowning while his head is out of the water, so our forerunner and head being in heaven on their behalf, he will assuredly draw all his living members to himself.[28]

Dear friends of Christ, because Jesus is exalted in heaven and we are united to Him, this means that we will not drown in our trials because we are secure in the exalted Christ. Our Head is above the water, and, one day, He will draw us up to Himself, rescuing us entirely from the experience of this sea of hardships. In the meantime, He has sent us gifts to strengthen and to encourage us as we live in the world but are not of the world (John 17:15–16).

His Gift(s)

Thus, Ephesians 4:8–16 declares Jesus to be the conquering King

Who leads captive those enemies of His people who would take them captive. Jesus triumphed openly over His and our enemies, and as with the Egyptians (e.g., Exodus 12:36), our victorious Lord showers upon us the spoils of war. Thus, the disciples of Christ in Luke 24:52 rejoiced because they now understood and believed that Jesus ascended to reign — and that His reign would be a true blessing for them. Not only did they rejoice for Christ's sake, but they rejoiced for themselves also. Christ's departure signaled His session as King in heaven, and this victorious King showered His people with gifts from heaven (e.g., Ephesians 4:8).

The greatest gift Jesus gave was the Spirit (e.g., John 14:16–19; cf. Luke 11:13). What greater gift could God give except Himself? The Spirit is Himself God sent to dwell in us in order to draw us and unite us to the Triune God. Thus, when you consider the language in Luke 24:49, for example (the Promise "upon" them and being "endued with power from on high" as they wait in Jerusalem), there can be no doubt whatsoever that Jesus promises to send upon them the Pentecostal Spirit, signified in the tongues of fire resting on them and clearly empowering them to preach the gospel (Acts 1:4–5; 2:1–4). As Norval Geldenhuys writes, "By this the Saviour means the Holy Ghost, who is the greatest of all gifts, through whom all good gifts are given."[29] This is the Helper Whom God would send in Christ's Name (John 14:26). The Spirit would comfort Christ's disciples. In fact, Christ would be with His disciples by His Spirit's presence. John Newton wrote, "While he pleads for them on high, by the power of his Spirit, he is present with them below."[30] When we say that Jesus dwells in our hearts, for example, we mean that Jesus, by His Spirit, indwells us.

By the Spirit of Christ, the people of Christ are equipped to persevere and prosper in God's Kingdom until our Lord Himself returns for us. Leon Morris explains what this promise of the Spirit (Luke 24:49) meant, namely,

The disciples are not to attempt the task of evangelism with their own meagre resources, but are to await the coming of the Spirit. The equipment He would provide is picturesquely described in terms of the disciples being *clothed with power from on high*. The note of power is significant, and *on high* reminded them (and reminds us) of the source of all real power for evangelism.[31]

John Calvin also observed that it was "as if he had said, though you feel yourselves to be unfit for such a charge, there is no reason why you should despond, because I will send you from heaven that power which I know that you do not possess."[32] In this case, the word "power" (not "authority") means that Christ's disciples were strengthened to live for Him while awaiting His return.

We have this same Spirit. We have the fullest measure of the Spirit of God empowering us and leading us into all truth also (John 14:17; 16:13). While the Pentecostal gifts have ceased, the work of the Holy Spirit continues.[33] In the Old Testament, the glory of God at first descended and filled the Temple palpably (so overwhelming was this glory cloud initially that the priests were driven out and could not minister there, e.g., 2 Chronicles 5:13–14). Later, this cloud receded and disappeared,[34] but Israel was to understand from that initial manifested presence that God dwelt there permanently, just as He promised to do (e.g., 1 Kings 8:10ff; cf. Exodus 25:8–9; 29:43–45). Likewise, when the Holy Spirit descended upon the apostles in tongues of fire, and they spoke in tongues, God signaled the arrival of the permanently present Holy Spirit in His fullest measure to date! While the palpable, overwhelming presence of the Spirit did not continue either, the church should recognize His continuing presence, nonetheless. The grand opening of a store may use many signs (such as large banners, inflatable animals, and wind dancers) to demonstrate the store is now open. However, the next week, when those signs are gone, you should know the store is still open. Likewise, the Spirit of God descended with visible signs, but, afterwards, you should recognize the Spirit is still working as powerfully as He did at Pentecost.

The questions for us are: Do we believe it? Do we believe the Spirit of God empowers us, dwelling in us? Do we believe the Holy Spirit guides us in all truth? Are we, therefore, emboldened to live for Christ? If the Holy Spirit dwells in us — the Spirit by Whose power the creation sprang into being, the Spirit by Whose power dead souls are made alive, the Spirit by Whose power cowardly apostles burst forth in almighty preaching — how could we ever be intimidated or afraid? Our Lord Jesus sent us the most precious gift of all: His Spirit. May we believe and walk in the Spirit! For, we have much to do as we await the return of Christ.

In fact, we have opportunities to serve Jesus in this life that we will never have again. In heaven, will you have opportunity to evangelize a lost soul? In heaven, will you have opportunity to wrestle against temptation and sin, prevailing to the glory of God? In heaven, will you ever be afflicted with a painful trial that you must endure, trusting in Jesus? Will you ever have opportunity in heaven to sing Christ's praises while struggling against lukewarmness or weariness? While we are on this earth, we have unique opportunities to glorify and serve Christ that we will never again have — not unto all eternity. Our Lord Jesus Christ has ascended to rule over all things for our good. He has sent us His Spirit to empower us to glorify Him. May we rejoice greatly in our exalted Lord Jesus and work diligently to honor Him, while we have unique opportunities to do so! For, soon, we will join Jesus in glory.

His Preparation

Jesus went to prepare a place for us (John 14:3). As we have seen above, when the exalted Lord of Glory ascended into heaven, He was returning home. Yet heaven is not only our Lord's home; it is ours also in and through Him! Accordingly, Jesus left, not to abandon His disciples, but to prepare a place for them to be with Him. What exactly does that mean?

You may have heard preachers say something like this, "If God created the world in six days, think of what He has been preparing for us in the last 2,000 years!" Yet, is that really what Jesus is doing — creating a new world for us like the original creation (*ex nihilo*, from nothing)? Is that what He means in John 14? How can Jesus mean such a thing, since this present world will be recreated, not *ex nihilo*, but renewed from the original creation (analogous to how we ourselves are called a new creation, e.g., 2 Corinthians 5:17). We are not recreated *ex nihilo*. We are recreated in the sense of redeemed and renewed. Likewise, the new heavens and new earth will be redeemed and renewed (not created out of nothing). In fact, in John 14:2, Jesus declares that there are many mansions (already). Thus, He does not say He will create or make a home for us; He says He goes to prepare them for us — to make those dwelling places ready to be our home.

What kind of preparation is Jesus making for us? On the one hand, Jesus prepared heaven for us by entering it at His ascension and by sitting at the right hand of God. As J. C. Ryle explains:

> He has prepared it by procuring a right for every sinner who believes to enter in. None can stop us, and say we have no business there. — He has prepared it by going before us as our Head and Representative, and taking possession of it for all the members of His mystical body. As our Forerunner He has marched in, leading captivity captive, and has planted His banner in the land of glory. — He has prepared it by carrying our names with Him as our High Priest into the holy of holies, and making angels ready to receive us. They that enter heaven will find they are neither unknown nor unexpected.[35]

On the other hand, we are not prepared to go to heaven now, are we? If we were, we would be there already. Even as Jesus prepared a home for us, so He must prepare us for that home. Therefore, since Christ is preparing us for heaven, let us be encouraged to prepare ourselves — working out our salvation while trusting in Him to work in us (e.g., Philippians 2:12–13). For, there remains glory for us to give to God now, while fighting sin within and temptations without. There remain sheep to be gathered into the fold, before we, as the church, are ready for heaven. Christ went to prepare a place for us; let us prepare to go to that place! For, in leaving us He did not abandon us (John 14:16–18). He went before us and He comes to us in the power of the Holy Spirit. He did not forget about us. He went to prepare a place for us — to which we will go, at the exact moment when all things are ready. Do you begin to see why the disciples rejoiced greatly when Jesus ascended?

Conclusion

Did Christ's closest disciples desire to have Jesus back on earth with them after He ascended into heaven? No, they rejoiced greatly at His departure. Should we long to return to the earthly life and ministry of Jesus Christ? No, that would be to reverse the work of Christ. Rather, we should desire to be with Jesus where He is now. We do not desire to see the work of Jesus reversed (back to an earthly ministry in this fallen world), but we desire to see Jesus and be with Him as He is — with the Conqueror seated above! We do not desire to bring Jesus down to us; we desire to go up to where He is! We do not desire to see Jesus re-humbled, but to remain exalted! To put it another way, why do we want to be there when Jesus ministered upon the earth? It is a legitimate desire, if we want to be with Jesus in order to see His glory and power. However, Jesus is now exalted as never before in His ascension and session. If we would see His glory and power, we should desire far more to be with Him where He is and as He is now. As Wilhelmus à Brakel wrote,

> Does your heart not will to be where your treasure is? Is not Christ your treasure, desire, life, and love? He is in heaven and it is the comfort of believers in this world that they will once be with the Lord (1 Thessalonians 4:17–18). ... Acknowledge yourself to be but guests and 'strangers and pilgrims on the earth,' and seek this country looking 'for a city which hath foundations, whose Builder and Maker is God' (Hebrews 11:13–16, 10) ... It is your Father's house (John 14:2) and your house ... This is where your brothers and sisters reside ... This is your inheritance, 'incorruptible, and undefiled, and that fadeth not away, reserved in heaven for you' (1 Peter 1:4).[36]

When we declare that we do not want Jesus back with us on earth now so that we can observe His earthly ministry, we do not deny in the least the glory and joy of that unique experience. Rather, we declare a surpassingly greater glory and joy — to be with our exalted Lord and Savior where He is now, in glory! Whether in death (being transported to heaven by angels, Luke 16:22) or at His second coming (being caught up in the air with Him, 1 Thessalonians 4:16–17), He will not come down to us; we will ascend to Him! Therefore, let us rejoice greatly that our Lord Jesus Christ has ascended into heaven and is seated at the right hand of God!

8

Christ and His Bride

An Exposition of Psalm 45

Michael Barrett

THERE IS NO MORE INTIMATE RELATIONSHIP ON EARTH THAN that between husband and wife. Adam, in his yet sinless state, expressed his understanding of the inseparable connection between himself and the partner God had made especially for him: "This is now bone of my bones, and flesh of my flesh" (Genesis 2:23). In his inspired commentary on and application of Adam's statement, Moses made it clear that the marriage bond took priority over every other human connection. "Therefore shall a man leave his father and his mother, and shall cleave unto his wife: and they shall be one flesh" (Genesis 2:24). In arguing for the sexual purity of believers, Paul used the theology of Moses to explain the relationship of the believer to Christ: "But he that is joined unto the Lord is one spirit" (1 Corinthians 6:17). He later said to the same group of believers that they had been espoused to one husband, Christ (2 Corinthians 11:2). In Ephesians 5, which is perhaps the most explicit passage expounding the gospel as it accords with marriage, the apostle goes back to Adam's confession when he describes the believer's union with Christ: "For we are members of his body, of his flesh, and of his bones" (5:30).

Marriage Analogy

It is not surprising that Scripture so frequently uses marriage as the choice symbol of the intimate and eternal relationship that exists between Christ and His bride, which is the church. The parallels are many and the theology illustrated is magnificent. In marriage God ordained that two become one flesh; in spiritual union the believer becomes one with Christ. In marriage two people traditionally share a name; in spiritual union Christians are called by His name. In marriage two people share one life; in spiritual union Christians, being one with Christ, are beneficiaries of the grace of His life. In marriage two people have in this life a common destiny: what God has joined together, man should not put asunder. Likewise, nothing can separate the Christian from the love of Christ. In marriage two people live in constant company and fellowship; so in spiritual union believers abide in Christ and He abides in them. In marriage two people share a mutual attraction and affection. Each sees something in the other that generates and feeds love. The Song of Solomon portrays a marriage that was a mutual admiration society consisting of two members. That is a good lesson for every marriage, but it transcends to the sublime when referring to the marriage relationship between Christ and the church. As the Bride of Christ, we are to look in adoration to Him who is altogether lovely and to Him who is altogether ours. It is astounding beyond comprehension that Christ views us with such love and desire. For Christ loved us first with a love that was not reciprocated. He loved us, but we saw no beauty in Him that we should desire Him (Isaiah 53:2), even though He is the altogether lovely One (Song 5:16). But His gracious spirit wooed us and drew us irresistibly to Him, and now we love Him because He first loved us (1 John 4:19). Here is the real mystery. He loved us not because we were lovely, but in spite of our ugliness and sin. His love for us is single, exclusive, and undivided. It is amazing that Jesus would love even me, but it is an overwhelming thought that in union with Him, Jesus loves especially me. As any bride is special to her husband, so are believers special to Christ.

Love Songs

Significantly, love and marriage have occasioned countless poems and lyrics throughout time; marriage is something to sing about. If that is true for human relationships, how much more should the spiritual union between Christ and His Bride be the theme of song. We turn now to consider such a love song. Psalm 45 provides outstanding evidence of the Old Testament's use of marriage as typical or prophetic of Christ and his relationship with his church. The inspired poet-prophet employs the marriage theme to spotlight the beauty of the spiritual union between the coming Christ and His people. It is not surprising that he begins the predictive poem with his confession, "My heart is overflowing with a good theme" (Psalm 45:1) and ends with his assurance that "the people shall praise You [the King] forever and ever" (Psalm 45:17). In between, the Psalm describes the King's beauty (45:2), His might (45:3), His throne (45:6), and His merit (45:2, 7). The Royal husband is precious to His bride (45:1); He protects and defends His bride (45:3, 5); He rules for the welfare of His bride (45:5); He shares His wealth and merit with His bride (45:9–15). A significant difference between understanding this text in the old dispensation versus the new is that we know the King's name is Jesus. God intended for them then and for us now to see in this wedding song what belongs to believers in union with Christ. It is a prophecy in poetic portrait.

The superscription labels Psalm 45 a "song of loves," which is most likely a plural of amplification; it is a song about intensely passionate love. The word occurs only here, but its connection to a root meaning "beloved" or "friend," suggests the existence of a relationship.[1] Even the fact that the song is directed to the sons of Korah, whose forefather was buried alive because of his rebellion against God's chosen mediator (Numbers 16), underscores the amazing nature of this love that extends to those from a most undeserving and unlovely stock. But that is the case for all who comprise the church, the Bride of Christ, who prior to being espoused to Christ were as vile and undeserving as Hosea's Gomer. This amazing love infinitely surpasses the Cinderella fairy tale motif in which a prince falls in love with an attractive peasant girl. Here is the King of glory setting His selective love on one with no inherent beauty or attractiveness. This love song is all about grace. There is something about singing that comes naturally to believers as a response to divine grace.

Throughout Scripture, those who are the beneficiaries of God's goodness and grace break out in song. After Moses led the children of Israel through the Red Sea, he became the first choir director as he led the nation in singing unto the Lord, "The LORD is my strength and song, and he is become my salvation" (Exodus 15:2). After Deborah delivered the nation from oppression, she broke out in song: "I, even I, will sing unto the LORD; I will sing praise to the LORD God of Israel" (Judges 5:3). After David testified of God's bringing him up from the miry clay and setting his feet on a rock, he declared, "And he hath put a new song in my mouth, even praise unto our God" (Psalm 40:3). Paul marked singing as one of the evidences of being filled with the Holy Spirit: "Speaking to yourselves in psalms and hymns and spiritual songs, singing and making melody in your heart to the Lord; Giving thanks always for all things unto God and the Father in the name of our Lord Jesus Christ" (Ephesians 5:19–20). On more than one occasion in his vision of things to come, John recorded the singing of the redeemed in heaven (Revelation 5:9; 15:3). Whether in the Old or the New Testament dispensations or in eternity, God's people express their worship in song. Singing is an effective means of stirring the heart and actively fixing the emotions and passions on the Lord. It is not surprising, therefore, that this celebration of the Royal Wedding and marriage is presented in the form of a song.

Messianic Psalms

Before going any further in my analysis of Psalm 45, I should say a few things to justify my taking this Psalm as referring to Christ and His Bride. That Christ is a prevalent topic of the Psalms stands without question, particularly since that was the testimony of Jesus Himself in His post-resurrection survey of the Old Testament (Luke 24:27, 44). But how to identify the messianic Psalms is the question. Essentially, identifying the messianic passages in the Psalms is no different from identifying them anywhere else in the Old Testament. What makes it a little more complicated is the fact that sometimes entire Psalms are uniquely messianic and sometimes only a part of a Psalm is. Recognizing the uniqueness of the former and the transitions in the latter are key elements in the interpretative process. It is paramount to stay on Christ-alert as you read the Psalms. Let me suggest some specific guidelines that should help in identifying the messianic texts.[2]

First, *be alert to messianic clues.* If you know whom and what you are looking for, you will know it when you see it. This approach involves the analogy of Scripture principle[3] and especially factors in all of the antecedent theology. When you see a clue word elsewhere associated with Messiah or some activity or attribute that other Scriptures have used or defined in terms of Messiah, you are warranted in linking it to the Messiah in the Psalms. For instance, when you notice Psalm 89's referring to the "seed" that will endure forever (89:29, 36), you should immediately identify that Psalm as messianic. "Seed" is a messianic word, a clue word that runs throughout the entire Old Testament beginning in Genesis.[4]

Second, *be alert to the "ideality" or uniqueness principle.* By this I simply mean that there are going to be statements that transcend any possible reference to mere men and that must find their sole application in Christ. For instance, when Psalm 72 talks about a King whose dominion is universal (72:8) and whose name is eternal (72:17), it is likely that David is not referring to himself, Solomon, or any other merely human sovereign. That is an ideal and unique reference to Christ. The same is true in Psalm 45 when the King, whose throne is forever and whose kingdom is righteousness, is addressed specifically as God (45:6). I'll have more to say about that in a moment.

Third, *be alert to the type-antitype connection.* Keep in mind the proper definitions of type and antitype.[5] Typology is not a hermeneutical ploy to rescue the Old Testament for Christian relevance. On the contrary, it is a divinely intended picture prophecy that is to be read out of the text (exegesis) not read into the text (eisegesis). A type is a real, historical person, thing, or event that conveys some key point of analogy to the future reality, the antitype.[6] By definition, a Psalm that is typical of Christ must have a direct reference to a real historical person or phenomenon. This is most common in what are often called the Royal Psalms, namely, those that deal with the theme of kingship (Psalms 2, 18, 20, 21, 45, 72, 89, 101, 110, 132, 144). All have their theological foundation in the Davidic Covenant (2 Samuel 7:11–16). For instance, Psalm 18 reviews God's faithfulness in delivering David from the dangers that threatened his rule. That was certainly David's testimony, but it found even greater fulfillment in David's greater Son, who experienced the preserving and protecting hand of the Lord throughout His earthly ministry, from His deliverance from Herod's slaying of the innocents (Matthew 2:16ff) to His deliverance from Hell's onslaught in Gethsemane (Luke 22:41ff; Hebrews 5:7). The Psalm ends with its own suggestion to take this reference beyond David: "Great deliverance giveth he to his king; and sheweth mercy to his anointed, to David, and to his seed for evermore" (18:50). The three clue words, "king," "anointed," and "seed," ought to start you thinking about the points of correspondence between David and Christ.

Fourth, *be alert to New Testament confirmations.* The cross-references in your Bible should help direct you to most of the New Testament parallels or fulfillments. I recognize that some regard reading the New Testament's interpretations back into the Old Testament to be the unpardonable hermeneutical transgression.[7] Yet I would argue that it always helps to have an inspired commentary on the Old Testament text. The New Testament, for sure, may find new significance or application to an Old Testament statement, but it does not change the meaning or intended sense of the Old Testament itself. A given truth can have multiple applications. If the New Testament marks a Psalm has being messianic, then we cannot ignore that evidence. It means that if I didn't see Christ in my initial analysis, then I was not analyzing the text correctly. I should remark as well that the fact the New Testament tends to focus on a particular part of the Psalm does not necessarily mean that that part is the only messianic statement in the Psalm. Maybe it is and maybe it isn't. If the New Testament confirms that at least one element in the Psalm is messianic, then study the whole context to see if or how the rest relates to Messiah.

The Messianic Wedding

Now back to Psalm 45. Psalm 45 is the Song of the Royal Wedding; it is a Royal and messianic Psalm. Remember that the Royal Psalms are those dealing with kingship that in some way touch on God's covenant with David regarding the perpetual occupation of his throne (2 Samuel 7:12–16; Psalm 89:4). Not all messianic Psalms are Royal Psalms (e.g., Psalm 22), but all Royal Psalms in one way or another are messianic, pointing to David's greater and Ideal Son, who is the Lord Jesus Christ. The question raised by each Royal Psalm is whether it is uniquely messianic, typically messianic, or an admixture of referents. Thoughts differ in Psalm 45 as to the identity of the husband and the bride, ranging from the absurd to the sublime. I think Spurgeon's assessment of this Psalm is right on point:

> Some here see Solomon and Pharaoh's daughter only — they are shortsighted; others see both Solomon and Christ — they are cross-eyed; well-focused spiritual eyes see here Jesus only, or if Solomon be present at all, it must be like those hazy shadows of passers-by which cross the face of the camera, and therefore are dimly traceable upon a photographic landscape. 'The King,' the God whose throne is for ever and ever, is no mere mortal and his everlasting dominion is not bounded by Lebanon and Egypt's river. This is no wedding song of earthly nuptials, but an Epithalamium for the Heavenly Bridegroom and his elect spouse.[8]

I cannot duplicate the old Baptist's eloquence, but I concur with his conclusion. I would argue that the Psalm is uniquely messianic for several reasons. There are some statements that preclude any other identity (the uniqueness principle), and there is no statement that cannot apply to Christ or His Bride. The New Testament, as we will see, quotes a portion of the Psalm and applies it directly to Jesus, which should settle the issue. Not that it would acknowledge fulfillment in Jesus, but the Aramaic Targum translates verse 2 "Your beauty, O King Messiah goes beyond the sons of men" (my translation) and then says that the spirit of prophecy was on his lips. Significantly, even the Jewish tradition recognizes the uniquely messianic focus of the Psalm's principal referent.

The Psalm does not seem to be structured with any obvious strophic design, but it clearly begins with a description of the Royal Husband and then transitions to a description of the Royal Bride. It is a song of mutual love. The inner being (heart) of the inspired songwriter was boiling as he was stirred regarding this good matter. His hot heart gave expression to these lyrics. So, may our hearts grow hot in meditating about Him. I want to develop my analysis of the Psalm under two heads: the Royal Husband and the Royal Bride.

The Royal Husband

On most wedding days in our culture, all eyes are on the bride; the groom is a just a necessary fixture in the ceremony. But in this royal wedding, the groom is the center of attention, and rightly so. This song highlights four aspects of Christ's person and work that should move the Bride to break out in song in adoration of Him.

His Beauty

First, attention is directed to the Husband's beauty: He is altogether lovely and precious to His Bride. His beauty is beyond description: "Thou art fairer than the children of men" (v. 2). The Hebrew word translated, "thou art fairer," is notoriously difficult to translate. It is derived from the root *yph*, which means, "to be beautiful." The repetition of the initial letters of the root have been explained with extremes (*yapyapita*). Some claim it is simply unintentional and meaningless dittography.[9] Others explain it as an extremely rare and anomalous mixed formation.[10] Some even propose a sort of grammatical rationalism, claiming that the doubling of the root signifies the doubling or intensifying of the meaning; thus, the reference is to extreme or superlative beauty.[11] Although the form is unique, the basic sense is undisputed. Even the LXX grasps the sense nicely, if not pedantically, with its translation, "beautiful with respect to beauty."

The stative or adjectival verb, "to be beautiful," is then followed by the comparative *min*. The Royal Groom is endowed with beauty beyond the sons of mankind; He is more beautiful than any other in the human race.

Notwithstanding Christ's incomparable beauty, only the eye of faith can perceive it (1 Corinthians 2:9–10). It has been said that love is blind. Human love is often blind to flaws that are obvious to others. That may be true for human relationships, but spiritual love is not blind. On the contrary, it is the unbelieving with their sightless eyes who are blind to the beauty of Christ (2 Corinthians 3:13–18). Ironically, Isaiah said that the Incarnate Servant did not have the visible ornaments of royalty that would attract the physical eye to him (Isaiah 53:2). But to His adoring Bride, He is precious beyond words to describe.

His precious beauty is not only beyond description, it is abundant: "grace is poured into thy lips" (v. 2). I suggest that the *beth* preposition is instrumental rather than locative. Grace is poured out by or through your lips, which is a way of saying that He speaks graciously. Similarly, the bride in the Song of Solomon describes the lips of her beloved husband as being like lilies dropping sweet smelling myrrh (Song 5:13). What bride does not delight in hearing affirmations of love from her husband? Those words "I love you" are good to hear. I have been married for 47 years, and I don't think there have been many days, if any, when I have not expressed my love for my wife and, happily, she usually responds in kind. It is not that we need to be assured daily of such love verbally, but there is something special about hearing those words. Admittedly, sometimes I've uttered them carelessly, thoughtlessly, or routinely, and I suppose there have been a few times over these last 47 years that I've said some things I regretted and confessedly more than once my tone has not been right. But it is not so with Jesus, who is the Ideal Husband. His lips are full of grace, and what He speaks to His Bride declares and affirms His love: my beloved, my sister, my spouse, my dove, my love — all words of tenderness. It is not surprising that those who actually heard Jesus speak were impressed "at the gracious words which proceeded out of his mouth" (Luke 4:22). His gracious speaking is all the more significant because He says what He says because His heart is what it is towards us. Jesus Himself said that it is "out of the abundance of the heart the mouth speaketh" (Matthew 12:34). Therefore, His speaking grace reveals His heart for His Bride. As His bride, may we have eyes to behold His beauty and ears to hear His grace.

His Might

Second, attention is directed to the Husband's might: He has the power and means to defend His Bride (vv. 3–5). The vocative, "O most mighty," appropriately designates this Royal Husband. Significantly, in the Old Testament the word has both human and divine referents (Goliath was the *gibbor*, the champion of the Philistines, 1 Samuel 17:51; Yahweh is strong and mighty, Psalm 24:8). Regardless of the referent, the word highlights power and/or valor. That power and valor is infinite when referring to God[12] since God is infinite, eternal, and unchangeable in all of His perfections. Not even Goliath-like strength compares to the Lord. "Hero" is a common gloss for the word, and I think that is a good way to refer to this Royal Husband, Christ. He is the Hero and Champion of His people.

How many young girls dream of finding their hero, that mythological knight in shining armor that will sweep them away to a fairy-tale life of uninterrupted happiness only to discover before long the chinks and rust in the armor? Sooner or later, the best of ordinary husbands will disappoint. Yet Christ never disappoints. Two thoughts stand out that warrant a legitimate and commendable Hero-worship of our spiritual Bridegroom.

First, His arsenal is imposing. I translate verse 3 like this: "Bind your sword upon your hip — your splendor and your majesty." Splendor and majesty stand in apposition to sword, which most likely is metonymical for the entire arsenal at His disposal to defend His Bride and to advance His kingdom. Wearing the ceremonial sword as part of His wedding attire would have been a great assurance to the Bride of His ability to protect her against any jeopardy to her safety. Interestingly, at this occasion the King's sword is sheathed as a symbolic deterrent against any would-be foe, whereas in Revelation 19 the wedding attire has given way to battle apparel dripping with the blood of the enemy with His sword unsheathed, wielding fury. His power is no empty show. Armed with such a weapon the Hero cuts through the enemy with irresistible ease. Theologically, the sword is His sharp and powerful word (hence, out of His mouth in Revelation 19:15) that can discern between the soul and spirit and slice open the heart (Hebrews 4:12). Here is a picture of the catechism's proposition: "Christ executeth the office of a king in subduing us to himself, in ruling and defending us, and in restraining and conquering all his and our enemies" (*Westminster Shorter Catechism*, Q. 26).

Second, His mission is successful: "Be successful, ride on" (v. 5). The juxtaposing of the two imperatives without using the conjunction "and" expresses a certain urgency or intensity. In addition to simply issuing commands, imperatives can be used to express the certainty or assurance that a particular action will occur. Putting both of these thoughts together gives the idea that the King will proceed successfully on His mission. His mission concerns truth, meekness, and righteousness. The particular word for meekness is a *hapax legomenon* (a word that occurs only once in the Bible), but its root connection to the word, "to afflict," suggests the notion of oppression resulting from the absence of justice. If that is the general sense, then the King's mission on behalf of truth, oppression, and righteousness points to the reversal of the state of affairs described by Isaiah: "And judgment (i.e. justice as the antidote to oppression) is turned away backward, and justice (i.e. righteousness) standeth afar off: for truth is fallen in the street, and equity cannot enter" (Isaiah 59:14). Isaiah also explains how this King will accomplish this guaranteed-to-be-accomplished mission: "But with righteousness shall he judge the poor, and reprove with equity for the meek of the earth: and he shall smite the earth: with the rod of his mouth, and with the breath of his lips shall he slay the wicked. And righteousness shall be the girdle of his reins" (11:4–5). The successful mission, which the prophet details, the poet encapsulates: "thy right hand (i.e. the instrument of powerful activity) shall teach thee (i.e. direct your actions) to do terrible things (i.e. awesome)." It is an awesome thought to know that all the injustice, wickedness, and falsehoods that so alarm us are destined for defeat by our Royal Husband, who will not fail in vindicating truth, advancing His kingdom, and defending His Bride.

Verse 5 graphically reiterates the success of the King's mission: "Thine arrows are sharp in the heart of the king's enemies." Every enemy will fall to the razor-sharp arrows that are aimed at the heart with fatal precision. Whether in love or in vengeance, Christ never misses His objective. With "Cupid-like" arrows He attracts His Bride to Himself and with the darts of justice He vanquishes every opposition. Remember the words of the catechism: "Christ executeth the office of a king, in subduing us to himself, in ruling and defending us, and in restraining and conquering all his and our enemies." (*Westminster Shorter Catechism*, Q. 26).

His Authority
Third, attention is directed to the Husband's authority. The affirmation of His royal authority could not be more remarkable or astounding: "Thy throne, O God, is for ever and ever: the scepter of thy kingdom is a right scepter. Thou lovest righteousness,

and hatest wickedness" (vv. 6–7a). The vocative, "O God," by which the Royal Husband is addressed is evidence enough that the One in view is the Messiah. It is one of the most explicit declarations in the Old Testament regarding the deity of the Messiah. There have been alternate translations suggested that attempt to avoid this theological high-water mark, such as the NEB's "Your throne is like God's throne, eternal." Yet the Hebrew is clear that God is used as a vocative. The LXX's rendering reflects that sense, and the New Testament's quotation of the LXX confirms its accuracy (Hebrews 1:8). In addition the application of the statement in the argument of Hebrews 1 is based on the implications of Christ's being God. The inspired commentary is irrefutable. This is one of those capital texts exuding theological significance. That the vocative *Elohim* refers to the Royal Husband specifically is settled by the fact that verse 7b continues to address this God yet distinguishes Him from "God, thy God." Here is the mystery: Absolute Deity in association with Absolute Deity. There is but one true and living God, yet this one true and living God is a Holy Trinity. Could it be that the reference to God's anointing God (the verb form of Messiah) with oil (a common image for the Holy Spirit) at least alludes to the Holy Spirit in this messianic ministry (see Isaiah 61:1)? Although this is not a full exposition or explanation of the Godhead, it certainly contributes to the database of biblical evidence for this essential truth. It is not surprising that Hebrews 1 includes this text as part of the Old Testament's testimony regarding the deity and superiority of Christ, God's Son.

In context, this statement develops a key theme that is integral to the marriage relationship. The throne and the scepter are metonyms referring to headship and authority. So, it is in the God-ordered marriage relationship that "the husband is the head of the wife" and that the wife is to submit to her husband (Ephesians 5:22–23). This *hierarchal* order is analogous to the ideal marriage between Christ and His church: "Christ is the head of the church: and he is the savior of the body" and consequently, "the church is subject to Christ" (Ephesians 5:23–24). As a godly church submits to Christ, a godly wife submits to her husband. In this sense, every Christian marriage should be a living sermon pointing to Christ.

The unhappy thing is that even in the best of human marriages submission becomes a struggle because headship is either weak or abusive. But in the ideal marriage with this Royal Husband, submission should be the happy response of the church because His rule is righteous. "The scepter of thy kingdom is a right scepter. Thou lovest righteousness, and hatest wickedness" (Psalm 45:6–7). The principal trait of His rule is justice; He never deviates from the perfect and proper standard of rectitude. David's inspired job description for rulers is ideally fulfilled in Christ: "He that ruleth over men must be just, ruling in the fear of God" (2 Samuel 23:3). Loving righteousness and hating wickedness are volitional statements. As Christ exercises His just authority, He consistently chooses righteousness (what is right) and rejects wickedness (what is wrong). In human marriages, sooner or later, husbands will disappoint their wives. But it is not so with Christ; He is perfect in every way. Whatever He does is right; He is incapable of disappointing His bride. His submitting Bride may not always understand the "whys" of His rule, but she does recognize the benevolence of it and should trust Him implicitly that He knows what is best. His objective is a "glorious church, not having spot, or wrinkle, or any such thing; but that it should be holy and without blemish" (Ephesians 5:27).

Another unhappy thing about human marriage is the inevitable death of one of the spouses. The marriage vow is until "death us do part," and sooner or later death arrives to dissolve what man cannot put asunder. "For the woman which hath an husband is bound by the law to her husband so long as he liveth; but if the husband be dead, she is loosed from the law of her husband" (Romans 7:2). Every human marriage is temporary. But the rule of the Royal Husband never ends: "Thy throne, O God, is for ever and ever." Earthly heads of state surrender their "scepter" at death, as a result of the voting box, or by force of rebellion. But Christ ever lives, and the perpetuity of His rule does not depend on the consent of the governed. His rule is unique, universal, and unending. That has far-reaching implications, but the context here highlights the indissoluble union between the Royal Husband and His Bride. Christ's conquering death guarantees that not even this last great enemy can sever the relationship between Christ and His people (Romans 8:38–39). Christ's Bride is bound to Him forever. It is not without significance that one of the inspired descriptions of eternity is the marriage supper of the Lamb (Revelation 19:9). The old hymn sums it well:

> His forever, only His;
> Who the Lord and me shall part?
> Ah, with what a rest of bliss
> Christ can fill the loving heart!
> Heav'n and earth may fade and flee,
> Firstborn light in gloom decline;
> But while God and I shall be,
> I am His, and He is mine.[13]

His Reward

Three "therefores" point to the merited exaltation of the Royal Husband. First in verse 2, because or in evidence of the fact He is fair and exudes grace, God has blessed Him. Second in verse 7, because or in evidence of the fact that He rules rightly, God has anointed Him. This anointing (the verbal root for the word "Messiah," that one who has been anointed) generally refers to the affirming, accrediting or setting apart an individual to function in one of the mediatorial offices of prophets, priests, or kings. However, the anointing here is not so much a symbol of consecration as it is celebration. This fits nicely the marriage motif for as Canticles says, the day of the king's espousals is "the day of the gladness of his heart" (Song 3:11). Third, verses 16 and 17 highlight a key messianic truth with significant theological implications: "Instead of thy fathers shall be thy children, whom thou mayest make princes in all the earth. I will make thy name to be remembered in all generations: therefore shall the people praise thee for ever and ever." Note that the masculine pronouns in verses 16 and 17 make it clear that the reference is to the Husband and not the Bride. Unlike most ordinary monarchs who can boast of the dynastic ancestry that perpetuated them to the throne, this unique King, who is David's greater and ideal Son, ascended the throne of a dynasty that appeared to be defunct and vacant for hundreds of years. But notwithstanding the centuries-old vacancy, God set His King upon the holy hill of Zion (Psalm 2:6–another Royal Psalm) and gave Him a people, His inheritance, His seed. These final verses parallel the prophet's revelation regarding Christ's reward for His atoning work: "he shall see his seed, he shall prolong his days, and the pleasure of the Lord shall prosper in his hand" (Isaiah 53:10). Scripture frequently imputes Christ's exaltation to His merits as Paul so explains in Philippians 2:5–11. Though Christ is equal with God, His incarnate obedience unto death led to His triumphant exaltation by receiving a name above all names.

The Royal Bride

This thought transitions to our next major consideration about the Bride. Significantly, the divine blessing and happy celebration in this context relates to the Royal Wedding and to the Bride, who shares in His dignity. In verse 8, the Husband comes forth in the expensive wedding attire to claim His queen, who experiences the benefits of His exaltation. This is the theological point: believers are united to Christ, and marriage is a choice symbol of that mystical and spiritual union between Christ and His church. The Scripture says that in marriage a man and wife become one flesh. So it is that Christ and His Bride are inseparably united, and His Bride benefits from His riches. It is not surprising that the Psalmist testified of a hot heart when writing of this glorious King. May it be that our hearts be aroused as well in adoration and love as we see Him, who is our Beloved.

This inspired love song highlights four views of the Bride, who enjoys a special and privileged position with her Royal Husband. Significantly, each of these depictions of the bride point to the gospel benefits experienced by all those united to Christ as His Beloved Bride.

Her Honor

First, the bride stands in an honored position: "Kings' daughters were among thy honorable women: upon thy right hand did stand the queen in gold of Ophir" (v. 9). The bridal party was itself impressive, but the queen stood in a unique place at the King's right hand. Throughout Scripture, the right hand is the place of honor and special privilege. Psalm 16:11 parallels being in God's presence with being at His right hand — a place to experience the fullness of joy and unceasing pleasures. Paul described this honored place as being in Christ in the heavenly places — a place to experience all spiritual blessings (Ephesians 1:3). Whether in lyrical imagery or didactic declaration, the point is amazingly clear that union with Christ puts the believer in a position of privilege to experience all the benefits of His lavished grace.

Her Attire

Second, the poet gives attention to the bride's glorious dress. This is not surprising, since the bridal gown is always a matter of keen interest. The dress highlights the beauty of the bride. This royal bride is dressed "in the gold of Ophir" (v. 9), "wrought gold" (v. 13); and "in raiment of needlework" (v. 14). She was a sight to behold. Dressed in this beautiful attire, she was "all glorious within" (v. 13). This most likely refers to her being within the palace, a place off limits where she had no right to be apart from the wedding garment, which was symbolic of the marriage union.[14] The theology in this portrait is profound and points to one of the most outstanding benefits of gospel grace. In describing the marriage of the Lamb, John said, "his wife hath made herself ready. And to her was granted that she should be arrayed in fine linen, clean and white: for the fine linen is the righteousness of saints" (Revelation 19:7–8). It is the wedding dress that identifies the bride. John makes it clear that that this attire was provided for her and not self-fabricated. The righteousness of saints, I would argue, is imputed and not enacted righteousness. For sure, Christ's imputed righteousness in justification demands the imparted righteousness of sanctification, but it is the righteousness of Christ that is the ground of acceptance. Isaiah, interestingly, compares the robe of righteousness and garment of salvation to wedding attire with which God has clothed the believer (Isaiah 61:10). Although not in a wedding setting, Joshua's provision of a splendid wardrobe in place of his filthy garments pictures the same remarkable truth, a key component in justification. The dirty garments were removed as an illustration of forgiveness; the new garments were given as an illustration of imputed righteousness (Zechariah 3:4–5). The only garment that gives entrance to the heavenly palace is the righteousness of Christ imputed to His Believing Bride. I can't put it any better than McCheyne: "When I stand before the throne, Dressed in beauty not my own ... Then, Lord, shall I fully know, Not till then how much I owe."

Her Loveliness

Third, the bride is the object of the King's delight: "So shall the king greatly desire thy beauty" (v. 11). In some ways, this is the most amazing line in the entire song. The *hithpael* form of the verb, "to desire," designates a most personal and internal craving

for and longing after something. It is intense and it can only be
satisfied with the possession of what is desired. This is equivalent
to the bride's assessment in the Song of Songs: "I am my beloved's,
and his desire is toward me" (7:10). That Christ desires his church
with this kind of passion is beyond comprehension. It is amazing
how the King perceives the bride: she is beautiful. In this sense,
beauty is in the eye of the beholder. Theologically, this beauty is
the consequence of Christ's redeeming love. Paul's exposition of
marriage in Ephesians 5 is to the point:

> Christ also loved the church, and gave himself for it; That he might
> sanctify and cleanse it with washing of the water by the word, That
> he might present it to himself a glorious church, not having spot, or
> wrinkle, or any such thing, but that it should be holy and without
> blemish (Ephesians 5:25–27).

Receiving this beautiful bride was part of the joy that
was set before Him as He endured the sufferings of the cross
(Hebrews 12:2).

Her Devotion

The fourth feature about this Bride is her unreserved devotion to
her Royal Husband. This devotion is expressed by two imperatives,
which underscore the duties that she performs willingly. First, she
is to forget her previous family ties: "forget also thine own people,
and thy father's house" (v. 10). To forget is a conscious refusal to
think about or to acknowledge something.[15] Marriage constitutes a
new family that takes precedence over the old one. This was Moses'
exposition of Adam's declaration regarding Eve that she was bone
of his bone and flesh of his flesh: "Therefore shall a man leave his
father and his mother, and shall cleave unto his wife: and they shall
be one flesh" (Genesis 2:23–24). Again, this poetic picture points
directly to the nature of the spiritual marriage between Christ
and his bride. With his theological astuteness, Paul applies this
statement directly to the great mystery of Christ and His church

(Ephesians 5:30–32). He plainly says elsewhere regarding those united to Christ, that "old things are passed away; behold, all things are become new" (2 Corinthians 5:17). Marriage to Christ is newness of life.

Second, she is to submit to Him: "for he is thy Lord: and worship thou him" (v. 11). The word Lord refers to a master, the one who exercises headship and authority. Worshiping him has the idea of submitting to and paying homage to him. In its ultimate sense, it refers to the worship that is reserved only for God, thus giving more evidence concerning the deity of this Royal Husband. God ordered this hierarchal order and it is integral to the marriage union. We have only to consider Paul's analogy to see the link to Christ: "Wives, submit yourselves unto your own husbands, as unto the Lord. For the husband is the head of the wife, even as Christ is the head of the church" (Ephesians 5:22–23). Therefore, "the church is subject to Christ" (Ephesians 5:24). This submission is not oppressive or burdensome in light of the love, admiration, character, and divine dignity of the husband. It is the happy response of the one who is living in the experience and reality of that love. What a sense of security to know that the church is loved and that it is special to God. This is part of why the gates of hell will never prevail against her (Matthew 16:18). This divine love affects individual believers in the church as well. When we are conscious of the love that binds us inseparably to the Savior, our response should be to reciprocate with mutual love to Him. Christ is our life and He should be our reason for living (Colossians 3:4). Pleasing Him should be our chief desire, and there is no more tangible way to please Him than submitting to Him in adoration and action.

Conclusion

In this analysis of Psalm 45 I have not attempted to exegete or expound every statement. There are sufficient commentaries available that provide that kind of analysis.[16] I have simply attempted to extract from the Psalm what it may tell us about Christ and His Bride. God has ordained marriage from the beginning to be a kind of pictorial sermon, which points from the purely human relationship to the spiritual. It is my opinion, along with Spurgeon, that this Psalm bypasses any mere human marriage – even of earthly royalty – and takes us directly to Christ and His glorious Bride, which is the church. May it be as we have reflected a little on this glorious theme that our hearts would burn and yearn and become hot with passion for Him. We can so love Him because He first loved us.

9

Christ the Exalted King

Joseph A. Pipa, Jr.

THE WESTMINSTER CATECHISMS DEVELOPED THE WORK OF THE
Incarnate Savior under three offices: prophet, priest, and king.[1]
These three offices actually represent three aspects of Christ's single
office as Mediator. The Savior possesses the title Christ/Messiah
because he was anointed to fulfill these offices. He exercised them
throughout his public ministry on earth (his estate of humiliation)
and he is now exercising them in heaven (his estate of exaltation).
Perhaps the office that most fully encompassed his earthly ministry
was priest, which includes his active and passive obedience and
continues now in his intercession. If this is true, then the office
that most fully characterizes his heavenly ministry is that of king.
As king, he is exercising the offices of prophet and priest. His
three offices of prophet, priest, and king inform and augment
one another in Christ's single office as Mediator. In his estate
of humiliation, he largely kept his kingly office veiled. He often
avoided the designations Messiah and Son of David (Matthew

22:41, 42; see also Matthew 1:1; 9:27; 20:30) because the people had warped views of the messianic king — one who would militarily deliver them from Rome. Of course, he demonstrated his kingly power in his miracles, exercising absolute authority over all physical and spiritual entities — physically, raising the dead (John 11:38–44) and spiritually, casting out demons (Luke 4:36; Matthew 12:28–29). Not until his triumphant entry (Matthew 21:1–11), however, did he make a public declaration of his royalty, which led to his execution. Upon his ascension and session, he was exalted as King of kings and Lord of lords (Philippians 2:9–11; 1 Timothy 6:15; Revelation 17:14; 19:16). In this chapter, it is my purpose to examine his work as king through the lens of Psalm 93.

Psalm 93 introduces this little section of psalms, which include Psalms 93 to 100.[2] I refer to them as messianic kingdom psalms. They are psalms that prophesy the coming of the Lord Jesus Christ as the judge of the earth and as the one who rules over all peoples on the earth. Therefore, all peoples are to serve and worship him.

In the broader context of the psalms, Psalm 93 is related to Psalm 92.[3] Psalm 92 is a psalm for the Sabbath. It was sung on the Jewish Sabbath. In particular, in verses 8 and 9, it reminds us of God's victory over his enemies and ours: "But You, O LORD, are on high forever. For, behold, Your enemies, O LORD, For, behold, Your enemies will perish; All who do iniquity will be scattered." Psalm 93 focuses on the reign of God in the midst of his people. In the minds of old covenant believers, these psalms were closely related. According to the Septuagint, Psalm 92 was sung on the Sabbath; Psalm 93 was sung on the day before the Sabbath to prepare the Israelites for the Sabbath.

When the exiles returned to the land and reflected again on Jehovah's position as their King, they sang this psalm.[4] The psalmist takes the historical occasion of Jehovah's re-established reign in Jerusalem to be prophetic of the reign of the future messianic king. The Lord Jesus Christ is the exalted king who rules over his church and all things forever; he is restraining and conquering his enemies so that we may serve him in holiness according to his word. The psalmist declares the reign of King Jesus, he demonstrates the victory of King Jesus, and he describes our response to King Jesus.

The Declaration of the Reign of the Lord Jesus Christ (vv. 1–2)

The psalmist begins by declaring the reign of Jehovah: "The LORD [Jehovah] reigns, He is clothed with majesty; The LORD has clothed and girded Himself with strength; Indeed, the world is firmly established, it will not be moved. Your throne is established from of old; You are from everlasting."[5] This is a declaration of triumph: Jehovah reigns. It is better translated as Jehovah has assumed his reign (Isaiah 52:7). God's people are to know that Jehovah God is the eternal king who reigns forever. As Isaiah announced the return from captivity, he used this expression: "Your God reigns" (Isaiah 52:7). Isaiah is announcing that God has assumed his kingship over his people. But, as I have pointed out, this psalm is particularly about the Lord Jesus Christ. How do we know that? This series of psalms is focusing on Jehovah reigning through his Son Incarnate, a special kingship, a special reign. Look, for example, at Psalm 96:10 and 13: "Say among the nations, 'The LORD reigns; Indeed, the world is firmly established, it will not be moved; He will judge the peoples with equity'" (v. 10). "Before the LORD, for He is coming, For He is coming to judge the earth. He will judge the world in righteousness And the peoples in His faithfulness" (v. 13). These psalms are prophesying the coming of Jehovah's appointed judge, who is the great deliverer, namely, Christ himself. He is the Son of God and our Savior. Earlier, in Psalm 2, this reign was prophesied. God placed his Son on the throne and gave him the nations as his inheritance. In Psalm 110, David prophesied: "The LORD says to my Lord: 'Sit at My right hand Until I make your enemies a footstool for Your feet.'" Christ instructs us that this was a messianic prophecy (Matthew 22:41–46). And so, the Scriptures tell us that God the Son Incarnate is going to come as a mighty king and he now has assumed that reign. We read in Revelation the description of him in 19:16, written on his robe, on his thigh, he has a name: "King of kings, and Lord of lords." In his resurrection and ascension, the Lord Jesus Christ is exalted on high as the glorious king. He has had that great victory parade into the throne room of heaven and is now enthroned at the right hand of God the Father forevermore. He reigns; he has assumed kingship as the glorified and exalted Messiah.

We may consider Messiah's reign under three phases. First, he reigned as the pre-incarnate Savior, to whom the Father gave his elect from eternity. In human history, God the Son has reigned as Mediator. Beginning in Genesis 3:15, when God promised the supernaturally provided deliverer who would defeat Satan, the promised Savior ruled over his church, providing for and protecting her. Berkhof wrote,

> The generally accepted position of the Church is that Christ received His appointment as mediatorial King in the depths of eternity, and that He began to function as such immediately after the fall (Proverbs 8:23; Psalm 2:6). During the old dispensation, He carried on His work as King partly through the judges of Israel, and partly through the typical kings.[6]

The second person of the Godhead is pictured ruling on a throne in Isaiah 6:1 (cf. John 12:41, where John says that Isaiah saw Christ in this vision).

The second phase began with his anointing in his baptism (Matthew 3:16, 17; Mark 1:9–11). Hence he preached: "'The time is fulfilled, and the kingdom of God is at hand; repent and believe in the gospel'" (Mark 1:15). In his earthly ministry, he began his work as king. But, as noted previously, in the state of humiliation it was veiled — an anointed king not yet inaugurated. David typified this twofold stage: after his anointing, he spent many years in humiliation before his inauguration as king (2 Samuel 2:1–4; 5:1–5). We noted Christ's miracles. Also, as the Son of Man (a messianic title), he claimed authority to forgive sin (Matthew 9:1–8). He responded to the title, Son of David, and healed people (Luke 18:35–42). He proclaimed himself king in his triumphal entry (Matthew 21:1–11). In fact, Matthew wrote his Gospel to demonstrate that Jesus of Nazareth was the messianic king (1:1–17). The Magi came seeking the King of the Jews (Matthew 2:2). He confessed his kingship before Pilate (Matthew 27:11) and Pilate declared him King of the Jews as he hanged on the cross (Matthew 27:37). Moreover, a large portion of his teaching was on the nature of the kingdom he had come to establish.[7]

The third phase of His mediatorial reign came to fruition with his ascension and session. This is what the psalmist alludes to in verse 1. Berkhof wrote, "He did not publicly and formally assume His throne and inaugurate His spiritual kingdom until the time of His ascension and elevation at the right hand of God (Acts 2:29–36; Philippians 2:5–11)."[8] The writers of *The Westminster Larger Catechism* described his elevation at the right hand of God (Q. 54):

> Christ is exalted in his sitting at the right hand of God, in that as God-man he is advanced to the highest favour with God the Father, with all fulness of joy, glory, and power over all things in heaven and earth; and doth gather and defend his church, and subdue their enemies; furnisheth his ministers and people with gifts and graces, and maketh intercession for them.

When one compares this statement with Q. 45 in *The Larger*

Catechism, it is clear that, in his session, he is exercising his office of king:

> Christ executeth the office of a king, in calling out of the world a people to himself, and giving them officers, laws, and censures, by which he visibly governs them; in bestowing saving grace upon his elect, rewarding their obedience, and correcting them for their sins, preserving and supporting them under all their temptations and sufferings, restraining and overcoming all their enemies, and powerfully ordering all things for his own glory, and their good; and also in taking vengeance on the rest, who know not God, and obey not the gospel.

As the psalmist declared this reign of Christ, he stated four things about the reign of King Jesus. First, it is a glorious reign: "He is clothed with majesty." Earthly monarchs demonstrated their glory by the garments they wore, garments often woven with special threads of gold and silver. They had crowns encrusted with precious jewels. They were waited on by courtiers also decked out in beautiful garments. Everything was designed to show their splendor and eminence. As one entered into their presence, every step of the way, there were greater displays of that majesty and splendor. Our Savior, as King of kings and Lord of lords, enthroned on high, also is clothed in great splendor and beauty. The splendor of his person is a splendor that is pictured in Isaiah 6:1: "In the year of King Uzziah's death I saw the Lord sitting on a throne, lofty and exalted, with the train of his robe filling the temple." He was surrounded by the seraphim who cried out incessantly, "Holy, Holy, Holy, is the Lord of hosts, The whole earth is full of His glory." Also consider the incomprehensible picture in Revelation 1:12–16:

> Then I turned to see the voice that was speaking with me. And having turned I saw seven golden lampstands; and in the middle of the lampstands I saw one like a son of man, clothed in a robe reaching to

the feet, and girded across His chest with a golden sash. His head and His hair were white like white wool, like snow; and His eyes were like a flame of fire. His feet were like burnished bronze, when it has been made to glow in a furnace, and His voice was like the sound of many waters. In his right hand He held seven stars, and out of His mouth came a sharp two-edged sword; and His face was like the sun shining in its strength.

This description pictures for us the majesty and glory with which our king is clothed. These figures depict him in his awful holiness and power. In his person, as the exalted God-Man, he is honored.

Moreover, we see his beauty in his great works. It is as the exalted king that he holds all things together by the word of his power (Hebrews 1:3). His beauty is further manifested in his attributes: for example, his wisdom, might, power, holiness, and eternality (Psalm 45:1–9). All of these things are the clothing of our Savior, given to us that we might with mind's eye gaze on him and be filled with wonder and awe at the beauty and splendor of our king, who indeed is the greatest of all kings. He is King of kings; he is Lord of lords (Psalm 45:17).

The realization of the beauty of the king will stimulate our worship. I mentioned that earthly kings will surround themselves with all the paraphernalia of majesty and power. My wife and I have visited Hampton Court Palace. In order to enter the throne room, one has to pass through a series of antechambers. Each chamber is more glorious, more splendid, more full of wealth than the previous. All of that is designed to overwhelm the visitor with the king's majesty before coming into his presence.

As you consider the majesty and splendor of Christ, you will be overwhelmed with his glory before entering into his presence. We begin in the outer chamber of this world and meditate on his power. We enter the chamber of providence and are filled with a sense of his wisdom and power. We enter the chamber of his angels, such wonderful creatures, all who point to his splendor and glory. We come close and consider his attributes and the extent of his rule. Then, our hearts will be beating with awe and wonder as we come to his throne and we bow in love, adoration, and thanksgiving. Our king is clothed with majesty.

Second, the psalmist taught that he is a powerful king: "The LORD has clothed and girded Himself with strength." Most kings today are what we call constitutional monarchs or parliamentarian monarchs, like the Queen of England. They possess a title and often splendor and wealth, but they have little power. They do not have the power of ancient kings. They do not have armies at their disposal. But we read here that our king is not a paper tiger; he is not some constitutional monarch. Our king is a mighty warrior. God declared to him in Psalm 2:8–9: "Ask of Me, and I will surely give the nations as Your inheritance, And the very ends of the earth as Your possession. You shall break them with a rod of iron, You shall shatter them like earthenware." And Solomon described him in Psalm 45:3–5: "Gird Your sword on Your thigh, O Mighty One, In Your splendor and Your majesty! And in Your majesty ride on victoriously, For the cause of truth and meekness and righteousness; Let Your right hand teach You awesome things. Your arrows are sharp; The peoples fall under You; Your arrows are in the heart of the King's enemies." Or, David in Psalm 110:2–7:

The LORD will stretch forth Your strong scepter from Zion, saying,

"Rule in the midst of Your enemies."
Your people will volunteer freely in the day of Your power;
In holy array, from the womb of the dawn,
Your youth are to You as the dew.
The LORD has sworn and will not change His mind,
"You are a priest forever

According to the order of Melchizedek."
The Lord is at Your right hand;
He will shatter kings in the day of His wrath.
He will judge among the nations,
He will fill them with corpses,
He will shatter the chief men over a broad country.
He will drink from the brook by the wayside;
Therefore He will lift up His head.

John saw the fulfillment of this powerful rule in Revelation 19:11–16:

> And I saw heaven opened, and behold, a white horse, and He who sat on it is called Faithful and True, and in righteousness He judges and wages war. His eyes are a flame of fire, and on His head are many diadems; and He has a name written on Him which no one knows except Himself. He is clothed with a robe dipped in blood, and His name is called The Word of God. And the armies which are in heaven, clothed in fine linen, white and clean, were following Him on white horses. From His mouth comes a sharp sword, so that with it He may strike down the nations, and He will rule them with a rod of iron; and He treads the wine press of the fierce wrath of God, the Almighty. And on His robe and on His thigh He has a name written, "King of Kings, and Lord of Lords."

Oh, Christian, this one is your king, exalted on high in all splendor and majesty, mounted on a white stallion, riding through the nations, conquering his and our enemies. As we look around the world today, we see tyrants and dictators exalting themselves against Christ and his church. But they have not dethroned him. He is on his mighty stallion, riding through the kingdoms of the earth, gathering his people to himself, and accomplishing his holy will. It is in the exercise of his kingly power that Christ, our king, subdues us to himself.

This leads us to the third thing about our king. His reign is a universal reign: "Indeed, the world is firmly established, it will not be moved. Your throne is established from of old" (Psalm 93:1b-2a). What does the psalmist mean? How does this world being firmly established relate to the rule of Christ? He is asserting that Christ, the king, reigns over the entire world. He reigns over the physical world, which means, as king, he controls all things: he controls the weather; he controls earthquakes, hurricanes, tsunamis, volcanos, droughts, and floods. There's not a thing that is beyond his control. All illness, all disease, all things are under the authority of Christ. Hence the world physically is firmly established; it cannot be moved apart from his holy, saving purposes. He swore that never again would the earth be inundated with a flood of water and all destroyed. But we also know that some meteor will not fall from outer space and wipe out our planet, and no great holocaust will take place physically and destroy a great portion of the human race because the king reigns and he's governing all things for the sake of his people. This is true over the earth geographically, politically, and nationally. The earth is firmly established. Not a thing is taking place in the entire history of mankind, there is nothing that you will read in the newspaper tomorrow that is true news which took place yesterday or this past week that King Jesus has not authorized. Not one man goes to a throne; not one battle is fought; not one ambassador is killed; not one embassy is burned; nothing can take place apart from the rule of King Jesus.

Furthermore, he is doing these things for the sake of his church. Paul wrote in Ephesians 1:22–23: "And He put all things in subjection under His feet, and gave Him as head over all things to the church, which is His body, the fullness of Him who fills all in all." He is directing all things physically, politically, spiritually, to accomplish the purposes of his kingdom. When you pray in the Lord's prayer, "Your kingdom come, Your will be done," you are praying for this active reign of Christ Jesus. There is not one dictator today who can lift up his hand and oppose the kingdom of Christ and succeed. If a tyrant succeeds, it is because it is the will of the king. The tyrant's victory is but temporary and that for wise and holy purposes. The principle holds true in your life. No cancer, no disease, no illness, nothing can come into your life apart from the king's good pleasure. And that's why Paul promised that all things work together for good to those that love God and are called according to his purposes (Romans 8:28). It is as this all-powerful king that he has subdued us to himself, that he rules and defends us.[9]

Fourth, our king's reign is eternal: "Your throne is established from of old; You are from everlasting" (Psalm 93:2). God the Son is from everlasting; he is eternal. But now the exalted God-Man is an eternal king. Yes, there'll be a day when he turns the mediatorial kingdom over to the Father, but he shall reign over us forever. We will delight in him as our king. Consider the comfort in this truth: he's unchangeable, absolutely unchangeable. All that you read about the king in the Old Testament, in the New Testament, demonstrates that he's the same. What he did for his people then, he does now. What he has done for his people in the history of his church, he will continue to do. He is the same yesterday, today, and forever. What a king! And he wants you to think upon him in his kingdom. He's not a king in waiting. He's not the Prince of Wales. He's not waiting for that day when he'll come back and establish some kind of kingship in Jerusalem. Matthew Henry states that next to the deity and power of God, his active rule is the most important thing for a Christian to know.[10] He rules today; he is king over you, over your family, over your work, and over your church. And he wants you to approach him as king.

The Demonstration of Victory (vv. 3–4)

Having declared the king's reign, the psalmist demonstrated the king's victory: "The floods have lifted up, O Lord, The floods have lifted up their voice, The floods lift up their pounding waves. More than the sounds of many waters, Than the mighty breakers of the sea, The Lord on high is mighty."

We are surrounded by awful powers; the world's system and Satan have set themselves against Christ and against his church. And they are powerful in their opposition. The psalmist was picturing this powerful opposition in verse 3. Flooding waters and mighty breakers are often used in Scripture to describe the power of the enemies of God's people. Isaiah used this figure to describe the opposition of the nations: "Alas, the uproar of many peoples Who roar like the roaring of the seas, And the rumbling of nations Who rush on like the rumbling of mighty waters! The nations rumble on like the rumbling of many waters, But He will rebuke them and they will flee far away" (Isaiah 17:12–13).

There are few things, physically, more powerful than water. You may have seen pictures of just a few inches of water sweeping a pick-up truck off a bridge or of houses floating down rivers. We know that floods or tsunamis have wiped out entire villages and towns. You may have stood on the beach and seen the mighty breakers roar with awful power. And we know that nothing can resist them. Anything that is in their way will be demolished. That is why the Bible refers to flooding waters and mighty breakers of the sea to remind us of the awful power that has set itself against King Jesus: "The kings of the earth take their stand And the rulers take counsel together Against the Lord and against His Anointed, saying, 'Let us tear their fetters apart And cast away their cords from us!'" (Psalm 2:2–3).

But in the midst of this raging storm and flow of water, one can hear the calmness that is greater than the sounds of many waters and the mighty breakers of the sea: "More than the sounds of many waters, Than the mighty breakers of the sea, The LORD on high is mighty." He is more powerful than the sea, than all its floods and breakers. He is the one who, having created the heavens and the earth and divided the sea from the dry land, has set a boundary. He has said to the sea, "You may come thus far and no farther."

There is a story, which is probably apocryphal, about Cnute, who was a great Christian king in eleventh-century England. The story is told that his courtiers were always flattering him, saying things like: "You are the greatest man that ever lived. There is nothing you cannot do. There can never be another as mighty as you. Nothing in the world would dare disobey you. You rule over the land and sea." The king grew tired of such foolishness. One day, as he was walking by the sea, he asked, "Do you think the tide will stop, if I give it the command?" They were puzzled, but dared not contradict him. "Give the order, O great king, and it will obey," one of them assured him.

He had his throne carried to the edge of the sea. With great vigor, he commanded the sea, saying, "You are part of my dominion, and the ground that I am seated upon is mine. No one has disobeyed my orders with impunity. Therefore, I order you not to rise onto my land, nor to wet the clothes or body of your Lord." But the sea carried on rising as usual without any reverence for his person, and soaked his feet and legs. Then moving away, he said, "All the inhabitants of the world should know that the power of kings is vain and trivial, and that none is worthy of the name of king but he whose command the heaven, earth, and sea obey by eternal laws." He removed his crown and never wore it again. Of course, our Savior fulfilled this literally; he walked on the sea as dry land; he commanded the waves, and they became as clear and smooth as crystal. God in his wisdom and power "tramples down the waves of the sea" (Job 9:8).

The storms of life are mighty and the waves pound against us. But he is mightier; his voice is mightier; his presence is mightier. He is enthroned on high over all of the opposition of life. He is the warrior king, restraining and conquering all his and our enemies.[11]

Reader, I ask you, "Have you bowed the knee to King Jesus?" You cannot beat him. If you refuse to bow the knee in grace and repentance, he will compel you to bow. He will smash you like a clay pot and cast you into hell forevermore. You can no more thwart his purposes than you can command the sea.

Some of you have not bowed the knee to King Jesus. You want nothing to do with him and his rule. You think you can live independently in rebellion against him. You need to note that every knee shall bow and every tongue will confess that Jesus Christ is Lord. You may bow to him in repentance and faith now. But, if you refuse, you will be crushed by his rod of iron and spend eternity in eternal damnation.

As Christians, we must not lose hope. Our king reigns and is conquering all his and our enemies. There are times when he allows his power to be unseen. But a day is coming when there will be a great shout and the blast of trumpets, and the king shall come with all the court of heaven and establish, for all time, his perfect reign in the midst of his people — the declaration of his reign, the demonstration of his victory.

The Description of our Response (v. 5)

In verse 5, God teaches us how we are to respond to the king: "Your testimonies are fully confirmed; Holiness befits Your house, O LORD, forevermore." Kings have charters, constitutions, and law books. Some wise kings have written very wise laws, but they are all imperfect and they are imperfectly enforced. But here we're told that our king has a charter that's perfect. His testimonies are perfect. Testimonies refer to the binding covenant law of our king, one of the many synonyms used for Scripture. The psalmist declared: "The law of the LORD is perfect, restoring the soul; The testimony of the LORD is sure, making wise the simple" (Psalm 19:7). And later in Psalm 119:160: "The sum of Your word is truth, And every one of Your righteous ordinances is everlasting." God's word contains no error; it perfectly expresses his will. For this reason, it serves as our only rule of faith and practice.[12] It is through this word that the king rules us. Do you want to know the will of the king? Read his word. Here, he exercises his prophetic office. By the word, he will rule you. In the word, he has appointed office-bearers to teach you the word and to rule the church according to his word. Through the word, the priest assures you of his intercession on your behalf and makes the sacraments effective in your life. *The Shorter Catechism* teaches that, as king, Christ rules and defends us. *The Larger Catechism* expands on this aspect: "... giving them officers, laws, and censures, by which he visibly governs them."[13]

Do you think about the Bible in this way? It is the word of your king. Do you cherish the word? Could you live without it? Would it be better to die than not to have a Bible? Would you willingly forfeit everything else rather than forfeit the word of God? And does your daily practice then demonstrate that? Are you in the word, listening to the voice of the king, learning his doctrines, his precepts, his promises, and his threats? Are you, men, leading your families in family worship of the king, instructing them in the charter of the king? And, above all, it is in preaching that the king himself utters with an unmistakable voice the powerful, life-changing truths found in his word. What a precious possession! Read it. Store it up in your hearts and live upon it for here the king speaks to us.

What, then, is the goal of the king in teaching us his word? The psalmist says, "Holiness befits your house, O LORD, forevermore." We are in the court of the king. We serve him as his servants and the distinguishing mark, the king's coat of arms, is holiness. He is garbed in beautiful holiness, and holiness is what befits him and his house. This means that we, his subjects, are to be holy. We are to possess a holiness that goes far beyond our outward acts, an external conformity to his law, although that is important. It is a holiness that must begin in our hearts — a desire for the king, for his glory, for his kingdom, a desire for his honor, love, and joy in the contemplation of him, and of serving him. And that's why we obey. Our obedience must come from our hearts, hearts subdued by the king, hearts aware that holiness is what befits the people of God and nothing else.

Are you consumed with a passion for holiness? A passion to be like your king? Do your sins cause you grief and do you mourn over them? Are you seeking daily to put them to death? Are you seeking daily to be conformed to the image of this glorious king, whose moral image looms large in the lives of his people? There's no other response that is fitting. He saved us that we might be a holy people. He saved us, not just to deliver us from hell and condemnation, but from our sins, to have a people for his own possession. And that must be your passion; it must be your desire; it must be the daily goal of your life because his testimonies are confirmed forever in holiness. Holiness befits his house forevermore.

This concept informs us of the necessity of holiness, if we are to worship the king well. Later the psalmist commands us to worship the king in holy attire or the splendor of holiness (Psalm 96:9). Of course, we are to approach him clothed in the perfect righteousness of Christ, but also clothed in personal holiness. Failure to do so nullifies our worship (Psalm 66:18; Proverbs 15:8; 21:27).

Conclusion

We have learned that Jesus Christ reigns over all things in majesty and might. The Lord Jesus Christ is the exalted king who rules over his church and all things forever. All that we have seen in this psalm is summarized in *The Larger Catechism* Q. 45:

> Christ executeth the office of a king, in calling out of the world a people to himself, and giving them officers, laws, and censures, by which he visibly governs them; in bestowing saving grace upon his elect, rewarding their obedience, and correcting them for their sins, preserving and supporting them under all their temptations and sufferings, restraining and overcoming all their enemies, and powerfully ordering all things for his own glory, and their good; and also in taking vengeance on the rest, who know not God, and obey not the gospel.

Behold your king in his preeminence! Love, adore, and serve him! Give yourself to support his rule among the nations. We are exhorted in Psalm 96:2b–3: "Proclaim good tidings of His salvation from day to day. Tell of His glory among the nations, His wonderful deeds among all the peoples."

Long and pray for the coming of his kingdom. *The Larger Catechism* teaches us how to pray for his kingdom:

> What do we pray for in the second petition?

> In the second petition, (which is, Thy kingdom come,) acknowledging ourselves and all mankind to be by nature under the dominion of sin and Satan, we pray, that the kingdom of sin and Satan may be destroyed, the gospel propagated throughout the world, the Jews called, the fullness of the Gentiles brought in; the church furnished with all gospel-officers and ordinances, purged from corruption, countenanced and maintained by the civil magistrate: that the ordinances of Christ may be purely dispensed, and made

effectual to the converting of those that are yet in their sins, and the confirming, comforting, and building up of those that are already converted: that Christ would rule in our hearts here, and hasten the time of his second coming, and our reigning with him forever: and that he would be pleased so to exercise the kingdom of his power in all the world, as may best conduce to these ends.[14]

Let us look to Christ our king to spread his kingdom in and among us, by his word and Spirit, to the glory of the Father.

"The Weak Things of the World"

The Enigma of Isaiah's Suffering Servant

Jonathan Gibson

How many are there whose eyes have been opened when reading this "golden passional of the Old Testament evangelist," as Polycarp the Lysian calls it! In how many an Israelite has it melted the crust of his heart! It looks as if it had been written beneath the cross upon Golgotha.[1]

The Wondrous Cross

One of the earliest surviving presentations of Jesus is a piece of Roman graffiti from the turn of the third century AD. The graffiti depicts a young man called Alexamenos worshiping a donkey-headed figure on a cross, with the inscription: "Alexamenos worships [his] God."[2] The graffiti was clearly meant to mock Alexamenos for his faith in the crucified Christ. In the first century, crucifixion spoke of weakness and defeat, of guilt and shame — hardly things that civil, educated people would boast in.

And yet Christians in the first century did just that: they boasted in
the crucified Christ. For them, at the center of Christianity was a
Christ on a cross, which made their faith seem, to the unbelieving
world, rather foolish — even preposterous. And yet, for Christians
then, and now, the image of the crucified Christ is not foolishness;
it is wisdom — the wisdom of God. As the apostle Paul wrote:
"But God chose what is foolish in the world to shame the wise;
God chose what is weak in the world to shame the strong; God
chose what is low and despised in the world, even things that are
not, to bring to nothing things that are" (1 Corinthians 1:27–28).
This is the enigma at the heart of the Christian gospel: what is
foolishness to the world — a crucified Jew on a cross — is wisdom
to the Christian. It is the wisdom of God. The cross of Christ is
not preposterous — it is wondrous. God's ways are not our ways,
and the crucified Christ is his surprising way of salvation.

Surprising Salvation

This was the lesson that Israel in the eighth century BC had to
learn, as they prepared to be sent into exile under God's judgment.
God was going to save them in a way that they would not have
expected. In the second half of his prophecy (chs. 40–66), Isaiah
tells Israel that God would save them in a surprising way, by
raising up a man called "Cyrus" to bring his people out of exile
and to help them rebuild the temple (44:28; 45:1). Later in biblical
history this "Cyrus" is identified as Cyrus, the "Great King" of
Persia (599–530 BC), who released Judah from captivity and sent
them back to their capital city to rebuild the temple (cf. Ezra
1:1–3). This was the surprise that awaited Israel in exile: "Cyrus
the Savior," an uncircumcised Persian, would bring them back to
Jerusalem.

Now, at one level, any eighth-century Israelite could live with a
pagan Persian being a pawn on God's chessboard in order to bring

them out of exile. But it is the allocation of certain messianic titles to Cyrus that heightens the surprise: "[W]ho says of Cyrus, 'He is my shepherd' … Thus says the LORD to his anointed, to Cyrus" (44:28; 45:1). The titles of "shepherd" and "anointed" were reserved only for the Davidic king, not for an uncircumcised sovereign from Persia! And yet, God declares that Cyrus would be the "shepherd-messiah" to save Israel: "'I have stirred him up in righteousness, and I will make all his ways level; he shall build my city and set my exiles free, not for price or reward,' says the LORD of hosts" (45:13). If Israel wanted to be saved, then they would need to be saved God's way, not their way. Indeed, anyone opposed to this way of salvation would receive the divine "Woe" (45:8–9).

Cyrus, however, could only ever bring Israel back to the land; he could not bring them back to God. The "exodus" needed to be more than territorial; it needed to be spiritual if Israel was to return and remain in the land. For that to happen, God would have to do a "new thing" (42:9; 43:19; 48:6). This new thing would be a "new exodus" (43:19), a motif that occupies much of the second half of Isaiah's prophecy (40:3–5; 41:17–18; 42:16; 48:20–21; 49:8–12; 51:9–10). In speaking of a new exodus, Isaiah makes various allusions to the first exodus, one of which is God's "arm" (cf. Exodus 6:6; 15:6; Deuteronomy 4:34; 5:15; 11:2; 26:8). At the first Exodus, God flexed his biceps, so to speak, and the world shuddered. Now Isaiah employs the same image of God's "arm" as the means by which this new exodus would occur (40:10; 48:14; 51:9; 52:10), only this time the "arm of the Lord" would be personified in the Servant of the Lord (53:1). God's "arm," his mighty power, would be seen in the Servant and his work. Here was the one who would do a new thing for God and enact a new exodus. Cyrus would bring them back to the land and help them rebuild Jerusalem and the temple; but the Servant would bring them back to God, enacting the real (spiritual) exodus and restoring true worship in Israel.

The Enigmatic Servant

Given the allusions in Isaiah to the arm of the Lord at the first Exodus, when the Servant is introduced, it is reasonable to expect a divine-like figure who saves Israel with public displays of terrifying power. After all, that is how God saved Israel out of Egypt through Moses, "by signs, by wonders, and by war, by a mighty hand and an outstretched arm, and by great deeds of terror" (Deuteronomy 4:34). Yet when the Servant appears in Isaiah's prophecy, in what are known as the four Servant Songs (42:1–9; 49:1–13; 50:4–11; and 52:13–53:12), he does not exactly fit the image of an arm flexed for battle. The Servant is more unimpressive than impressive — and this is what creates the enigma surrounding him.[3]

The first Servant Song (42:1–9) announces that the Servant will bring justice to the nations (v. 1); yet he will not make a song and dance of it as he does so. He will not cry aloud or lift up his voice in the streets (v. 2); his ministry will be understated, involving gentleness and care: "[A] bruised reed he will not break, and a faintly burning wick he will not quench"; and yet "he will not faint or be discouraged until he has established justice in the earth" (v. 4). His ministry will be discreet, yet determined. And so the enigma begins: this Servant is the "arm of the Lord," and yet he does not perform "signs and wonders" as there were at the first Exodus.

The second Servant Song (49:1–13) begins to shift perspectives. The Servant is introduced as an agent of war: his mouth is sharp like a sword; he is made into a polished arrow (v. 2). He is also given the name "Israel," an embodiment of what the nation ought to be, and the one through whom God will be glorified (v. 3).[4] However, in his calling he seems despondent at times: "I have labored in vain; I have spent my strength for nothing and vanity" (v. 4a). And yet, despite this, he still trusts that his cause is just and his recompense is with God (v. 4b). His purpose, even from the womb, is to bring Jacob (Israel) back to God and to bring salvation to the nations (vv. 5–6). Herein lies the enigma: although he will be "deeply despised, abhorred by the nation" and "the servant of rulers" (v. 7), God will make him "a covenant to the people" (v. 8).

The third Servant Song (50:4–11) advances the enigma: the Servant will be wise with his words, because he is first one who is taught by God; his teaching ministry will sustain the weary (v. 4); and he will be obedient before God (v. 5). Yet his obedience will entail giving his back to those who strike and his cheeks to those who pull out the beard; it will involve not hiding his face from disgrace or spitting (v. 6). And so the enigma grows: the Servant is supposed to be the mighty and powerful "arm of the Lord," and yet he will be despised and beaten and spat upon — in a word, defeated. How then can he possibly accomplish a new exodus for God's people, if the first Exodus was accomplished by the powerful arm of the Lord (cf. Deuteronomy 4:34)?

The fourth Servant Song (52:13–53:12), described by one commentator as "the jewel in the crown of Isaiah's theology,"[5] does nothing to lessen the enigma; if anything, it heightens it. The Song is divided into five distinct stanzas (52:13–15; 53:1–3, 4–6, 7–9, 10–12). The first stanza (52:13–15) serves as the overture for the rest of the Song and introduces us to the enigma: the Servant will succeed in bringing salvation to many nations, but he will do so through his suffering not his strength. And yet, this suffering Servant will be called "the arm of the Lord" (53:1). This is the enigma at the heart of Isaiah 53. The second and fourth stanzas (53:1–3 and 7–9) state simple facts about the Servant, while the third and fifth stanzas (53:4–6 and 10–12) state the significance of those facts.[6] As we move through stanzas two to five, the Servant moves from being passive to active, though, interestingly, the Servant never speaks in the Song. Each stanza builds upon the other, bringing the enigma of the Servant to a climax.

Stanza 1 — The Overture: Success through Suffering (52:13–15)

The song begins with the Servant's future success and exaltation (vv. 13 and 15) set in contrast to his intervening humiliation (v. 14). In one moment, he is said to be "high and lifted up," exalted like a king; in the next, people are said to be appalled at him because of his disfigurement.[7] Yet this marred, mangled man will "sprinkle many nations," like a priest sprinkling blood on an altar to atone for people's sins.[8] The Servant will also stun kings into silence. In the ancient world, kings were viewed as sages (think of Solomon, for example). Yet kings will submit in silence before this disfigured man, which brings us full circle to his position of exaltation and authority. The enigma, which has been building in each of the Servant Songs, now comes into sharp focus: the one mangled will be the one magnified, the one humbled will be the one exalted. But the Servant's magnification, his exaltation, will not come in spite of his suffering; it will come because of his suffering. He will succeed through suffering: he will sprinkle the nations and stun kings into silence through his own suffering — in silence (53:7, 9).

The next four stanzas in chapter 53 reveal four things about this Servant and his work.

Stanza 2: He Was Despised by Us (53:1–3)

The second stanza opens with words spoken by a collective group of witnesses ("us," v. 1; "we," vv. 2–3). When the "us" in v. 1 (the proclaimers of the Servant and his work) is connected to the "we" in vv. 2–3 (the despisers and rejecters), it becomes apparent that a profound change occurred in these witnesses — something with which every witnessing believer can identify. At first, we were not attracted to the Servant: "[H]e had no form or majesty that we should look upon him, and no beauty that we should desire him" (v. 2); the disinterest then turned to rejection: "[H]e was despised, and we esteemed him not" (v. 3). But later we experience a little of that rejection ourselves through our own identification with the Servant: "Who has believed what he has heard from us? And to whom has the arm of the Lord been revealed?" (v. 1) The questions are rhetorical. Yet they carry an element of surprise, given that this is the arm of the Lord we are speaking about. The last time the arm of the Lord was flexed for God's people, Pharaoh and Egypt and the surrounding nations saw it, and shuddered. Some, even as far away as Jericho, heard about it and believed, such as Rahab the prostitute (Joshua 2:10–13). So why such a poor response this time around? Why did more people not see the arm of the Lord revealed in this Servant? The simple answer is that the arm of the Lord was veiled behind the Servant's unattractive appearance and people's rejection of him.

The Servant's life, however, did not begin with rejection. He had a promising start in life, growing up before God like a tender plant, even though the environment in which he grew up was difficult (v. 2). Indeed, while his background was one of poverty and obscurity, it was nevertheless one of royalty. The mention of the "young plant" and the "root" recalls chapter 11 where Isaiah spoke of a "shoot from the stump of Jesse" (v. 1) and the "root of Jesse" (v. 10) — royal terms for a royal son. So why did people not believe the message about this royal son? Because, as he entered public life, there was nothing attractive about him, "no beauty that we should desire him" (v. 2b) — which is a surprise, given his royal heritage. As the "root of Jesse," this Servant was a direct descendant of David and Solomon, both of whom are described as handsome men. David, we are told, was a "man of form" (1 Samuel 16:18), yet this Servant had "no form" (Isaiah 53:2).[9] If we saw him in a crowd, we would not take a second look at him — not because he was necessarily ugly, but because he was so average looking as not to merit even a second glance. Yet people did not just ignore him — they despised and rejected him. Maybe it was after his face became marred beyond human semblance that he was despised, or maybe the marring was the fruit of his rejection. In either case, the fact is that this despising, this rejection, would ultimately end in his death. No wonder then that he is described as a "man of sorrows" and "acquainted with grief" (v. 3). This does not mean that he was generally a sad man, but rather that he experienced in his life the debilitating effects of sin (not personally in his own life, but socially in the world around him). He bore the burdens of humanity in his humanity. And, as if all this was not enough for one poor soul to carry, he experienced all of it alone: He was "one from whom men hide their faces" (v. 3). The "face" in Hebrew thought speaks of favor, approval, acceptance — basic requirements for a human personality to grow and develop.[10] Yet they were not afforded him, even from his own people: "[H]e was despised, and we esteemed him not" (v. 3). And so we come full circle: the proclaimers of the Servant, who began this section with their testimony, were first despisers of the Servant.

This is the first thing we see about this enigmatic Servant: the fact of his rejection. The one who would be high and lifted up was first despised by us.

Stanza 3: He Was Punished Because of Us (53:4–6)

The third stanza moves from the fact of his rejection to its significance. Here faith, as it were, converts the facts into their significance, seen in the emphatic use of "surely" and "he" commencing verse 4: "*Surely he* has borne our griefs and carried our sorrows..." The words recall verse 3 and serve to show the significance of this Servant being a man of sorrows and acquainted with grief: the weaknesses experienced through suffering as a result of sin and the sorrows that naturally accompany them, he bore; that which burdens us in this broken, sin-filled world, he made his own — which is all the more remarkable considering what we did to him. We despised him, yet he bore our griefs; we rejected him, yet he carried our sorrows. Verse 4 underlines the point that he did this while we "esteemed him stricken, smitten by God, and afflicted." We were like Job's friends: "No smoke without a fire! No punishment without a crime! He must have done something to be smitten by God and afflicted like this!" Yet now, with the eye of faith and the perspective of time, we see things differently: "But he was pierced because of our transgressions, he was crushed because of our iniquities; the punishment that brought us peace was upon him, and by his wounds he healed us" (v. 5).[11] The language speaks of a violent death. There are, however, different kinds of violent death. Religious leaders have suffered violent deaths that set examples for their communities; martyrs of a cause have suffered violent deaths that draw out sympathetic commitment from their followers. But this Servant's death was neither. He died to pay the penalty for the sins of his followers; he died to bring them peace and healing. In short, his death was a penal substitutionary atonement.

Verse 5 captures so much of this fact. The language of "piercing," "crushing," "punishing," "wounding" points to the penal nature of his death. The double use of the prepositional phrase "because of" provides the reason for his penal death: our transgressions and our iniquities.[12] The substitutionary nature of the death is seen in the matching of the pronouns: "he, him, his" correspond exactly to "our, we, us." This is a Servant who does something for us. A great exchange took place, a substitution, as verse 6 makes clear: "All we like sheep have gone astray; each of us have turned to his own way, but the LORD has laid on him the iniquity of us all."[13] God was like a high priest, as it were, entering the fray and placing his hands on his Servant's head, transferring all our iniquity to him. "From north, south, east, and west, from past, present, and future, the divine hand gathers in the sins of all sinners he proposes to save, and personally conducts them to a solemn and holy spot

— the head of his Servant."[14] This is the atoning nature of the Servant's death, and yet this understanding creates some irony: we once thought the Servant stricken and smitten and afflicted by God (v. 4), and now we realize that *he actually was* — just not for his own sins! It was for our sins, because "all we like sheep have gone astray ..."

This is the second thing we see about this enigmatic Servant: the significance of his penal substitutionary atoning death. To the outward eye, he was simply a man despised by us; to the inward eye of faith, he was a man punished because of us.

Stanza 4: He Was Innocent Unlike Us (53:7–9)

The fourth stanza returns again to a simple statement of fact, mainly in the passive voice. The Servant's submissive innocence is seen in the image of a sheep going to the slaughter, of a young lamb going before its shearers (v. 7). The image of the sheep carries over from verse 6, only now this particular sheep is innocent: he did not go astray; he did not wander off the way. Instead, he submitted himself to those who would slaughter him — and in silence, too. Twice we are told that he did not open his mouth (v. 7), and when he did open it, there was no deceit found in it (v. 9). Why the emphasis on the mouth? Because mouths reveal hearts, as Isaiah himself had learned (cf. 6:5). Yet under the most intense pressure of oppression and injustice, this Servant uttered no angry protests, no words of revenge — no deceit. His silence revealed his innocence; his muteness, his righteousness. Same with his actions: he did no violence (v. 9). Even when they beat him, he did not turn his face away (cf. 52:14). He did not hide his face from disgrace and spitting; instead, he gave his back to those who struck him, and his cheeks to those who pull out the beard (cf. 50:6). Alec Motyer nicely sums up the Servant's innocence: "Together violence and deceit embrace the total guiltlessness of the Servant; in neither outward behaviour nor inner person, in neither deed nor word, could a charge be justly levelled."[15]

The Servant's silent restraint in the midst of such intense persecution established the basic fact of his innocence. It is clear for all to see — and hear. However, the witnesses are not the ones to declare his innocence. Stanza 4 introduces us to a new speaker — the Lord himself — as the reference to "my people" (v. 8) suggests.[16] From this point on in the Song, the divine perspective dominates. The Servant was innocent, not just before men, but, more importantly, before God. And yet, "by oppression and judgment he was taken away ... stricken because of the transgression of my people" (Isaiah 53:8). Here is the penal substitutionary nature of the Servant's death, from the divine perspective: the lamb without blemish became the wrath-appeasing sacrifice for sheep full of blemishes. This too is an enigma. To the unbelieving eye, he was not innocent; he was like the sheep of verse 6, going astray, and thus they buried him in a grave with the wicked. That is, since he was numbered with transgressors (v. 12), he was buried with them in death. And yet, the Lord will not allow this blind, unbelieving perspective to be the last word. Yes, the Servant went into the grave, as do all the wicked (plural), but in his death he was also associated with a rich man (singular).[17] In the ancient world, to be buried in a rich man's grave was a symbol of honor. Thus we have a dilemma. If we take the references to "grave" and "death" to be synonymous (as the parallelism would suggest) then the Servant died and was buried in apparent disgrace and honor. This raises a question: so was he guilty or innocent? Buried with the wicked suggests guilty; buried with a rich man suggests innocent. The Lord will not allow the question to remain open, and so the stanza ends with a clear declaration of innocence from on high: yes, he was associated with the wicked in his death, but he also died with the honorable, "*because* he had done no violence and there was no deceit in his mouth" (v. 9b).[18]

This is the third thing we see about this enigmatic Servant: the fact of his innocence, seen in his silence. To the outward eye, he was simply a man despised by us; to the inward eye of faith, he was a man punished because of us, even though he was innocent unlike us.

These three truths about the Servant are not unconnected to each other; rather, the logic of the one builds upon the other, culminating in *the* theodicy question of the whole Bible:[19] if this Servant was despised by us, and punished because of us, yet was innocent unlike us, how could God — a God of justice — enact punishment upon him, as verse 6 indicates: "*But the LORD* laid on him the iniquity of us all"? The answer is found in the fifth and final stanza.

Stanza 5: … So that He Might Justify Us (53:10–12)

The final stanza does not immediately provide us with an answer to the dilemma over the justice of this Servant's death. In fact, it intensifies the theodicy question at first by stating, with emphasis, "*Yet the LORD* delighted to crush him; he caused him grief" (v. 10).[20] We know already that the Lord was the key agent in bringing the punishment upon the Servant: "*But the LORD* laid on him the iniquity of us all" (v. 6). The question is, "How could he delight to do so?" The rest of verse 10 begins to move us toward an answer: "[W]hen his soul makes an offering for guilt, he shall see his offspring; he shall prolong his days; the will of the LORD shall prosper in his hand." The "will of the LORD" at the end of verse 10 matches the Lord's "delighting" at the beginning of verse 10,[21] revealing that the Lord's delight in the crushing of his Servant was not an end in itself. It was a means to another end: the posterity, longevity and prosperity of the Servant and his people.

This helps to solve the dilemma of the Lord delighting in crushing his Servant, but it does not solve the dilemma of the just nature of that crushing. How can it be just for God to punish an innocent third party on behalf of a guilty party? Some have called this "cosmic child abuse"[22] — and it would be, if the Servant was crushed against his will. But he was not. He voluntarily submitted himself to the crushing, and so removed any problem of theodicy. The will of the Lord to crush his innocent Servant was in fact the Servant's own will to be crushed for the sins of his people. He willed what God willed. This has already been implied in the fourth stanza. Verse 7 can be read in a tolerative sense: "He let himself be oppressed, he let himself be afflicted." This is complemented by the image of the sheep before its shearers — silent and submissive. And verse 10 may be read "when his soul makes a sin offering,"[23] which also conveys the voluntariness of the Servant. Thus we see that the Servant's will and the Lord's will were hand in hand as the Servant made his fatal journey into death, eliminating any problem of injustice. The Lord willingly crushed his Servant, and the Servant willingly received it. This may appear something of a paradox to us, but there is no tension here — only a mysterious harmony.

To what end was the Lord's delighting in the Servant's death? What accounts for the Servant's willingness to die? Verse 11 provides the answer: "Out of the anguish of his soul he shall see and be satisfied; by his knowledge shall the righteous one, my Servant, make many to be accounted righteous, and he shall bear their iniquities".[24] The verse is richly packed with various aspects of atonement theology, but, in short, the death of the One led to the justification of the many. This is why the Servant could will such a death upon himself, and the Lord could delight in such a death, because of what the death would achieve: "making many to be accounted righteous."

Connecting the four stanzas (2–5), we see the following flow of thought: the Servant was despised by us, punished because of us, even though he was innocent unlike us, so that he might justify us. This was the end goal of the Servant's suffering. His death would not be in vain: when his soul made an offering for guilt, he would see his offspring; he would prolong his days; the will of the Lord would prosper in his hand. Out of the anguish of his soul he would see and be satisfied (vv. 10–11). But when would he see his offspring? When would he see his work and be satisfied? Perhaps in the moment of his death he was given divine foresight into his posthumous achievements. And yet mention of his "prolonged days" suggests otherwise. Indeed, after he poured out his soul to death, he would be given a reward from God, which he would then administer to others: "Therefore I shall divide him a portion with the many, and the strong he shall divide as spoil" (v. 12).[25] The Servant is portrayed as a victorious warrior dividing up the spoils of his bounty, something he could not do if he was still dead. This is the final thing we see about this suffering Servant: although the Lord delighted to crush him, it was not the end of him. After death, he would live — a resurrected and rewarded man — justifying many and making intercession for transgressors.

"Behold, My Servant Jesus"

The fourth and final Servant Song ends where it began, with the exaltation of the Servant (cf. 52:13, 15). In doing so, the Song presents a particular movement to the Servant's life: from rejection to exaltation through suffering. This is the heart of the enigma surrounding the Servant: he would succeed, but only after he had suffered. This is what distinguishes him from the "messianic" figure of Cyrus, the Persian king. Cyrus would bring Israel back to the land at no personal cost to himself; the Servant would bring Israel (and the nations) back to God at great personal cost to himself. This raises the question: so just who is this Servant? The secularist answer is: who cares? The liberal answer is: an unidentified individual in the Old Testament, the proposals being

Moses, Job, Jeremiah, Zerubbabel, Jehoiachin, Meshullam, Isaiah, "Second" Isaiah; or the Servant represents a group of people, either Israel, the prophets, a godly remnant within Israel, or teachers of the law.[26] The Jewish answer is: the Messiah who is yet to come.[27] The Christian answer is: the Servant is Jesus Christ, who has come.

Blaise Pascal once commented that "Prophecies are the greatest proof of Jesus Christ."[28] This is no truer than when it comes to the prophecy of Isaiah 53. A number of features in the Song help to identify the Servant with Jesus Christ. Besides some of the connections already alluded to, Christ's three offices of prophet, priest, and king are present. The prophetic office of the Servant is perhaps the subtlest in the fourth Servant Song, though it is clearly established in the second and third Songs. The Servant's mouth would be like a sharp sword (49:2), and he would receive the tongue of those who are taught by God (50:4). In the fourth Song, the prophetic office of the Servant may be implied from the revelation of the "arm of the Lord" (53:1), but also from the basic fact of the Servant's suffering. Of all the offices in Israel, the *prophetic* office received the most opposition and persecution (cf. 2 Chronicles 24:21; Matthew 23:37; Hebrews 11:37). The *priestly* office is seen in the Servant's sprinkling of the nations (52:15), his offering of himself as a guilt offering (53:10), and his intercession for transgressors (53:12). In this regard, the Servant is both priest and sacrifice. The *kingly* office is there in the "root" imagery, which recalls the royal lineage from Jesse (cf. 11:10), and also in the fact that the will of the Lord will prosper in his hand. In the theocracy of Israel, the king served as God's vicegerent to administer his will among the nation. The Servant is thus portrayed as a conquering king, through whom God accomplishes his purposes. In sum, we have in this Servant's life the three offices of Christ, of prophet, priest and king.

Additionally, in Isaiah 53 key moments in the Servant's life and ministry foreshadow Christ's earthly and heavenly ministry: there are his early years growing up before God as a tender plant (v. 2a), his life of rejection by men (vv. 2b–3), his violent death (vv. 4–6) and humble submission thereunto (v. 7), his burial with the wicked (plural) and a rich man (singular) (v. 9), his resurrection onto prolonged days with a posterity following after him (v. 10), his ascension (v. 12), his administration of spoil to many (v. 12), and his intercession for transgressors (v. 12). Various New Testament passages, such as Matthew 26:57–27:61, Philippians 2:6–11, 1 Peter 2:21–24 and Hebrews 7:25, reveal that we are not reading such prophecies into Isaiah's final Servant Song. Rather, they are organic to the Song itself. Isaiah penned a song in which we hear the Father say to us, "Behold, my Servant Jesus," and by the grace of the Spirit's illuminating work, we see God's wisdom — we see our Savior on a cross. And with Alexamenos, we bow and worship our God.

> Stricken, smitten, and afflicted,
> See him dying on the tree!
> 'Tis the Christ by man rejected;
> yes, my soul, 'tis he, 'tis he!
> 'Tis the long-expected Prophet,
> David's Son, yet David's Lord;
> by his Son God now has spoken:
> 'tis the true and faithful Word.
>
> Tell me, ye who hear him groaning,
> was there ever grief like his?
> Friends thro' fear his cause disowning,
> foes insulting his distress;
> many hands were raised to wound him,
> none would intervene to save;
> but the deepest stroke that pierced him
> was the stroke that Justice gave.

Ye who think of sin but lightly
nor suppose the evil great
here may view its nature rightly,
here its guilt may estimate.
Mark the sacrifice appointed,
see who bears the awful load;
'tis the Word, the Lord's Anointed,
Son of Man and Son of God.

Here we have a firm foundation;
here the refuge of the lost;
Christ the Rock of our salvation,
his the Name of which we boast.
Lamb of God, for sinners wounded,
sacrifice to cancel guilt!
None shall ever be confounded
who on him their hope have built.   (Thomas Kelly, 1804)

11

Seeing Him as He Is

Christ's Return and Growing in Godliness

Ryan M. McGraw

Is CHRIST'S RETURN AN INTEGRAL PART OF OUR CHRISTIAN lives?[1] I have heard pastors say frequently from the pulpit that we do not think about the return of Christ as often as we should. After hearing this numerous times, I began to ask, "Why not?" Christ's return is vital to the message of the Bible and it is a central theme of the Christian hope. Christ's return means resurrection for the Christian and resurrection brings both the perfection of believers and the transformation of heaven itself. Christ is the sun of heaven shining in his power and illuminating the faces of his saints. The rays of his glory penetrate our hearts through the darkness of this world now, but his shining face will dissipate all darkness when he returns in glory and we see him as he is. This is why his return is not, and cannot be, an afterthought in the Scriptures. If Christ's second coming is not an indispensable part of our daily Christian living, then we are likely trying to navigate the Christian life by candlelight rather than by sunlight.

Christ's return marks the aim of Christian faith, the fulfillment of Christian hope, and the culmination of Christian love. It both gives us direction and leads us to maturity in walking with God. 1 John 2:28–3:3 illustrates how our future hope of Christ's return should drive us to foster personal godliness through faith and love in the present. We must hope, negatively, not to be ashamed before him at his coming because, positively, we long to see him as he is and to be made like him. After introducing the influence of Christ's return on our personal holiness in Scripture broadly, this chapter amplifies this theme through the lens of 1 John 2:28–3:3. This gives us direction in the Christian life, drives us to maturity in him, and brings our hope to resolution in light of his second coming.

Direction: Christ's Second Coming and Personal Godliness in Scripture

Many have observed that young men are often aimless in our current culture.[2] People are marrying later and young men often do not know what they want to do with their lives well into their thirties. Life often becomes a prolonging of childhood and many young men are occupied with video games and other pursuits instead of laboring to establish homes and families. Whether men or women, if our lives are without direction, then we will likely lack drive, focus, and passion in serving Christ in anything that we do. As a result, life can pass us by with nothing to show for it.

Christ's second coming in Scripture gives direction to the Christian life. Seeing Christ in glory and being made like him is what Christians want to do and be when they "grow up." Christ's return keeps our walk with Christ in this present world grounded and it sets the goal toward which we as believers are moving.

Christ's second coming is like the rising of the sun illuminating the Christian pilgrimage to the Celestial City.[3] It is the focal point of our comfort at death and beyond. Even though believers hope to be with Christ at death, they are not satisfied with being disembodied spirits. We are body-soul creatures who long to worship the Father as whole people. The same Spirit who raised Christ from the dead will also give life to our mortal bodies (Romans 8:11). Death is likened in Scripture to removing a garment. Yet we do not want to be unclothed, but further clothed (2 Corinthians 5:4). We hope that our lowly bodies will be transformed to the likeness of his glorious body (Philippians 3:21). Christ is the firstfruits of the resurrection of the dead. His resurrection is the ground of the full harvest of the resurrection of his people in him (1 Corinthians 15:23). The return of Christ in Judgment should not be a dreadful prospect for the saints. It is the Day in which he will resurrect our bodies and openly acknowledge and acquit us on the Day of Judgment.[4] When we think of Christ's return, can we say with Paul, "therefore comfort one another with these words" (1 Thessalonians 4:18)?

Christ's return is a prime motive for persevering in the Christian life (Philippians 3:14). It flows like refreshing streams sustaining us in the pursuit of personal holiness as we long to see the risen Christ and be like him in glory. Ministers must labor soberly, faithfully, and joyfully because they hope to give a good account to Christ at the Last Day (2 Corinthians 5:9–11). We must all keep our lamps burning, waiting for the Bridegroom to return (Luke 12:35; Matthew 25:1–13). Since everything around us will be dissolved at the return of the King, what manner of persons ought we to be in holy conduct and godliness (2 Peter 3:11)? Because Christ is raised, he shall raise us by the Spirit to the glory of the Father (Romans 8:11). Yet we have died to sin and we are alive in Christ now (Colossians 3:3). We have died to sin in Christ and we walk in new life in Christ, presenting our bodily members as slaves to obey God through faith in him (Romans 6:1–14).

The eternal life that we have now will reach its glorious perfection at the return of our Lord (1 John 5:11; Colossians 3:4). As we live the Christian life, though we struggle with remaining sin, we are shining from one degree of glory to another (2 Corinthians 3:18). The righteous shine like the sun, shining ever more brightly until the perfect day. (Proverbs 4:18; Matthew 13:43). The Spirit of God and the bride of Christ, which is the church, say, "come Lord Jesus!" (Revelation 22:17). We should long for the coming of Jesus because we love Jesus who is coming (1 Corinthians 16:22). Though we have compassion on those who are lost and we should plead with them, and weep over them, to come to the Lord while it is the day of salvation (2 Corinthians 6:2), are we not simultaneously indignant over every sinful affront to Christ's glory remaining in ourselves and in others? This led Paul to write, "If anyone does not love the Lord Jesus Christ, let him be accursed! Even so come Lord Jesus!" (1 Corinthians 16:22). Our citizenship is in heaven, from which we eagerly await the Savior (Philippians 3:20). When Christ, who is our life appears, then we also shall appear with him in glory (Colossians 3:4).

Christ's return is the finish line of the race of the Christian life. While we face many evils in this life, the greatest evil that afflicts us is sin.[5] Christ's return means an ultimate end to sin in us and the ultimate removal of sin from the world through judgment. This is why Christ's return is, in Scripture, a primary motive for personal holiness. Do we long to see Christ as he is in glory? Do we long to worship him with pure, undistracted, sinless devotion? How can we say that we hope to go to heaven if we do not like the character of heaven's King and the holiness of his subjects? Every believer in Christ longs to be made "perfectly blessed in the full enjoying of God to all eternity."[6] Every step in killing sin by the Spirit now

(Romans 8:13) and all putting on the fruit of the Spirit in place of the works of the flesh now (Galatians 5:16) is a confession that we hope to be made like the Savior in righteousness when he comes. We must kill sin and practice righteousness because we love Christ. One of the reasons for Christ's coming is to give us what we desire. We must trust in Christ apart from our own works if we would be saved from the wrath to come (Romans 3:28), but if we are born of the Spirit of Christ then the Spirit is painting Christ's image in our hearts and lives. Does Christ's second coming make you long for the completion of your sanctification in glory? This question comes close to asking, "Are you a Christian?" We were saved to wait for the Savior to appear from heaven (1 Thessalonians 1:10).

All of this reminds us that it is more important how we live our lives and who we live them for than what the Lord calls us to do. We cannot control the outcome of our labor. Ministers do not know what fruit they will have from their sermons, nor do authors from writing books. Crops can be lost and companies can fail. Houses gain and lose value. For some of us, the Lord gives children and he takes them. The wicked often become rich while the righteous struggle in poverty (Psalm 73:1–3). Christ's second coming will not only make all wrongs right. When he returns, he will say, "Well done, good and faithful servant, ... Enter into the joy of your master" (Matthew 25:21). Is this what makes your labors and trials worth it? Do you change diapers to the glory of God? Do you educate your children because you long to see the King come in majesty and beauty? Do you preach, teach, and write because it is your joy and privilege to do all things well for him who did all things well for your salvation? Do you consider that the sufferings of this life are not worthy to be compared with the glory that shall be revealed? (Romans 8:18). For believers, Christ's return should lead us to say, "I know that nothing is better for them than to rejoice, and to do good in their lives, and also that every man should eat and drink and enjoy the good of all his labor

— it is the gift of God" (Ecclesiastes 3:12–13). This sets the stage for understanding John's appeal to Christ's return in his exhortation to personal holiness.

Maturity: Christ's Second Coming and Personal Godliness in 1 John 2:28–3:3

1 John 2:28–3:3 focuses our attention on a single point in relation to Christ's second coming. We are all like growing children in the Christian life. John addressed his readers affectionately as "little children" (1 John 2:1, 12–13, 18, 28). Yet even in this life, believers show different levels of maturity in Christ. Some are children in the faith while others are young men and fathers (1 John 2:12–14). This is true of women in Christ as well as it is with men.

Regardless of our level of growth and maturity in the Lord, the same goal should define our lives and the same things should drive us forward. According to John, our future hope of Christ's return drives our present pursuit of godliness by faith and love.[7] This presses us towards maturity in Christ in this life.

The Goal of Hope: That we Might Not be Ashamed Before Him at His Coming

Exhortation (1 John 2:28)
Our future hope in Christ's return should drive us to foster personal godliness. We must "abide in him" because we do not want to be "ashamed before him at his coming" (1 John 2:28). Abiding in him involves feeding on the Son of God by faith (John 6:54–58), hoping in his mercies, and loving him who first loved us (1 John 4:19). Abiding means bearing fruit as branches from a vine (John 15:1–8).

Our family once heard a sermon on abiding in Christ while visiting another church. In spite of preaching exclusively on abiding in Christ, the pastor said almost nothing about Jesus.

Instead, he urged his hearers to put their emotional lives in order by learning to "abide" in Jesus. Hearers were left wondering what abiding in Christ meant.

By contrast, Philip Henry (1631–1696) reduced abiding in Christ to four things: First, we must abide in Christ's truth by holding him fast through faith and not letting him go. Second, we must abide in Christ's righteousness by faith, not trusting in our own righteousness. Third, we must abide in Christ's love by obeying his commandments. Fourth, we must abide in Christ's fellowship by using the means of grace that he has appointed.[8]

This gives shape to John's exhortation here. Abiding in Christ means persevering in faith in him, obeying him, and fostering hope by using the means that he has appointed to promote these ends. Such means include diligently using the Word, the sacraments, and prayer, both in private and in public worship.

Aim (1 John 2:29)
John's aim relates to Christ's appearing and our hope of appearing before him. He argues in this passage that our personal righteousness must precede appearing boldly in Christ on the Day of Judgment. Unless we are first justified by faith in Christ alone, without the deeds of the law, (Romans 3:21–26, 28), then we remain liable to God's wrath (Romans 1:18; 5:10; 1 Thessalonians 1:10). John argues elsewhere in this epistle that our faith is the victory by which we overcome the world (1 John 5:4). Yet in 1 John 2:29, John was concerned with the practice of righteousness in our lives. Earlier in the chapter he wrote,

> Now by this we know that we know Him, if we keep His commandments. He who says, 'I know Him,' and does not keep His commandments, is a liar, and the truth is not in him. But whoever keeps His word, truly the love of God is perfected in him. By this

we know that we are in Him. He who says he abides in Him ought himself also to walk just as He walked (1 John 2:3–6).

Though we cannot be saved by our good works we have been saved for good works (Ephesians 2:10). The grace of God teaches us to deny ungodliness and worldly lusts (Titus 2:11–12). God loved us and predestined us "to be conformed to the image of his Son" (Romans 8:29). John argues that he who believes that Jesus is the Christ has been born of God (1 John 5:1). Yet the new birth entails new life. Eternal life begins in us now and continues into eternity. This life expresses itself through faith in and obedience to God, in Christ, by the Spirit. We know that we are the children of God "when we love God and keep his commandments" (1 John 5:2). Loving God means that "his commandments are not burdensome" to us (v. 3). We "overcome the world" by believing that "Jesus is the Son of God" and by continuing to trust in Christ throughout life (v. 4–5). We cannot be saved by Christ without being changed by Christ. We have the imparted as well as the imputed righteousness of Christ.[9] This means that we must love the law of God and delight in it in the inner man (Romans 7:22). While God does not accept those practicing righteousness because they practice righteousness, only those who practice righteousness are "born of him" (1 John 2:29). This amounts to saying that those who are born of the Spirit live to God through Jesus Christ.

Faith gives rise to hope, which is the focus of this section. John's aim is that "we may have confidence and not be ashamed before him at his coming" (1 John 2:28). Practicing righteousness is evidence of the new birth and of our union with Christ. John teaches us that we know that Christ is righteous and that "everyone who practices righteousness is born of him" (v. 29). We cannot continue in sin because there is no sin in Christ, to whom we are united, and with whom we have fellowship. We have also been born of the Spirit, who works righteousness in us. "The Son of

God was manifested that he might destroy the works of the devil," which includes the gradual eradication of the remnants of sin in us (1 John 3:7–9). Though we were once darkness, we are now light in the Lord (Ephesians 5:8). Therefore, the darkness is passing away in us and the true light is already shining (1 John 2:8).

The conclusion from these thoughts is that we must aim to appear blameless in righteousness before Christ at his return. We must be counted righteous in Christ through faith and we must become righteous in Christ by the same faith. Do we persevere in faith? Does our faith work by love? (Galatians 5:6). Do we practice righteousness because we have been born of God? A fish does not and cannot breathe air. It must breathe water. So Christians live and breathe through the Spirit of Christ, who is the fountain of living waters (John 7:37–38). We must not depend on our good works to earn God's favor. But God also does not save us without good works. Christ's return must drive us forward in hope so that "when he appears, we may have confidence before him and not be ashamed at his coming."

The Drive of Faith and Love: That We Might See Him as He is and Be Made Like Him

Our future hope to appear blameless at Christ's return should promote zeal for moral purity by means of fostering our faith and love. Though I have divided this passage by stressing hope, faith, and love, respectively, it is not easy to separate these ideas in John's thought. John's meditative and cyclical style is harder to outline than Paul's logical progressions. 1 John 3:1–3 reiterates the themes of 2:28–29 by pushing them in a more positive direction:

> Behold what manner of love the Father has bestowed on us, that we should be called children of God! Therefore the world does not know us, because it did not know Him. Beloved, now we are children of God; and it has not yet been revealed what we shall be, but we know that when He is revealed, we shall be like Him, for we shall see Him

as He is. And everyone who has this hope in Him purifies himself, just as He is pure.

Our hope to appear blameless before him at his coming is, more specifically, hoping or expecting to be like him when we see him as he is. As we have seen above, we can only pursue Christian living and overcome the world by faith. Yet John stresses that hope drives faith and that obedience flows from faith. Both proceed from the Father's love to us and they end in our love to the Father. John presses home personal godliness here by directing us to meditate on our adoption, to remember our alienation from the world, and to anticipate the consummation of our faith, hope, and love in Christ's appearing.

Adoption

Meditating on our adoption by God is a great means of promoting godliness. Some authors have noted that adoption is virtually a summary of all of the benefits of the gospel.[10] We were once children of wrath even as others (Ephesians 2:3). Yet now, in Christ, God has given us the Spirit of adoption through whom we cry, "Abba, Father" (Romans 8:15; Galatians 4:6). This highlights the greatness of God's love to us.

Our adoption is the legal ground of our heavenly inheritance, in light of which we are "heirs of God, and joint heirs with Christ" (Romans 8:17). Edward Leigh (1602–1671) wrote, "It is the gracious sentence of God the Father on a believer, whereby for Christ's sake he calls believers his children, and really admits them into the state and condition of children."[11] Our adoption in Christ is a present reality that awaits its full consummation in glory (Romans 8:23). Adoption in Christ expresses our legal right to our inheritance in him. Through adoption, "we are received into the number, and have a right to all the privileges, of the sons of God."[12]

This inheritance includes our glorification, which entails our

perfection in holiness at the Last Day (Romans 8:30). Adoption
is not itself transformative, but it is a primary motive and ground
of our transformation in Christ, both in this life and in the
next.[13] Leigh notes that by adoption we receive the Spirit of
sanctification.[14] The Spirit of adoption, who resides in our hearts,
enables us to serve God as sons rather than as slaves (Galatians
4:6–7). God gives as many as receive Christ the right to be called
the sons of God (John 1:12). These promises apply to God's
daughters as well as to his sons, highlighting the fact that men and
women in Christ all enjoy the privileges reserved for a firstborn son
in the ancient world.

Alienation

Reconciliation with God results in alienation from the world.
John wrote, "Therefore the world does not know us, because it
did not know him" (1 John 3:1b). This condenses Jesus' teaching
on this subject from John 15:18–16:4 into a single statement. Jesus
taught there that the world would hate his disciples because it
first hated him (15:18). He chose his people out of the world so
that, while they remain in the world, they would not be of the
world (v. 19). He informs us what to expect from a world that is
alienated from God, reminding us that, as servants, we are not
greater than our Master, who suffered and died for us (v. 20–21).
Yet the unbelieving world is without excuse for rejecting Christ
and for persecuting his people (v. 22–24). All of these things
fulfill the predictions of Scripture as well (v. 25). The remedy to
such problems lies in the gift of the Holy Spirit, who will enable
his people to testify to the truth in spite of opposition (v. 26–27).
Jesus warned us about these things in advance so that we might
not stumble when we are "hated by all" for his sake (16:1–4). If we
are friends with the world, then we are at enmity with God (James
4:4). John is, as it were, putting our adoption by God in Christ
on one side of the scales and the animosity of the world on the

other side, showing that belonging to God's family outweighs all opposition that faces us.

Anticipation

Adoption and alienation lead to anticipation in this passage. John begins with our hope in Christ in this life, then, he lifts us up to the heights of heaven, before bringing us crashing back to earth so that we might hit the ground running. We are the children of God now. This gives us hope by which to expect greater things. A better and fuller hope awaits us in the future.

The Scriptures persistently refuse to answer speculative questions about our future state in heaven. What will our fellowship with other saints be like? How much continuity and discontinuity will there be with this present life? Will we continue to enjoy our favorite labors and recreations in glory? Instead, it holds out hope of a new heavens and new earth, "in which righteousness dwells" (2 Peter 3:13). Whatever burdens believers bear in this world and whatever opposition they face from their enemies, their greatest burden will always be their own indwelling sin. This is why John says that "it has not yet been revealed what we shall be, but we know that when he is revealed, we shall be like him, for we shall see him as he is" (1 John 3:2).

The unveiled glory of Christ is the heaven of heaven to believers and heaven would not be heaven without him in their estimation. Our greatest hope is that we shall see him in his glory and be perfectly renewed in God's image in him. John concludes by bringing us from the heights of glory back to earth in order to run the race set before us. Christ is righteous and everyone who practices righteousness is born of God. As a result, "Everyone who has this hope in him, purifies himself, just as he is pure' (1 John 3:3). Hope of seeing Christ and being like him means that we cannot stand the sight of sin in ourselves now. Anticipating this blessed sight of Christ leads to purifying ourselves as Christ is pure.

We do this by the Spirit of adoption who is at work in us as we walk by faith, cling to hope, and grow in love.

We must place seeing Christ at his return at the heart of our pursuit of holiness. Aiming at anything less will not take us to the heights of heaven. John describes here what the church has ordinarily called the Beatific Vision. This is the blessed transformation that comes when the pure in heart see God (Matthew 5:8) in glory. John teaches us that Jesus Christ is the focal point of the Beatific Vision.[15] In a sense, all growth in grace comes through "seeing" Christ (2 Corinthians 3:8). Now we see him and know him through the eyes of faith (1 John 3:6). We see Christ in the picture that the Spirit paints of him, both in Word and sacrament, and in our hearts. Yet now we see darkly as through a glass (1 Corinthians 13:12). We walk by faith and not by sight (2 Corinthians 5:7). Yet as Thomas Manton (1620–1677) wrote, "Christ is the living Bible; we may read much of the glory of God in the face of Jesus Christ. We shall study no other book when we come to heaven."[16] John presents to us a Christological Beatific Vision.[17] This means that we can, and we must, pursue holiness as adopted children of God as we abide in Christ.

Resolution: Walking in Faith, Hope, and Love in Light of Christ's Return

If Christ's return gives us direction in life, promoting maturity in Christ, then what is the resolution of these things? Christ's return should drive us to walk in faith, hope, and love by prioritizing his return in our Christian lives and by using the means that God has appointed to remind us of his second coming. This leads to some needed exhortations, which serve as a conclusion to this essay as well.

Prioritize
I began this chapter by asking whether or not Christ's return is

integral to our Christian lives. In light of the teaching above, should it not be? This question is related to asking whether or not Christ himself is central to our Christian lives. Sinclair Ferguson observed,

> It is a disheartening fact that evangelical Christians, who write vast numbers of Christian books, preach abundant sermons, sponsor numerous conferences and seminars, and broadcast myriad TV and radio programmes, actually write few books, preach few sermons, sponsor few conferences or seminars, and devote few programmes to the theme of Jesus Christ and him crucified. We give our best and most creative energies to teaching God's people almost everything except the person and work of our Lord and Saviour. This should cause us considerable alarm, for there is reason to fear that our failure here has reached epidemic proportions.[18]

Thinking of Christ and his return as the culmination of our faith, the substance of our hope, and the object of our love may become a means of putting Christ himself back in his proper place in the church today.

If we neglect thinking frequently about Christ's return, then have we not lost something of the faith, hope, and love of the New Testament church? It has been said that J. C. Ryle would look out his window every morning and say, "maybe today Lord," and every evening and say, "maybe tonight Lord." As we go about our daily lives, this kind of thinking does not always come naturally. We need to meditate more on the blessed hope and glorious appearing of our great God and Savior, Jesus Christ (Titus 2:13). This should be a primary reason why we deny ungodliness and worldly lusts (v. 12). Christ gave himself for us to redeem us from every lawless deed, purifying us to himself to be his own special people who are zealous for good works (v. 14). The first step to restoring Christ's return to its proper place in the Christian life is recognizing its importance in Scripture. Do we do so?

Use Means

Thankfully, the Lord has given us several means to ensure that Christ's return is a regular part of our Christian faith and lives. In addition to reflecting on the general teaching of Scripture on the subject, the sacraments and the Sabbath stand out as divinely appointed helps to keep Christ's return at the center of our faith, hope, and love.

Our baptism in the name of the Triune God (Matthew 28:19) points to Christ's present victory over all his and our enemies so that we might serve him with clean consciences (1 Peter 3:21–22). It is also a picture of salvation from and through God's judgment of the world (v. 18–20).[19] Look to your baptism in order to point to the Day when Christ will bring salvation and judgment to their final consummation. We should do this especially, but not exclusively, when we witness the baptism of others.[20]

In the Lord's Supper as well, we "proclaim the Lord's death till he comes" (1 Corinthians 11:26). The Lord's Supper directs us to look back to what Christ has done, to look to what he is doing at present in communion with his church, and to look forward to the Day when he will eat and drink with us in the Kingdom (Matthew 26:29). In this way, the very words that Christ used to institute the Lord's Supper direct us to the consummation of his kingdom when he returns in glory. The Lord's Supper should make meditating on Christ's return inescapable every time we observe it. Use the Lord's Supper to meditate on Christ's return.

The Sabbath is a weekly reminder that a future rest in glory awaits the people of God (Hebrews 4:9–11). Just as Christ rose from the dead on the first day of the week and met with his disciples on that day repeatedly, so he continues to do in the assemblies of his saints today. The Sabbath is a pledge that the Lord sanctifies us to be his people (Exodus 31:13). It is also a weekly pledge that he will give eternal rest to his people in Christ.

Embedding a weekly reminder of Christ's return into our calendars is one of the greatest advantages God has given to help us long to appear with Christ in glory at the last Day. It is one of the greatest tragedies in the church at the present day that so many have reduced the Sabbath merely to avoiding work on that day, and that many more have neglected it entirely. The Sabbath is a great means of promoting self-denial in our churches and families as we remember Christ's finished work in his resurrection and as we look to the consummation of his work when he comes again. Delight in the Sabbath to point to the eternal rest that begins when Christ returns.

Conclusion

In his book, *The Great Divorce*, C. S. Lewis gives a picturesque view of the perspectives currently in hell and in heaven on the future. Both groups see the sun on the edge of the horizon. From the perspective of those in hell, the sun is about to set, while for those in heaven the sun is about to rise.[21] Christ's return will be like the sunset for unbelievers, in which all hopes and joys come to an end. However, his return will be like the sunrise for believers, in which faith gives way to sight and hope is eclipsed by love. Let us learn to prioritize Christ's second coming in our Christian faith and lives and let us use the means that he has given us to help us do so.

Notes

Introduction

1. John Owen, *The Works of John Owen, D.D.*, ed. William H. Goold (Edinburgh: Johnstone & Hunter, 1850), 1:304.
2. Sinclair B. Ferguson, *Some Pastors and Teachers: Reflecting a Biblical Vision of What Every Minister Is Called to Be* (Banner of Truth, 2017), 709.
3. Francesca Aran Murphy, ed., *The Oxford Handbook of Christology* (New York: Oxford University Press, 2015).
4. Isaac Ambrose, *Looking unto Jesus: A View of the Everlasting Gospel, Or, The Soul's Eyeing of Jesus as Carrying on the Great Work of Man's Salvation from First to Last* (London, 1658), 3.

Chapter 1: Christ Our Prophet

1. Embodying deity in a human form; both divine and human.
2. John Calvin, *Institutes of the Christian Religion*, Library of Christian Classics, Volume XX, Eds J. T. McNeill and F. L. Battles (Philadelphia: Westminster Press, 1960), XV.1, p. 494.
3. Calvin, *Institutes*, 495–496.
4. St Augustine, *Homilies on the Gospel of John* (Christian Classics Ethereal Library), Tractate XXX.III.5. See Patristic Bible Commentary, *Augustinus Hipponensis In Iohannis euangelium tractatus XXX.III*.

Chapter 2: The Lord from Heaven

1. In this chapter, I have restricted myself largely to focusing on John 8:58, as I was given a mandate by the conference organizer to preach from an individual text with considerable application rather than approach the topic given to me in only a topical and more academic manner. In addition to a variety of biblical texts in John's Gospel, there are numerous texts that teach

the doctrine of the Son of God's pre-existence, including Matthew 18:11; 20:28; Mark 1:1–3; 12:1ff.; Romans 8:3; 1 Corinthians 10:4; 2 Corinthians 8:9; Galatians 4:4; Philippians 2:6; Colossians 1:15–17; 1 Timothy 1:15; 3:16; 2 Timothy 1:10; Hebrews 1:1–14; 7:3; 1 Peter 1:20. Thanks to Ray Lanning for his research assistance. Unless otherwise noted, all Scripture citations are taken from the KJV.

2. For helpful treatments on the subject being addressed in this chapter, see Robert Letham, *The Work of Christ* (Downers Grove, IL: InterVarsity Press, 1993), especially chapter 3; Donald Macleod, *The Person of Christ* (Downers Grove, IL: InterVarsity Press, 1998), especially chapter 3.

3. William Hendriksen, *New Testament Commentary: Exposition of the Gospel According to John* (Grand Rapids: Baker, 1975), 111.

4. *The Psalter* (Grand Rapids: Eerdmans, 1927), no. 332:1.

5. *The Psalter*, no. 348:2, 3.

6. B. B. Warfield, *Biblical and Theological Studies* (Phillipsburg, NJ: P&R, 1968), 87.

7. Cf. John 6:35, 48, 51; 8:12; 9:5; 10:7, 9, 11, 14; 11:25; 14:6; 15:1; 18:5, 6, 8.

8. Michael P. V. Barrett, *Beginning at Moses: A Guide to Finding Christ in the Old Testament* (Greenville, SC: Ambassador International, 2001), 148.

9. This material on the Angel of the Lord is largely drawn from Joel R. Beeke, et al., *The Reformation Heritage KJV Study Bible* (Grand Rapids: Reformation Heritage Books, 2014), 361. For a more in-depth treatment, see Vern S. Poythress, *Theophany: A Biblical Theology of God's Appearing* (Wheaton, IL: Crossway, 2018).

10. Barrett, *Beginning at Moses*, 154–60.

11. Charles Hodge, *Systematic Theology*, 3 vols. (New York: Scribner, Armstrong, & Co., 1877), 1:483. See also two recommended essays from B. B. Warfield, "The Divine Messiah in the Old Testament" (*Biblical and Theological Studies* [Phillipsburg, NJ: P&R, 1968], chapter 4, 79–126) and "The Person of Christ according to the New Testament" (*The Person and Work of Christ* [Phillipsburg, NJ: P&R, 1968], chapter 2, 37–70).

12. "Form for the Administration of the Lord's Supper," *The Psalter*, 136.

13. John Murray, *O Death, Where Is Thy Sting: Collected Sermons* (Philadelphia: Westminster Seminary Press, 2017), 7.

14. Charles Hodge, *An Exposition of the First Epistle to the Corinthians* (New York: Robert Carter & Brothers, 1860), 175.

15. Psalm 73:23–25; *The Psalter*, no. 203:1–3.

Chapter 3: Cur Deus Homo: Why God Became Man

1. The title of this address comes from the title of a book by Anselm of Canterbury in the eleventh century AD.

2. Unless otherwise noted, all Scripture citations are my own translation.

3. This appears to confirm that Daniel 7:13–14 includes an allusion to Genesis

22:18, especially since Genesis 22:17–18 is the only reiterated promise that also contains the phrase, "possessing the gate of your enemy," which is a major theme in Daniel 7 related both to the "Son of Man" and to the Israelite saints. The allusion to the Adamic commissions, especially Genesis 22:18, in Daniel 7 is further confirmed from observing that the precise phrase (in the old Greek) "all the nations of the earth" (*panta ta ethnē tēs gēs*) occurs only five other times in the Old Testament, two of which are Genesis 22:18 and 26:4, which are among the repetitions of Adam's commission. See further in this respect on note 32 below.

4. Joyce G. Baldwin, *Daniel* (TOTC; Leicester: Inter-Varsity, 1978), 143, 150. Cf. also N. T. Wright, *The Climax of the Covenant* (London: T. & T. Clark, 2004), 23.

5. The remainder of this section is dependent on G. K. Beale, *A New Testament Biblical Theology* (Grand Rapids: Baker, 2011), 396–401.

6. The scope of this essay does not allow me to substantiate this view fully. See R. T. France, *Jesus and the Old Testament: His Application of Old Testament Passages to Himself and His Mission* (Downers Grove: InterVarsity, 1971), 227–239, for a persuasive argument of the quotation of Daniel 7 in Mark 13. If this view is correct, then it may be that the AD 70 coming of Christ in judgment as portrayed by the Gospels is a typological foreshadowing of his final coming in judgment. On the other hand, the traditional view that the coming of the Son of Man in the synoptic eschatological discourse refers to Christ's final coming is certainly a plausible view. This issue is a thorny problem that still deserves much more study. Certainly, there is abundant testimony to Christ's final coming as the conclusion of history elsewhere in Acts, Paul and the remainder of the New Testament.

7. Note that Daniel 7:13–14 refers to "one like a son of man was coming ... and to him was given dominion, glory and a kingdom" (MT). Likewise, see Matthew 19:28, which is probably an allusion to the same Daniel passage.

8. See J. D. G. Dunn, "The Danielic Son of Man in the New Testament," in *The Book of Daniel: Composition and Reception*, edited by J. J. Collins and P. W. Flint (Leiden: Brill, 2001), 529–530, who sees that three key elements from Daniel 7:13 in some cases are enough to recognize a clear allusion (e.g., "son of man" + "coming" + "on/with the clouds"), though he says when only "son of man" + "coming" occurs, "the case for literary dependence is less clear".

9. Though here Jesus may be looking forward imminently to inaugurating the fulfillment of the kingdom prophesied in Daniel in Mark 9 at the Mount of Transfiguration (cf. esp. 9:3, 7, 9; note reference to Jesus' future resurrection in v. 9) and probably continuing especially through the resurrection and ascension and perhaps even up through the destruction of Jerusalem. See likewise also Matthew 10:23, which has "you shall not finish going through the cities of Israel, until the Son of Man comes," which may refer to Christ's resurrection or ascension or, perhaps, his AD 70 coming.

10. Here applied to the coming eschatological king of Israel.

11. Here applied to the coming eschatological Davidic king of Israel.

12. While Wisdom, Jubilees, and Sirach are not a part of the Old Testament scriptures, they offer relevant support for understanding Israel as God's son.

13. See further references in this respect in Louis Ginzberg, *The Legends of the Jews*, trans. Henrietta Szold, 7 vols. (Philadelphia: Jewish Publication Society, 1909–38), 1:332 (and see n. 89 therein).

14. See likewise, though negatively stated, *Pesiq. Rab. Kahana*, Piska 15.1: "As with Adam, said God, so with his children: I brought them into the Land of Israel, I gave them commands, but they transgressed My commands."

15. The remainder of this section is a summary of the seminal though brief study of S. Kim, "The 'Son of Man'" as the Son of God (WUNT 30; Tübingen: Mohr [Siebeck], 1983), 1–37.

16. See Kim, "Son of Man," 20–22, for further discussion of the links between Daniel 7 and 4Q246.

17. Kim, "Son of Man," 27–29, also mentions other Jewish apocalyptic visions that refer to heavenly figures both as "a man" and as a "son of God" or "firstborn."

18. Kim, "Son of Man," 99.

19. Following W. Austin Gage, *The Gospel of Genesis* (Winona Lake: Eisenbrauns, 1984), 27–36.

20. I have found support for this link in J. Cohen, *"Be Fertile and Increase, Fill the Earth and Master It": The Ancient and Medieval Career of a Biblical Text* (Ithaca/London: Cornell University Press, 1989), 18, who also cites James Barr and Claus Westermann in support.

21. So also W. J. Dumbrell, *The Search for Order* (Grand Rapids: Baker, 1994), 24–26.

22. See my *The Temple and the Church's Mission* (NSBT 17; Downers Grove: InterVarsity, 2004), 66–70, and other secondary sources cited therein, for the argument that Adam was a king-priest serving in the Edenic temple.

23. See further Allen P. Ross, *Creation and Blessing* (Grand Rapids: Baker, 1988), 134–135, who observes three changes in the original wording of Genesis 2:16–17 as it is cited in Genesis 3:2–3.

24. G. J. Wenham, *Genesis 1–15*, Word Biblical Commentary (Waco: Word, 1987), 38, who also says, "If the other parts of creation were designed for man's benefit, so too was the Sabbath."

25. This cannot be argued in depth here, but for the fuller argument see William N. Wilder, "Illumination and Investiture: The Royal Significance of the Tree of Wisdom," *WTJ* 68 (2006), 56–69, for the significance of investiture with clothing and clothing as symbolizing inheritance with respect to Adam and Eve, and which I find compatible with my discussion of the significance of clothing in Colossians 3 and Genesis 3 in chapter 14 of my *New Testament Biblical Theology* (see in Wilder for numerous secondary sources on which he partly depends for his discussion). See, in addition, pp. 51–56 of Wilder's

article for other possible escalations of blessing that may be reflected in Genesis 1–3, including references to early church commentators as well as later ones who hold that Adam was designed to receive greater blessings than he had been created with.

26. The preceding section on Adam's role in Genesis 1–3 is a summary of Beale, *A New Testament Biblical Theology*, 29–58.

27. The italic print in the following biblical citations represents verbal and unique conceptual parallels with Genesis 1:28. Broken italic print represents broader conceptual parallels.

28. Notice that the ruling aspect of the commission is expressed to Abraham elsewhere as a role of "kingship" (Genesis 17:6, 16), and likewise with respect to Jacob (Genesis 35:11).

29. G. J. Wenham, *Story as Torah* (Edinburgh: T&T Clark, 2000), 37.

30. Wenham, *Story as Torah*, 37; so also Dumbrell, *Search for Order*, 29–30.

31. M. Fishbane, *Text and Texture* (New York: Schocken, 1979), 112.

32. This appears to confirm Daniel 7:13–14 as an allusion to Genesis 22:17–18, especially since 22:17–18 is the only reiterated promise that also contains "possessing the gate of your enemy," a major theme in Daniel 7 concerning the "son of man" and the Israelite saints. Also the son of man's rule of sea beasts (portraying the enemy) also reflects Adam's original commission to do the same. The allusion to the Adamic commissions, especially Genesis 22:18, in Daniel 7:14 is further confirmed from observing that the precise phrase (in the old Greek) "all the nations of the earth" (*panta ta ethnē tēs gēs*) occurs only five other times in the Old Testament, two of which are Genesis 22:18 and 26:4, which are among the repetitions of Adam's commission; two more occur in Deuteronomy 28:10 and Joshua 4:24, likely also a part of allusions to the earlier phrases in Genesis (though Zechariah 12:3 appears not to be an allusion). Other case forms of the phrase also occur in Deuteronomy 28:1, which together with the same expression in 28:10, directly following mention of repeated blessings, and the phrase "the Lord will multiply you for good in your offspring" in 28:11 would enhance the two Deuteronomy 28 phrases as allusions to the earlier Genesis texts. The phrase occurs also in Jeremiah 33:9 and 51:8, which do not appear to be allusions to Genesis.

33. The preceding section on the reiterations of the Genesis 1:28 Adamic commission elsewhere in the Old Testament is based on Beale, *A New Testament Biblical Theology*, 46–52.

34. Which I have also elaborated on in my book on *The Temple and the Church's Mission*, 395–402.

Chapter 4: Spotless Lamb of God

1. John Shelby Spong, *Why Christianity Must Change or Die* (San Francisco: HarperCollins, 1999), 84.

2. Ibid., 95.
3. William G. T. Shedd, *Dogmatic Theology*, 659.
4. Herman Bavinck, *Reformed Dogmatics* (Grand Rapids: Baker Books, 2006), 3:314.
5. Ibid. 3:315.
6. Shedd, *Dogmatic Theology*, 662.
7. Ibid. 665.
8. Isaac Watts, "Not All the Blood of Beasts," 1709.
9. Charles H. Spurgeon, *The Metropolitan Tabernacle Pulpit*, 63 vols (Pasadena, TX: Pilgrim Publications, 1975), 31:438–439.
10. Isaac Watts, "Jesus, My Great High Priest," 1709.
11. Spurgeon, *The Metropolitan Tabernacle Pulpit*, 31:436–437.

Chapter 5: Jesus the Obedient Son

1. Joel R. Beeke, *Living for God's Glory: An Introduction to Calvinism* (Orlando: Reformation Trust, 2008), 385.
2. All Scripture quotations are taken from, or based upon, the New King James Version (Thomas Nelson, 1982).
3. For helpful studies on this subject, drawn from for this chapter, see Birger Gerhardsson, *The Testing of God's Son (Matt. 4:1–11 & Par): An Analysis of an Early Christian Midrash*, trans. John Toy (Eugene, OR: Wipf & Stock Publishers, 2009); Gregory S. Smith, *The Testing of God's Sons: The Refining of Faith as a Biblical Theme* (Nashville: B & H Academic, 2014); Brandon D. Crowe, *The Obedient Son: Deuteronomy and Christology in the Gospel of Matthew*, *BZNW* 188 (Berlin: De Gruyter, 2012).
4. John Owen, *Exposition of the Epistle to the Hebrews*, vol. 6 (repr. Edinburgh: Banner of Truth, 1991), 310.
5. Mark Jones, *Knowing Christ* (Edinburgh; Carlisle: Banner of Truth, 2015), 106.

Chapter 6: Christ's Resurrection

1. Richard Gaffin, *Resurrection and Redemption: A Study in Paul's Soteriology* (Phillipsburg, NJ: P&R, 1987), 12, note 2.
2. John Murray, *The Epistle to the Romans* (Grand Rapids: Eerdmans, 1968), 7.
3. Murray, *Romans*, 7.
4. Murray, *Romans*, 11.
5. The following five points are based on John Murray's extended comment in *Romans*, 156–157.
6. John Bunyan, *Grace Abounding to the Chief of Sinners* (Glasgow: William Collins, 1863), paragraph 229, 90.
7. Gaffin, *Resurrection and Redemption*, 34.
8. Gaffin, *Resurrection and Redemption*, 35.

Chapter 7: Rejoice! The Triumphant Lord Jesus

1. I am indebted to R. C. Sproul, whose sermon provided me the idea for this introduction. R. C. Sproul preached on the Ascension in his Renewing Your Mind (Dust to Glory) series (preached on October 20, 2012). Found at: https://www.sermonaudio.com/saplayer/playpopup.asp?SID=1020121630325. Accessed 2/9/2018.

2. Of course, men besides priests have blessed others, and rightly so. Nonetheless, ordinarily, and as instituted by God, the priests were especially called to bless God's people on a regular basis. This was part of their regular priestly duties (e.g., Leviticus 9:22 and Numbers 6:22ff). Thus, when Jesus raised His hands (as the priests did) and pronounced a blessing as part of His ministry, the clearest and most obvious reference point would be the priestly blessing.

3. In the sacrificial system, the priest put his hand on the head of the atoning sacrifice to transfer the worshiper's guilt upon that substitute (e.g., Leviticus 1:4; 3:2, 8, 13; 4:4, 15, 24, 29, 33; 8:14, 18, 22; 16:21). In this case, the priest puts his hand on the congregation in order to transfer God's blessing. In both cases the act is "sensual," perceived by man's senses. Thus, should not the act be viewed as for man's sake, for man's senses?

4. John Calvin, *Calvin's Commentaries: A Harmony of the Evangelists: Matthew, Mark, and Luke*, trans. William Pringle (Grand Rapids: Baker Books, 1979), 17:392.

5. Norval Geldenhuys, *Commentary on the Gospel of Luke, The New International Commentary on the New Testament* (Grand Rapids: Eerdmans, 1993), 645–646.

6. William Hendriksen, *New Testament Commentary: Luke* (Grand Rapids: Baker Books, 2002), 1076.

7. Calvin, *Commentary on a Harmony of the Evangelists: Matthew, Mark, and Luke*, 392

8. Matthew Henry, *Matthew Henry's Commentary on the Whole Bible: Wherein Each Chapter Is Summed up in Its Contents: The Sacred Text Inserted at Large in Distinct Paragraphs; Each Paragraph Reduced to Its Proper Heads: The Sense Given, and Largely Illustrated with Practical Remarks and Observations.* (McLean, VA: MacDonald Pub. Co., 1970), 5:846.

9. Westminster Divines, *The Westminster Confession of Faith* (Banner of Truth Trust, 1990), 155–156.

10. Part of the authoritative ministry of the Word is pronouncing the benediction, following the example of the apostle Paul: 1 Corinthians 16:23; 2 Corinthians 13:14; Ephesians 6:23–24; Philippians 4:23; Colossians 4:18; 1 Thessalonians 5:28; 2 Thessalonians 3:18; 1 Timothy 6:21; 2 Timothy 4:22; Titus 3:15; Philemon 25.

11. The benediction is a pronouncement from God to His people. Prayer, however, is a request to God from His people. Both in the declared

benediction to man as well as in prayer requests to God, Christ intercedes for our blessing.

12. Derek Prime, *The Shout of a King: The Ascension of Our Lord Jesus Christ and His Continuing Work Today* (Epsom: DayOne, 1999), 61. Prime notes that some theologians deny Christ speaks vocally for us. These theologians understand Christ's intercessions to refer only to "Christ's presence at the Father's right hand, and not a matter of vocal supplication." Prime includes John Calvin on this list of theologians (e.g., John Calvin, *Institutes of the Christian Religion: In Two Volumes* [2]. ed. John Thomas McNeill, trans. Ford Lewis Battles (Philadelphia: The Westminster Press, 1960), 3.20.20). However, *Westminster Larger Catechism* Q. 55, clearly states that Christ's intercessions include "declaring his will to have [his meritorious sacrifice] applied to all believers" and "answering all accusations against them." This suggests speaking, not merely presenting Himself.

13. John Bunyan, *John Bunyan's The Holy War: A Modern English Version*, ed. Thelma H. Jenkins (Darlington: Evangelical Press, 2003), 49.

14. Charles Hodge, *Systematic Theology* (Grand Rapids: Eerdmans, 1989), 2:634.

15. Psalm 18:10ff; Psalm 97:2–4; Psalm 104:3; Isaiah 19:1; Nahum 1:3.

16. E.g., Matthew 24:30; Matthew 26:64; Mark 13:26; Revelation 1:7.

17. Carl Friedrich Keil and Franz Delitzsch, *Commentary on the Old Testament* (Grand Rapids: Eerdmans, 1981), 9:235–236.

18. Isaac Ambrose, *Looking Unto Jesus: A View of the Everlasting Gospel; Or, The Soul's Eyeing of Jesus, as Carrying on the Great Work of Man's Salvation, from First to Last* (Harrisonburg, VA: Sprinkle Publications, 1986), 494.

19. Leon Morris, *The Gospel according to St. Luke: An Introduction and Commentary*, The Tyndale New Testament Commentaries (Leicester: Inter-Varsity Press [u.a.], 1986), 345.

20. While Jesus was born the Messiah (and thus has always been King, e.g., Matthew 2:2; John 18:37), nonetheless, when Jesus ascended to be seated, His established rule began its fullest and final step — which will end in the new heavens and new earth. Thus, He ascended to be established as the King Who rightly rules from heaven.

21. Does this mean every blessing prior to Christ's death and resurrection was unjust? Does this mean Christ was not a true King before His death, unable, therefore, rightly to bless His people? No, of course not. Christ is the Lamb slain before the foundation of the world (Revelation 13:8). Thus, His Kingdom has always been built from this eternally accepted work. Nonetheless, as God works out this perfect redemption in time and space, after Christ died and was raised, this work was finished, and, now "all authority" was given to Christ. Just as you were predestined in love before the foundation of the world (e.g., Ephesians 1:4), but you are actually regenerated in time and space (e.g., John 3:3; cf. WCF 10.1), so, too, does Christ exercise that authority He earned on the cross before the foundation of the world, but He actually earns this

authority in time and space. And, when that work of Christ was finished, the authority — not in an anticipatory manner — but in full was granted to Him!

22. E.g., Psalm 110:1; Matthew 26:64; Mark 14:62; Mark 16:19; Luke 22:69; Ephesians 1:20; Colossians 3:1; Hebrews 1:13; Hebrews 8:1; Hebrews 12:2.

23. William Cowper, "God Moves in a Mysterious Way," *Trinity Hymnal* (Philadelphia: Great Commission Publications, 2008), 128.

24. Remember that Christ exercised His rule prior to the cross. However, that rule was in anticipation of the cross.

25. Edward Dorr Griffin, *The Life and Sermons of Edward D. Griffin* (Edinburgh; [Carlisle, PA]: Banner of Truth Trust, 1987), 2:126.

26. Augustus M. Toplady, "A Debtor to Mercy Alone," *Trinity Hymnal*, 463.

27. Derek Thomas, *Taken up into Heaven: The Ascension of Christ* (Darlington: Evangelical Press, 1996), 14–15.

28. John Newton, *The Works of John Newton* (Edinburgh; Carlisle, PA: Banner of Truth, 1985), 4:299.

29. Geldenhuys, *Commentary on the Gospel of Luke*, 642.

30. Newton, *The Works of John Newton*, 4:300.

31. Morris, *The Gospel according to St. Luke*, 343–344.

32. Calvin, *Commentary on a Harmony of the Evangelists: Matthew, Mark, and Luke*, 378–379.

33. Richard B. Gaffin, *Perspectives on Pentecost: Studies in New Testament Teaching on the Gifts of the Holy Spirit* (Phillipsburg, NJ: Presbyterian and Reformed Pub. Co., 1993).

34. How do we know the cloud disappeared? The cloud or pillar of God's glory did follow the Tabernacle in the wilderness so that whenever God moved, the people could follow His visible presence (e.g., Numbers 9:15–23). However, we have no indication this cloud was visible once the Tabernacle came to rest in Israel. In fact, later, when the Temple was built and consecrated, the cloud of God's glory again appeared and filled the Temple (e.g., 2 Chronicles 5:11–14), suggesting the cloud was no longer present prior to the Temple's establishment. However, this time, the cloud need not remain over the Temple (as it did over the Tabernacle at one point) because the people no longer followed the moving cloud. The Temple that was built in a fixed location in Jerusalem was the permanent dwelling place of God. Thus, we hear nothing of this cloud's visible presence after 2 Chronicles 5:11–14. In fact, the cloud had (at least) to recede, if the priests were to enter and minister there after this initial outpouring. And, if the cloud of God's presence was constantly hovering over the Temple, surely it would have been noted from time to time. In fact, later, when the Second Temple was built, we hear nothing of the cloud appearing (e.g., Ezra 6:15–22). Yet, the people should have understood, nonetheless, that God, faithful to His promise, answered Nehemiah's prayer and dwelt in Jerusalem with His people who returned from the Exile (Nehemiah 1:8–9). For, the original appearance of God's glory cloud

in the first Temple was enough to signal God's continued presence there at the second Temple. The cloud remaining visibly over the Temple was not expected and not necessary in order to indicate that God dwelt there.

35. J. C. Ryle, *Expository Thoughts on the Gospels* (Grand Rapids: Baker Book House, 2007), 4:52.

36. Wilhelmus à Brakel, *The Christian's Reasonable Service: In Which Divine Truths Concerning the Covenant of Grace Are Expounded, Defended against Opposing Parties, and Their Practice Advocated, as Well as the Administration of This Covenant in the Old and New Testaments*, ed. Joel R. Beeke, trans. Bartel Elshout (Grand Rapids: Reformation Heritage Books, 1992), 1:646.

Chapter 8: Christ and His Bride

1. See F. Brown, S. R. Driver, and C. A. Briggs, *Hebrew and English Lexicon of the Old Testament* (Oxford: The Clarendon Press, 1972), 187.

2. For a more detailed discussion of identifying messianic texts in all the Old Testament, see my *Beginning at Moses: A Guide to Finding Christ in the Old Testament* (Greenville, SC: Ambassador Emerald International, 1999). See also O. Palmer Robertson, *The Flow of the Psalms* (Phillipsburg, NJ: Presbyterian and Reformed Publishing, 2015). Likewise, find helpful clues in C. Hassell Bullock, *An Introduction to the Old Testament: Poetic Books; revised and expanded* (Chicago: Moody Press, 1988), 138.

3. "The analogy of Scripture refers to the exegetical use of texts earlier than the one(s) under consideration that 'inform' the later passages by giving background, depth, and poignancy to the words used. They include technical terms; direct quotations; indirect citations; allusions to previous events, persons, or institutions, or previous covenants." Walter C. Kaiser Jr, and Moisés Silva, *Introduction to Biblical Hermeneutics* (Grand Rapids: Zondervan, 2007), 240.

4. Walter Kaiser notes that there are certain textual clues that are identified through antecedent theology. "The use of certain *terms* which have already acquired a special meaning in the history of salvation and have begun to take on a technical status (e.g., 'seed,' 'servant,' 'rest,' 'inheritance')." *Toward an Exegetical Theology* (Grand Rapids: Baker Book House, 1981), 137. See as well my development of the "seed" in *Beginning at Moses*, 119–144.

5. "A *type* is an object lesson, a symbol, that foreshadows or predicts the actual, future realization or fulfillment of the pictured truth. ... An *antitype* is the future realization to which the type points; it is the fulfillment of the picture prophecy. Types are divinely inspired analogies whose salient points not only correspond to but also predict the reality, the antitype, the main topic of the revelation." *Beginning at Moses*, 248. Similarly, A. Berkeley Mickelsen says that in typology there is "a correspondence in one or more respects between a person, event, or thing in the Old Testament and a person, event,

or thing closer to or contemporaneous with the New Testament writer. It is this correspondence that determines the meaning in the Old Testament narrative that is stressed by the later speaker or writer. The correspondence is present because God controls history, and this control of God over history is axiomatic with the New Testament writers." *Interpreting the Bible* (Grand Rapids: Eerdmans, 1974), 237.

6. See my *Beginning at Moses*, 269–292 for a detailed discussion of examples of people, events, and things that God used as types.

7. Kaiser claims that using the New Testament or even "subsequent" Old Testament texts "to interpret (or even worse yet, to reinterpret) the old material" is "an outright act of rebellion against the author and his claim to have received divine authority for what he reports and says ..." *Toward an Old Testament Theology* (Grand Rapids: Zondervan Publishing House, 1978), 19.

8. C. H. Spurgeon, *The Treasury of David*, vol. I, (reprint, Grand Rapids: Zondervan, 1977), 315.

9. A. E. Cowley, ed., *Gesenius' Hebrew Grammar*, 2nd Edition (Oxford: The Clarendon Press, 1970), ¶55 e, 152.

10. Ludwig Koehler and Walter Baumgartner, *The Hebrew and Aramaic Lexicon of the Old Testament*, vol. I (Leiden: Brill, 2001), 423.

11. "The fact that this beauty is superlative is made evident by the repetition ..." H. C. Leupold, *Exposition of Psalms* (London: Evangelical Press, 1959), 354.

12. "The word *gibbor* by itself does not necessarily indicate deity, but when it is joined with the divine name *El* ('God'), as it is in one of the four names Isaiah 9:6 gives to the Messiah, it is a title of majestic proportions." Walter C. Kaiser, *The Messiah in the Old Testament* (Grand Rapids: Zondervan Publishing House, 1995), 128.

13. "Loved with everlasting love" by George W. Robinson.

14. See *The Reformation Heritage KJV Study Bible* (Grand Rapids: Reformation Heritage Books), 799.

15. Whereas the English notions of remembering and forgetting are involuntary acts of the memory, the Hebrew words are primarily acts of the will. To remember is to think about something on purpose; to forget is to refuse to think about something on purpose. The volitional component of these words is clear from the fact that they often occur as imperatives, that form of the verb that is directed to the will (see Deuteronomy 9:7).

16. See, for instance, the three volume set of Allen Ross, *A Commentary on the Psalms*, part of the Kregel Exegetical Library and Willem A. VanGemeren's commentary on Psalms in the Expositor's Bible Commentary.

Chapter 9: Christ the Exalted King

1. See *Larger Catechism* Q. 45 and *Shorter Catechism* Q. 26.
2. H. C. Leupold, D. D., *Exposition of the Psalms* (Grand Rapids: Baker Book

House, Second Printing 1972) 663–67. Allan M. Harman, *Commentary on the Psalms* (Ross-shire, Scotland: Christian Focus Publications, 1998), 315–16. Derek Kidner, *Psalms: An Introduction and Commentary* (Downers Grove, IL: IVP, 1975). O. Palmer Robertson, *The Flow of The Psalms: Discovering Their Structure and Theology* (Phillipsburg, NJ: Presbyterian and Reformed Publishing Co., 2015), 153–60. Dr. Robertson makes a good case to include Psalm 92 as well as part of this section.

3. Some have Psalm 92 beginning this section. See Robertson, *Flow of Psalms*, 157–60.

4. The Septuagint ascribed this Psalm to David, "when the land was settled, a praise song to David." Many commentators maintain that it was post-exilic, written in anticipation of the people back in the land. C. F. Keil and F. Delitzsch, *Commentary on the Old Testament*, vol. 6, Psalms (Grand Rapids: Wm. B. Eerdmans Publishing Co., 1988), 74.

5. Unless otherwise noted all quotations are from the NASB, 1995.

6. Louis Berkhof, *Systematic Theology* (Edinburgh: Banner of Truth Trust, 1958), 409, 410.

7. Charles Hodge, *Systematic Theology* (Grand Rapids: Wm. B. Eerdmans Publishing Co., 1952), 598.

8. Berkhof, *Systematic Theology*, 410.

9. See *Shorter Catechism* Q. 26.

10. Matthew Henry, *Commentary on the Whole Bible* (McLean, VA: MacDonald Publishing Co., 1970), 594–95.

11. See *Shorter Catechism* Q. 26.

12. See *Larger Catechism* Q. 3 and *Shorter Catechism* Q. 2.

13. *Larger Catechism* Q. 45.

14. *Larger Catechism* Q. 191.

Chapter 10: "The Weak Things of the World"

1. C. F. Keil and F. Delitzsch, *Isaiah, Commentary on the Old Testament* 7 (Peabody, MA: Hendrickson, 2001 [1866–91]), 500.

2. B. Hudson McLean, *An Introduction to Greek Epigraphy of the Hellenistic and Roman Periods from Alexander the Great Down to the Reign of Constantine* (University of Michigan Press, 2002), 208.

3. My thinking on the enigma of the Servant was first stimulated by Alec Motyer, *The Prophecy of Isaiah: An Introduction and Commentary* [Leicester: IVP, 1999], 424.

4. In 41:8, the Servant is first identified with national Israel ("my Servant"), which raises the question of whether the Servant is to be understood corporately as Israel the nation. However, as Isaiah outlines the sins of national Israel (42:18–25; 48:1–22), it becomes clear that national Israel could not possibly fulfill the role of a Servant in whom God's soul delights (42:1).

Moreover, as the Servant and his work is developed, the possibility of the corporate identity with the nation fades and an individual comes to the fore.

5. Barry G. Webb, *The Message of Isaiah*, The Bible Speaks Today (Leicester: IVP, 1996), 209.

6. Henri Blocher, *Songs of the Servant: Isaiah's Good News* (London: IVP, 1975), 61, with credit given to E. J. Young.

7. "The thought is not that the Servant suffered more than any other individual or more than other humans but that he experienced disfigurement 'from [being] an individual … from [belonging with] humankind', so that those who saw him stepped back in horror not only saying 'Is this the Servant?' but 'Is this human?'" (Motyer, *Prophecy of Isaiah*, 425).

8. The translation "sprinkle" (ESV), as opposed to "startle" (NRSV), may seem obscure in the context, but it is the best rendering of the Hebrew and requires no conjectural emendation, unlike "startle." Moreover, Isaiah's choice of "sprinkle" anticipates the language of sacrifice near the end of the Song (53:10–11), and serves to increase the enigma of the Servant, which marks the opening stanza (cf. Motyer, *Prophecy of Isaiah*, 426).

9. Edward J. Young, *The Book of Isaiah*, Volume 3: Chapters 40–66 (Grand Rapids: Eerdmans, 1972), 342, makes a similar observation.

10. Blocher, *Songs of the Servant*, 63–64.

11. Author's own translation.

12. Keil and Delitzsch, *Isaiah*, 509, commenting on the Hebrew preposition *min*, make a helpful distinction: "[T]he meaning is not that it was our sins and iniquities that had pierced Him through like swords, and crushed Him like heavy burdens, but that He was pierced and crushed on account of our sins and iniquities."

13. Author's own translation.

14. Alec Motyer, "'Stricken for the Transgression of My People': The Atoning Work of Isaiah's Suffering Servant," in *From Heaven He Came and Sought Her: Definite Atonement in Historical, Biblical, Theological, and Pastoral Perspective*, ed. David Gibson and Jonathan Gibson (Wheaton: Crossway, 2013), 254–55.

15. Motyer, *Prophecy of Isaiah*, 436.

16. Most commentators think that the speaker here is Isaiah, but I find this unconvincing, since there is no obvious break between the personal reference in verse 8 "(my people") and that of verse 11 ("my Servant").

17. Motyer, *Prophecy of Isaiah*, 435: "… if Isaiah intended a simple contrast between a shameful and sumptuous burial he would have used two singulars, but the use of a plural and a singular can only mean that he is not talking about classes but about persons. He seems to be saying that in the burial of the Servant, wicked people and a rich man were somehow involved."

18. Author's own translation, with emphasis. The Hebrew preposition '*al* may be taken as concessive ("although"; so ESV; cf. Job 10:7; 34:6), but it is rare

(Young, *Isaiah: Chapters 40–66*, 353). The causal use is more common and makes more sense here.

19. Theodicy concerns the vindication of God, especially in his sovereignty and goodness, as he relates to the existence of evil or injustice.

20. Author's own translation.

21. Same root word in Hebrew.

22. Steve Chalke and Alan Mann, *The Lost Message of Jesus* (Grand Rapids: Zondervan, 2004), 182.

23. See Motyer, "Stricken for the Transgression of My People," 259–60, on three possible translations of this text.

24. The reference to knowledge connects us back to 52:13 where we read of the Servant acting wisely.

25. This translation follows Motyer, *Prophecy of Isaiah*, 443: "the 'kings' fall silent because they are in the presence of the stronger than the strong, they are spoil at his disposal."

26. Both lists are provided by Edward J. Young, *Isaiah Fifty-Three: A Devotional and Expository Study* (Grand Rapids: Eerdmans, 1953), 84, as he comments on liberal interpretations.

27. See Targum Jonathan, *ad loc.*, or the *Babylonian Talmud: Tractate Sanhedrin* (98b), for example. Interestingly, the reading of Isaiah 53 in synagogue worship eventually led to such confusion that the Rabbis chose to remove it from the Haftarah, select readings from the Prophets that follow the reading of the Torah.

28. Cited in Blocher, *Songs of the Servant*, 59.

Chapter 11: Seeing Him as He Is

1. This chapter has been published previously as a booklet and is reprinted here with permission of the publisher. See Ryan M. McGraw, *How Does Christ's Return Promote Godliness?* (Grand Rapids: Reformation Heritage Books, 2018).

2. For example, Leonard Sax, *Boys Adrift: The Five Factors Driving the Growing Epidemic of Unmotivated Boys and Underachieving Young Men* (New York: Basic Books, 2016).

3. This imagery comes from John Bunyan, *The Pilgrim's Progress: From This World to That Which Is to Come* (London: 1778, n.d.).

4. *Westminster Shorter Catechism* Q. 38.

5. Jeremiah Burroughs, *The Evil of Evils, or the Exceeding Sinfulness of Sin*, ed. Don Kistler (Grand Rapids: Soli Deo Gloria Publications, 2008).

6. *Westminster Shorter Catechism* Q. 38.

7. For an excellent treatment of the interrelationship between faith, hope, and love, see Mark Jones, *Faith, Hope, Love: The Christ-Centered Way to Grow in Grace* (Wheaton, IL: Crossway, 2017).

8. Philip Henry, *Christ All in All: What Christ Is Made to Believers* (Grand Rapids: Reformation Heritage Books, 2016), 28–29.

9. See *Westminster Larger Catechism* Q. 77: "Although sanctification be inseparably joined with justification, yet they differ, in that God in justification imputeth the righteousness of Christ; in sanctification of his Spirit infuseth grace, and enableth to the exercise thereof; in the former, sin is pardoned; in the other, it is subdued: the one doth equally free all believers from the revenging wrath of God, and that perfectly in this life, that they never fall into condemnation; the other is neither equal in all, nor in this life perfect in any, but growing up to perfection."

10. Edward Leigh, *A Systeme or Body of Divinity Consisting of Ten Books, Wherein the Fundamentals and Main Grounds of Religion Are Opened* (London, 1654), 511.

11. Leigh, *Body of Divinity*, 511.

12. *Westminster Shorter Catechism* Q. 34.

13. In slight contrast to David B. Garner, *Sons in the Son: The Riches and Reach of Adoption in Christ* (Phillipsburg, NJ: P&R Publishing, 2016), 307.

14. Leigh, *Body of Divinity*, 511.

15. For Christ as the heart of the Beatific Vision, see John Owen, *Meditations and Discourses on the Glory of Christ, in His Person, Office, and Grace with the Differences Between Faith and Sight: Applied Unto the Use of Them That Believe* (London, 1684), 14–15; Thomas Manton, *The Complete Works* (London: Nisbet, 1870), 11:94.

16. Manton, *The Complete Works*, 10:123.

17. Suzanne McDonald, "Beholding the Glory of God in the Face of Jesus Christ: John Owen and the 'Reforming' of the Beatific Vision," in *The Ashgate Research Companion to John Owen's Theology* (Burlington, VT: Ashgate, 2012), 141–58.

18. Ferguson, *Some Pastors and Teachers*, 731.

19. J. V. Fesko, *Word, Water, and Spirit: A Reformed Perspective on Baptism* (Grand Rapids: Reformation Heritage Books, 2010).

20. See *Westminster Larger Catechism* Q. 167.

21. C. S. Lewis, *The Great Divorce* (New York: Harper One, 1973).